In memory of Mum and Dad
And for Keith

PAPERING OVER THE CRACKS

MY SPIRITUAL JOURNEY THROUGH TRAUMA TOWARDS A PLACE OF FORGIVENESS AND FULFILMENT

COLIN MURRAY

Matador
5 Weir Road
Kibworth
Leicester LE8 0LQ, UK
Tel: (+44) 116 2792299
Email: books@troubador.co.uk
Web: www.troubador.co.uk/matador

British Library Cataloguing in Publication Data.
A catalogue record for this book is available from the British Library.

ISBN 978 1848764 026

Typeset in 11pt Sabon by Troubador Publishing Ltd, Leicester, UK
Printed and bound in Great Britain by TJ International Ltd, Padstow, Cornwall

Matador is an imprint of Troubador Publishing Ltd

CONTENTS

FOREWORD

In our modern world we can't escape the "big talkers". You know the type – they make bold promises, massive plans, engaging statements, convincing stories, but with no real intention of fulfilling their words – hollow and empty verbal diatribe. Some just enjoy making a noise, being the centre of attention. It's not about action but reaction, and maybe even the betrayal that follows is what motivates them; then again, they like saying one thing and doing another.

Most people prefer to tell the truth, and to exercise their right to know the truth. Our author, Colin Murray, who in his first book tells how he "papered over the cracks" from his childhood until he discovered and acknowledged Jesus Christ to be his Saviour in his mid-life, both knows the truth and tells the truth.

As a companion on his journey in recent years, I can affirm Colin's blossoming as a Christian as he follows in the footsteps of Christ – he still suffers and falls, but not so frequently; he rejoices in the many talents which God has given him but does so with quiet humility and humour. He continues to ask meaningful and searching questions, with the wit to find joy in testing situations, but never at the expense of anyone's dignity as a person. Loving neighbour and God is now integrated into the depth of his being.

This is no ordinary testimony. In this book is found not only a frank, honest story of Colin's life, but also boldly painted is a vivid picture of situations and characters encountered both in a changing community in the North East of Scotland, and on his travels beyond the "safety" of home in his quest for personal fulfilment. Read it for yourself, and draw your own conclusions

Reverend John Woodside
Christmas 2009

ACKNOWLEDGEMENTS

This book would not have been completed within this time scale and in its final format but for the help of a small group of valuable friends. I will be forever deeply indebted to them for their selfless commitment during the writing of this publication.

Julia Dickson gave wonderful encouragement and helped instil a resolute belief in me that not only was this the right thing to do, but also that I was capable of doing it.

I was then led to Sandra Bain, a warm, patient and Godly lady whose wisdom and guidance, particularly in the early chapters, was extremely important to me.

Grant and Edith Smith made an invaluable contribution when my writing needed fresh impetus. Edith offered meticulous editing skills whereas Grant encouraged me to adopt a more descriptive and contemporary writing style, which we hope will be more appealing to a wider reader base.

He also deserves the credit for enlightening me on the virtues of 'Bizet's Opera'!

Paulina Smith-Honig truly embraced the spirit of my vision and was responsible for the proof reading and final formatting. Countless e-mails, phone calls and face-to-face discussions between us eventually pushed this daunting but exhilarating undertaking over the finishing line!

I offer immense gratitude to my good friend Rev John Woodside for accommodating me with more time than I could have reasonably expected. John not only affirmed my belief that I had a story worth sharing, but also wholeheartedly accepted my request to write a foreword.

I also thank those who reviewed and commented on parts of the manuscript, particularly Liz Bowie, Jan Steyn, Linda Riach and Carol Thornton.

PROLOGUE

How often has someone said to you, 'I know how you feel?' Our first reaction is to think: 'No you don't'. Suffering is so personal, no one could envisage our pain. Yet the truth is that we all suffer. We will all experience pain – a deep dark loss that leaves us breathless, curled up in bed, curtains closed, losing the willpower ever to face the world again.

When our child, friend, partner, or parent dies suddenly, robbing us of the opportunity to even say goodbye or say sorry, it's then that we know suffering, and it's then that we feel we are entitled to question whether or not there is a God.

The reality is that any one of us can at any given moment be trapped in this chasm of hopelessness, sorrow, guilt, anger, shame, unforgiveness, and confusion through having to deal with such an unforeseen cataclysmic life-challenging trauma.

Sir Alex Ferguson, in the dedication of his biography *Managing my life*, thanks the Lord for such a happy childhood in which, he states, he can still feel the warmth of the love of his parents and surrounding family.

He also suggests: 'We are basically what our parents are'.

I am led to endorse that same feeling of warmth that Sir Alex felt for his parents in my own life, but I would argue that we can choose to accept, reject, or even modify any influence they have had on us.

Parents remain precious to us even after death. In a way, they are still both absent and present. Such is the capriciousness of life that when I do right or wrong I inevitably try to imagine how my parents would have viewed things; whether they would have reacted with typical parental pride or perhaps with a private lecture, relating it to another one of my erroneous decisions.

It would be fair to say that this publication has had a gestation period in my heart, lasting several years, before it was birthed. When the time came, I resisted the temptation, or perhaps even logic, of employing a professional ghostwriter. So, with no acknowledged literary ability, I embarked on my most daunting life-challenge in the spring of 2006.

There were occasions when feelings of self-doubt and inadequacy almost overwhelmed me, but as I began typing the words my desire and sense of calling was so strong that I discarded the notion that any personal deficiencies or lack of book-writing experience were going to hold me back.

Having read countless biographies over the years, I can now say with conviction that if the publication has had any lasting impact on me, the author has stripped himself naked of all pride, vanity, and pretence, with the risk of feeling vulnerable, so that the reader can see a real, transparent person who is not hiding behind a mask of infallibility, justification and flawlessness.

I trust that my willingness to do just that will be seen as this narrative's most noble attribute.

This is not the writing of a fundamentally religious man or a formally trained philosopher. It is simply the story of an ordinary guy who, through assorted and diverse life experiences, feels a strong calling to open up his heart in order to help, comfort, challenge, and inspire others in this complex and troubled world. This contemporary first person account covers an eventful and varied 46 years of my life, with the main focus on several pivotal life-transforming experiences.

You will undoubtedly move through a gamut of different emotions, while reading the early chapters of this book, as my random life splinters off in several directions. These may range from horror to hilarity and from pathos to puzzlement.

In the second half of this narrative, which is more contemplative and reflective, I endeavour to integrate both my own views and experiences with the perspective of others whom I greatly respect, to offer encouragement, hope and inspiration to any reader.

As you journey with me through my life, you will witness me wearing an assortment of stereotypical hats: the hat of the wise cracking bar fly, the guilt-ridden wrongdoer, the compulsive business builder, the passionate protagonist, or even the wronged dupe.

It's worth remembering that between all these stirring incidents and unlikely scenarios there were long periods of silence with little to record except the same multitude of petty burdens that weigh heavily on most of us from day to day.

Attempting to explain my spiritual pilgrimage has been extremely difficult, because so much of my journey involves the mystical inner feelings that lie beyond the horizon of words. The complicated paths and winding roads we follow are vast and varied.

We all chase meaning and purpose in life.

We are all seekers.

We all desire lives of significance, profound with meaning.

Our pursuit is often an unconscious one. Surely, if there is a purpose in life at all, not only must there be a place for success and accomplishment, but also a purpose in suffering and dying.

Each of us must figure it out for ourselves and, just as importantly, each of us must accept the responsibility our own answer prescribes.

We all reach a time in our lives when we want to know, at the deepest level, if our existence and our Soul are compatible.

This book simply chronicles my quest for this fundamental truth.

SCARRED FOR LIFE

I drew up to his house feeling my usual apprehension about entering.

I jogged up the garden path and opened the front door with trepidation; the same foreboding I had felt on many occasions since my mother's death, almost four years before.

I went through to the living room where I noticed that the kitchen door was ajar.

Strangely, I cannot now remember whether I shouted on him or not ...

I had always dreaded the possibility of finding my father, lying slumped on his bed or in a chair, having died from a massive heart-attack or alcohol poisoning. However, I was not at all prepared for the scene that met me as I tentatively entered the kitchen that evening.

It was Tuesday the 9th of June 1992, around 5pm. I had been working at the local Boyne Hotel and my intention was to go and visit my father, then return to finish a ceiling I had been papering.

The two of us had disagreed the previous evening and we had not parted on the best of terms. This was not unusual when he was drinking heavily, but it made no difference to a promise I had given him that I would see him every day.

What confronted me left an indelible imprint on my life that I will carry with me all my days: My father was hanging from the hatch in the ceiling.

He was dead.

Total panic engulfed me. I didn't know what to do next. My whole body felt completely numb. It was like walking in space. Everything felt surreal; as if it was happening to someone else. In a corner I noticed an opened whisky bottle.

Then my mind seemed to go on to automatic pilot, and in an incoherent daze I scanned the kitchen, frantically searching for a suicide note.

Nothing ...

Hysterically, I ran out of the house and into the street where I met one of my neighbours.

'It's my father! It's my father! ... He's in there ... In the kitchen ... He's taken his own life! Please do something ... Please!'

Taffy, my neighbour, must have thought I had gone mad.

Most of my recollections after that are hazy. Nothing seems to be in sequence. Many pieces are missing. The next thing I remember is being in my neighbour's house.

A young policewoman and my family doctor came into the room. The policewoman pulled out a notepad and pen and started asking me questions.

'How was your relationship with your father?'

'Just cut that out now,' snapped Dr Taylor angrily, 'I know the family well – there is no foul play involved here.'

'Sorry, I am really sorry,' the policewoman timidly replied.

Even in my state of shock and from my slightly dissociated perspective, I could see that this was an ordeal for the young policewoman. In spite of the turmoil of the moment, I felt a tinge of sympathy for her predicament as she was only carrying out her duty.

Through the numbness I had flashbacks to my childhood, but in the confusion only two emotions seemed to alternate through my mind. Primarily there was anger, as I remembered my father's words, four years ago, when he told me that my mother was dying: 'Don't worry about me. I'll be all right.'

How could he have been so selfish?

2

Secondly, there was guilt. Guilt, because I would now never get the chance to make amends for the previous night, when harsh words were spoken between us.

My brother Keith came in some time later – I can't exactly recall when – but we barely spoke. There were no visible signs of distress from either of us, just stunned looks of disbelief. It was as if we had not only been confronted by the stark brutality of the situation but also by its bleak inevitability.

But the ordeal was not quite over yet, for later that evening we had to go to Banff to officially identify the body. This really stung me. I had already identified the body once. How much more painful was this day going to be?

'Aye, that's him,' was all I could muster, as I glanced down at my father's body in the mortuary.

I was in my late twenties, but still very much 'a little boy lost'.

CLOSE SHAVES AND THRILLING ESCAPADES

If there was such a thing as a typical Portsoy family in the 1960s it was probably ours, the Murrays.

My father, Bill, the second of a family of eight, came from the village of Sandend, two miles west of Portsoy, a small town of less than 2000 inhabitants, situated 55 miles north-west of Aberdeen along the Moray Firth coast.

Portsoy was once a vibrant, thriving fishing port. A bustling trade was done throughout the 18th and 19th centuries, when the herring fleets would come and go from its two harbours.

The dawning of the 20th century brought a decline in Portsoy's maritime importance but the town faced these challenges over future decades by toiling admirably to reinvent itself. This culminated in the completion of extensive restoration work in the 1960s whereby the buildings around the old harbour were renovated to complement the popular open air swimming pool, as well as the camping and caravan site at the links, as the town established itself as a fashionable coastal holiday resort.

Portsoy was also famed for its marble, cut from a rich vein of blue and green serpentine rock which ran across the braes to the west of the town. This unique marble was so appreciated for its beauty that it was used for parts of the construction of the opulent Louis XIV's Palace of Versailles.

My mother, Margaret, the eldest of four, was born in Blyth, Northumberland. She came to Portknockie, another Moray Firth fishing village, to stay with her grandparents, at the outset of World

War II. Like many of her fellow evacuees, she became so attached to her grandparents that she did not want to go back home to live – and she never did.

My parents were married in Portsoy in 1962. They set up their first home in Chapel Street, renting a small one-bedroom flat. My arrival came a year later and we resided there for a few more years before moving to a larger two-bedroom council house at the other end of the town, following the birth of my brother, Keith, in 1967.

We were not practising Christians but the way we were brought up was certainly within the parameters and boundaries of a Christian family. There was no bad language or back-chat tolerated, by my father in particular, who came across as a strict disciplinarian. Mum, on the other hand, seemed softer and more flexible in how she dealt with situations. Although my dad was never a regular Churchgoer, he used to display a level of reverence for the Sabbath by always wearing a shirt and tie.

We could hardly be classed as an affluent family but we wanted for nothing, with my father always commanding a decent wage as a foreman joiner and the family income supplemented by my mother's wages from part-time work at the school canteen and later at the geriatric hospital, close to where we lived.

Keith and I became familiar figures in the town because of our bright ginger hair, inherited from both sides of the family.

I didn't really get off to a comfortable start in life as I had a bad stammer and lacked confidence. In addition, I was a slow learner and ended up in a remedial class during Primary 1 and 2.

However, as much as I struggled with knowing my right foot from my left and remembering the most basic of things, I used to look forward to our daily milk ration whereby we all received 1/3rd of a pint of the creamy pasteurised drink in a glass bottle. The sub-zero winters of the 1960s would quite regularly freeze the milk, leaving a layer of ice inside the bottle. This all changed with the introduction of milk in plastic bags, which meant that the unpleasant taste of the plastic was more distinct than that of the milk!

Like all the other boys in my class I had to wear short trousers in Primary 1. These were held up by a "snake belt", consisting of an elasticated strip, fastened at the front with an S-shaped metal hook-buckle fashioned as a snake; it was obviously this feature of the belt which gave it its popular name. However, it did not take me long to find that it had other practical uses, most notably to defend myself against an older boy who was bullying my friend and me as we walked home from school, and also for a more light-hearted moment when I used it to tighten a towel I had placed on my head to imitate an Arab ... with freckles, of course!

My mother made sure I attended Sunday School. It would be wrong to suggest that she pushed me out of the door kicking and screaming but I could have come up with a multitude of more exciting things I would rather have done with my time.

My strongest recollections of Sunday School are of singing 'Away in a Manger' at Christmas time, and 'There is a Green Hill far Away' at Easter.

The strange thing was that as much as I found Sunday School a chore, these seasonal favourites always provoked an emotional response from me.

I just loved the meals at Primary School. I would sit in class, stare out the window at the grey Massey Ferguson tractor that was ploughing the field in the distance, dreaming of eating my favourite sausage-meat flan with mashed potatoes, topped, of course, with a unique hot cherry-red coloured sauce.

I would devour anything that was placed in front of me; from spam fritters to liver casserole. The desserts may often have looked vile and off-putting but sago or tapioca with prunes, and Swiss roll with pink custard were culinary delights, as far as I was concerned.

At home, my mother could have fed me nothing except spaghetti hoops and I would have been entirely satisfied. She only needed to allow me to make my own special Creamola Foam powder-based drink of erupting raspberry fizziness, totally tantalising my taste buds, to complete what would have been my perfect meal!

Our Sundays were usually spent visiting either my mother's relatives in Portknockie or my father's in Keith, a distillery town 18 miles south of Portsoy, well-known as 'The Gateway to the Malt Whisky Trail', with many other distilleries in the surrounding area. Portknockie, a cliff top village with a steep rugged coastline, was a welcome change, giving me a fresh lease of life from the familiarity of my home town. Part of its unique charm for me was a 50 meter rock, called 'The Bow Fiddle', situated just off the shoreline, only a short distance from my relatives' house. The quartzite rock appeared white in colour from the layers of bird droppings left, over the years, by seagulls that nested there, and was shaped like a violin – unlike anything I had ever seen before.

As I wallow in halcyon nostalgia while typing these early chapters, I find myself having a vague recollection of travelling with my mother to Portknockie in a steam train – just prior to the transport secretary Lord Beeching's short-sighted railway termination plan that left Portsoy and countless other towns and villages all over the country without a railway system.

Part of the freedom that growing up in a small North-East community brought was the ability to roam about freely with minimal parental supervision. My generation also had little in the way of entertainment devices, so we had to create our own imaginary worlds, which led to frequent misadventure. There was an incident when I was seven that I remember vividly as showing the fine line between life and death.

Keith and his best friend, Steven, had been playing in the fields near our house when they came across a donkey. Apparently, Keith went into the field and was tormenting the donkey. The near-fatal result was that the donkey turned on him and gave him a violent mauling. With the help of Steven, he somehow managed to get back to the house – bloodied from head to toe, with the thick padded yellow jacket he was wearing almost torn to ribbons.

He recovered, but poor old Neddy, who was minding his own business until Keith came along, had to be put down. I remember the doctor telling my mother that if he hadn't been wearing such a protective padded jacket my brother would probably have been killed.

Just a few months later it was my turn to have a close call. I was taken along on a fishing trip with my father and my uncle Alan. Being prone to calamities from an early age, it was no surprise that I fell into the deepest and widest stretch of water in the Boyne Burn, one mile east of Portsoy. I remember flapping about and shouting frantically – over my head in water.

I was convinced I would drown but my father jumped in after me and, in spite of my frenzied struggling, managed to pull me out. Needless to say, they never invited me to go trout fishing with them again.

My main passion was football. Dad was not really interested, preferring fishing, but I became fanatical about anything related to the game. If I wasn't playing I was watching it or reading about it. And I collected anything associated with it, such as chewing-gum cards, coins from the petrol station and old football programmes.

Strongly influenced by my mother's cousin, Sandy Laing, who lived in Portknockie, my team was Glasgow Rangers. Sandy gave me two Rangers LP records when I was about seven years old. One was called 'Glory Glory', with a large red, white and blue rosette on the front cover; the other was named 'Follow Follow' and featured the current Rangers team.

From then on I became entrenched in all things Glasgow Rangers. My mates were all big football fans and we seemed to be fairly even split between Rangers and Celtic supporters. Aberdeen was our local team but they never had the same appeal although, arguably, they had a finer team than Rangers around that time.

In those days everyone seemed to have a nickname and I became one of several *Cocos* who had Colin as a first name. Keith was given an equally unoriginal one when he was christened *Keish* by one of my friends.

We made go-karts or "Karties" out of Silver Cross prams and old fish boxes, complete with personalised number plates. My ambition was to own a whole fleet of them!

Home life was pretty settled. Mum and Dad had the occasional falling-out but I always found them a compatible couple, although diametrically opposed in nature and personality. Dad was quiet, almost introvert, sometimes appearing aloof. He was not very talkative at home but became more alive when he'd had a few drinks. My mother, on the other hand, was outgoing and chatty and she did a lot of my father's talking for him.

Dad liked to unwind by having a social drink with his friends at the weekend and my mother, although almost teetotal, never seemed to mind. I quite liked it when Dad came back from the pub because he seemed more relaxed and easier to speak to; I think alcohol was a crutch for him to overcome his natural shyness. On the outside I appeared to be more like my mother by nature, being excitable, talkative and comfortable with people, but I also had a tendency to be intense and serious like my father.

My dad was a joiner but he really always wanted to be a fisherman, like two of his brothers. He did go away on a trip with a skipper he knew but suffered badly from sea sickness.

Out of his whole family he was closest to his brother Alan, who was twelve years his junior. They decided to build a boat, and my father spent several months building a sixteen-foot one inside a polythene canopy he had erected in our back garden. I remember the day he went up to the fishing village of Burghead, near Elgin, to purchase an outboard engine. His boat and this 7.5 Mercury engine were his pride and joy, and his trips out fishing and laying creels were the ideal distraction from the rigours of the building sites.

Although he caught mainly mackerel, and the odd codling, my father's favourite catch was lobster, which he viewed as a delicacy. As a young boy, I vividly recall being horrified to see my father boil the lobster alive in a large pot. I could never fathom out how someone who was such an avid watcher of nature programmes could possibly do such a thing.

By the time I reached Primary 5 I felt I was holding my own at school regarding the different subjects we were taught. This was an improvement.

I liked all my Primary School teachers but the one I recall with most fondness was Miss Davidson. I was a little frightened of her at first, for she came across as very strict and demanding, but once I got used to her old-fashioned style of teaching I really grew to respect her and her methods, which were always consistent and fair.

She was a stern, diminutive lady in her 50s and I will always have this picture of her in my mind, standing in front of the class with a long wooden pointer in her hand, asking us to repeat the names of all the 'Firths' on the coast of Scotland as she pointed to them on a large scrolled map that was hanging on the wall.

My father was frequently bragging to me about how fit he was when he was my age, recounting stories of regularly swimming the two miles from the new harbour in Portsoy to his home community of Sandend.

His once slender physique had now given way to a more chubby build – mainly due to his weekend beer drinking – and his jet-black wavy hair was turning grey and thinning on top, yet he still reckoned he could beat me over a 60 yard sprint. So, when he challenged me to a race one weekend at Aviemore, I felt it was time to put him in his place by beating him easily. I did beat him, but only by a whisker, proving to me that many years previously he would have been a real whippet!

For the Murray family, the two-hour car journey to Aviemore was always something to be eagerly anticipated. Aviemore became famous in the late 1960s as one of the first established ski-resorts in the United Kingdom. The resort blossomed when the 'Aviemore Centre' complex opened, with such innovative facilities as an ice rink, and a heated indoor swimming pool that made artificial waves. These futuristic recreational amenities only began to grab my attention when I had outgrown the small electric cars that ran on 6d (sixpence) coins.

Sadly, Scotland's answer to Chamonix rapidly deteriorated into a hideous eyesore during the 1980s and early 90s when ski enthusiasts chose instead to go to the Alps and Pyrenees, where real snow was guaranteed!

Although I was never much interested in reading as a child, I clearly recall being transfixed when I first read *The Last of the Mohicans* when I was about 10, and became fascinated with that story after receiving the book from my great-aunt in Portknockie.

Why, I thought, was Uncas allowed to die, rather than his father, Chingachcook, which meant that the Mohican tribe could not continue? Even at that young age I felt a shiver going down my spine when I saw the spectacular coloured pictures in my book, depicting unspoiled nature and wilderness. Though it certainly owes much to the romantic style it had been written in, as a young boy I was getting so intrigued by the characters and events described by the author, James Fenimore Cooper, and my imagination set off by the plot in such a powerful fashion that even the Sunday evening television dramatisation of that time did not come close.

Growing up in Portsoy in the 1960s and '70s could not be described as boring. As I have said, we had no shortage of pastimes in the days long before iPods, mobile phones and home computers.

A vibrant open air swimming pool and two harbours were some of the places we frequented, as well as a massive playing field, only a stone's throw from my house, where we would go and play football for hours on end with seemingly boundless energy.

And my idea of recycling consisted of returning empty lemonade bottles to the shop and getting a few pennies back on them. In those days, it was quite acceptable for friends to share a can of coke without getting germs!

Something that struck me as a kid was the sheer optimism of the time.

Even with the constant Cold War threat of nuclear destruction and with memories of the 2nd World War still vivid in most adults' minds, many people seemed to believe that the future was brighter than the past.

On February 15th, 1971, the long awaited Decimalisation came with little fuss involved. On that day, the United Kingdom changed from the centuries-old custom of using 12 pence to the shilling and 20 shillings to the pound to a new decimal 100 new pence to the pound. However, of far more importance to me was a tragic event that happened just six weeks earlier.

I clearly recall watching Grandstand that Saturday afternoon, when grainy black and white images and newsflashes of the Ibrox disaster started filtering through that would cause a whole nation to mourn.

New Year bells had been ringing less than 48 hours before; the old year had died, and the new had been birthed. In the last dying moments of the annual New Year 'Old Firm' game, Jimmy Johnstone had scored for Celtic and Colin Stein had equalised for Rangers.

As the crowd was leaving the ground, barriers on Stairway 13 gave way, causing a massive chain-reaction pile-up of spectators. The tragedy resulted in the loss of 66 lives, many of them teenagers, including five schoolboy pals from the small town of Markinch, in Fife. Most of the deaths were caused by compressive asphyxia, with bodies being stacked up to six feet deep in the area.

More than 200 other fans were injured.

I read this perceptive observation regarding the disaster:

> 'Tragedy is never genuinely portrayed in this post-modern society unless seen through the lens of a television camera but this disaster in Glasgow, nearly 40 years ago, was almost concealed from public view.
>
> Unlike the more recent Bradford, Heysel and Hillsborough tragedies, there are no graphic images of the Ibrox disaster to be hauntingly replayed. When those 66 fans died on staircase 13, it was only just one horror beyond the horizon for the cameras covering the match.'

I was too young to grasp the full magnitude of the tragedy, but not too young to forget the unfolding events of that horrendous day. Ironically, soon after, my father took me to see my beloved Rangers play for the first time.

Rangers' opponents were Aberdeen that bitterly cold Saturday afternoon in January and walking to the match amongst thousands of football supporters, mostly grown men, was a daunting experience for me. Even holding my father's hand did little to quell the strange mix of anxiety and excitement that I felt.

This was in the days before all-seated stadiums, and crowds at the smaller grounds, like Pittodrie, often exceeded 30 000 when the big Glasgow teams came to visit.

Nothing was what I had expected. As we huddled like sardines behind the Rangers' goal the atmosphere was tense and hostile – and the noise deafening. I could hardly see a thing; everyone else was massive.

I recall turning round to see a guy – barely able to stand due to drunkenness – urinating on the back of another man's coat. He stumbled forward and knocked me off balance.

'Hey pal, watch the wee laddie,' came a voice from somewhere. I looked over and a man of about my dad's age said, 'Are you okay, son?'

It was good to hear a voice of sanity amongst all the mayhem and madness. I looked up at Dad. I could see he was tense; ill at ease with the whole experience.

Later in the game, another intoxicated man, in a grey pin-stripe suit, tapped my father on the shoulder and slurred, 'Gies a fag there, Jim' – noticing him taking a cigarette out of his packet. My father just gave a deep sigh of resignation and disgust before handing him a cigarette, without even giving him a second glance. I was baffled at the man calling my father 'Jim' and a thought went through my mind at that moment: Should I tell him his name is Bill, not Jim?

I cannot remember much more about the game other than that it was a relief to get out of the ground at full time, for I felt intimidated by the whole experience. And I know it had been an ordeal for my father who never really liked football anyway.

The score was 1-1, and in many ways it was an anti-climax, but

I had seen Rangers 'live' for the first time and that was all that mattered.

Keith and I were fortunate in that we, as a family, went on camping holidays every year, and they were always something to look forward to months in advance. We travelled to such non-tropical destinations as Ireland, Skye, or Devon and Cornwall. Our camping holidays were consistent in their lack of frills but it was always great to hear the rain battering against the canvas tent through the night, then wake up to the fresh smell of dew on the grass.

The only downside for me was being a passenger in our car, in the middle of July, suffering from motion sickness, with my father, smoking cigarette after cigarette, seemingly oblivious as to how I was feeling.

I still remember the thrill when we purchased our first colour television. My father had promised us one for the 1974 World Cup and, true to his word, it was delivered on the eve of the tournament. I had only seen fleeting glimpses of colour TV before then, and it was a fantastic feeling to watch Scotland play reigning World Champions Brazil in colour, from an armchair in our own house.

I was also a big 'Star Trek' fan and seeing an episode in colour for the first time was truly amazing – discovering that Spock had a blue jersey, Captain Kirk a yellow one, and that Scotty's was red.

Although my father had the final say on what we watched on TV, we had our own favourite programmes that we dared not miss. While he loved Tom and Jerry cartoons, nature programmes, and Spaghetti Westerns, my mother would never miss Bruce Forsyth's 'Generation Game' on a Saturday night. I would regularly see her tense with excitement near the end of the programme, when the cuddly toy and coffee percolator passed along the conveyor belt as predictable prizes for the contestants.

I myself was hopelessly addicted to 'The Banana Splits' on Saturday mornings. As I recall, the show's live action included 'Danger Island' – a cliffhanger serial running alongside the animated segments of 'The Arabian Knights' and 'The Three Musketeers'.

Football, of course, was a *must watch* – especially if it meant staying up really late to watch the extended highlights.

Around the age of twelve or thirteen Gary, my regular partner-in-crime, and I were involved in an unforgettable lark that could well have had tragic consequences.

While playing in a room in the Boyne Hotel, owned by Gary's parents, we came across an unopened bottle of whisky. Never having had alcohol before, we thought we would taste it to see what it was like. We decided, in our folly, to go up to a large bathroom in the new wing of the hotel. We grimaced at the horrible taste as we took our first sip. However, that was no deterrent for us and we continued drinking.

After a short while I blacked out, but I do remember being in the bath and unable to get out. I heard someone knocking on the door and then Gary's father bellowing, 'What's all that noise about?'

Gary replied, 'It's only Colin. He's in the bath pretending to be drunk.' Even at that early age he could hold his consumption of alcohol.

The next recollection I have is waking up in one of the hotel beds, with an aching head and feeling extremely sick. I also had a badly grazed face; a painful legacy of an apparent fall that I'd had somewhere outside that I could not remember. I still cannot believe how stupid and dangerous a stunt that was.

After a while I "progressed" from the more mundane misdemeanours. Stealing apples, and 'Ding Dong Dash' were no longer enough to excite and challenge someone like me who craved any pointless pursuit to achieve a cheap adrenalin rush.

This inevitably led to a more shameful misadventure involving me and two friends spray-painting graffiti on various walls around Portsoy. This senseless exploit resulted in a visit and a caution from the police and was the first of several brushes with authority I was to have throughout my formative years.

Despite these odd examples of wrongdoing I have to say that on the whole I was contented and happy. Any trouble I found myself in was more a reflection of my own compulsive nature and desire to be popular rather than any disharmony in my home life.

Gary and I decided to go for a more legitimate type of adventure by joining the local army cadets. Playing with real rifles seemed like a good idea but requiring to have our hair cut was not! I never really excelled as a cadet; I found the rifles too heavy and difficult to manage and I did not take kindly to the discipline that was part and parcel of the training. However, I did like the cross-country running, and at a camp in Inverness I was picked for the North of Scotland football team, playing against teams from other regions.

I remember pleading with my mother to let me stay up to watch Alfred Hitchcock's famous suspense thriller 'The Birds'. She knew I would probably suffer recurring nightmares, due to its gruesome content and frightening storyline, but she relented when I convinced her that all my friends were allowed to watch it.

After the inevitable restless night with the light on I found myself being a bit more wary and respectful of any flock of birds I came across in the following weeks. A real life plague did appear during what felt like a sub-Sahara heat-wave in the mid seventies when the entire ladybird population of the British Isles seemed to descend on Portsoy. These apocalyptic swarms of bugs meant that I couldn't even eat an ice cream outdoors or ride my bike with my mouth open – unless, of course, I wanted an undesirable free snack!

I vividly recall being involved in an aborted attempt to communicate with dead spirits through the ritual of a séance. I was in the company of two friends, Micky and Allan, when Allan hatched the idea of having a séance – he'd participated in one with another two friends and was keen to pass his experience and knowledge on to us. Micky was the son of the local doctor and he lived in a large house, so we decided to go up to Micky's bedroom and give it a go.

As we did not have a Ouija board, we decided to cut out the letters A to Z, the numbers 1 to 10, and the words yes and no, which we divided evenly round a table. The light was switched off and we placed a glass upside down in the middle of the table.

This was all new to me but I found the whole thing exciting and scary in equal measure. Each of us tentatively put a finger on the glass. We closed our eyes – well almost closed them – and one of us asked a question about a dead relative in as spooky and haunting a voice as possible. We did this several times and although the glass moved a few times, I was never quite sure if it was being pushed or not. Suddenly, a loud, sharp, shrill voice came from downstairs demanding us to, 'Stop that damned s... in this house, Mick!' Camilla, Micky's older sister, had obviously overheard us and as we looked at each other in total shock we realised that our supernatural experience had come to an abrupt end.

October 1976 saw the first real tragedy in our family with the death of my uncle Alan from injuries sustained in a car crash. He had been travelling to Keith to watch a football match when the car in which he was a passenger skidded off the road into a field. Alan, or Nipper as he was better known, died in hospital a few hours later. He left a wife and two young daughters.

I saw my father cry – for the first time that tough exterior he often portrayed to us showed signs of vulnerability.

FROM STINGING HANDS TO NEW WAVE BANDS

I liked primary school but Banff Academy was different. It was a much larger school with almost three hundred pupils in my year alone. I was never all that comfortable there. I may have appeared outgoing but I was not relaxed out-with my own group of friends and there were always a few adolescent hard men about to make things difficult.

Although I did reasonably well at some subjects, like English and Geography, the only subject I really enjoyed was PE where we often played football. With some of my friends I hatched a plan to form our very own football team and we knew enough boys from the surrounding area to fix up matches against.

There was little or no organised football available in the 1970s, except if you were good enough to play for your school team. I was a moderate player, quite skilful, with an abundance of stamina, but lacking in the physical side of the game, so the best I could do was play the occasional game for the school team. This team was rather exceptional, with about half the players going on to play in the Highland League and some of the others holding their own in the local junior league.

At a hastily arranged meeting in a friend's garage we decided we were going to be a five-aside or a seven-aside team, so that we would be eligible to play in the summer gala competitions that were held in local towns, without disrupting our team.

We agreed that we should be called 'Portsoy Spartans', after the semi-professional team of my mother's birthplace, 'Blyth Spartans'. I also had more sentimental reasons for wanting our team to be called 'Spartans', because it was while attending a Blyth Spartans home game that my grandfather collapsed and died at the age of 39, four years before I was born.

Next, we had to choose the colour and style of our strip and as there were more Rangers fans in our team, I felt it was only fair that we should play in blue, red and white! We decided on a replica Manchester City away strip, which was royal blue in colour with a round neck and two diagonal red and white stripes. Most of us owned a pair of white shorts and our socks could be any colour – apart from green!

My father made a set of wooden goal frames, suitable in size for seven-aside games, and we managed to acquire enough green fishing net to cover them. I 'borrowed' camping pegs from my parents to keep the nets in place.

Our squad consisted of around twelve players, including three goalkeepers! We played various teams – from the sublime and talented to a bunch of clumsy bruisers who spent more time kicking us than making contact with the ball. But what I liked about the Spartans was that we were just a team of mates who loved playing football. We had no superstars, no prima donnas and no one who refused to pull their weight to play as a team.

Our mothers would take turns driving us to and from away games where we had no changing rooms and no after match warm showers to look forward to! We played regularly for a year or two, until the novelty wore off and we started to focus our attention on under-age drinking – and other less innocent pursuits.

The mid-70s were confusing years for kids growing up in the UK, for there was a strong sense of national malaise. Worker unrest and images of street violence on television were the backdrops to our lives.

As a kid, I never felt directly affected by these social breakdowns, yet there was a sense of social reality closing in –

perhaps because, in my mid teens, it was entering my consciousness. National Front Skinheads were becoming an ugly symbol of a culture that could best be defined by terror, menace and racism.

Being very much a non-aggressor by nature, I was more wary than impressed by this movement, started by those Skinheads, who were non-civillized youths on the look-out for "aggro" (aggravation).

They had hair cut to the skull, were dressed in jeans, held up with braces and with the legs rolled up high. Skinheads wore big industrial boots that earned them the name 'Bovver Boys' or 'Boot Boys'.

By this time football-affiliated fights were becoming a familiar sight on TV and the periodic electricity blackouts, as well as water shortages, signified that all was not running smoothly in the country.

For a gullible teenager like myself such incidents were viewed as adventure rather than anxiety. I was too young to really pay much attention of the 'Glam Rock' phenomenon that was developing in the UK in the post-hippie era of the early 1970s, whereby singers and musicians performed wearing outrageous clothes, make up, hairstyles and platform-soled boots.

Bands like Mud, T Rex and Slade were regularly featured on 'Top of the Pops', but it wasn't until the sensational almost overnight emergence of a young Scottish band in the mid-seventies that I became influenced in any way by popular music.

I hate to confess this, but I got carried away on the tartan tidal wave of 'Rollermania' that seemed to engulf the whole of Scotland for a relatively brief but fervent period as The Bay City Rollers became one of the most popular musical acts of their time. Incredibly, they even sparked off scenes of teeny bop hysteria on a scale not seen since the heady days of Beatlemania, more than ten years earlier.

The Bay City Rollers were very much the ultimate heartthrob group for young girls from age 8 to 16, so you can see where my embarrassment comes from! Their youthful, clean-cut image, distinct style – featuring tartan-trimmed outfits – and cheery, catchy sing-along pop hits helped the group become an overnight worldwide sensation.

The 'Rollers' wore denim shirts trimmed with tartan at the collar, tartan cuffs and trouser hems – trousers being worn at calf length with multi-coloured striped socks showing. I must admit, this outlandish patriotic rig-out appealed to me more than their actual music and although I was never brave enough to wear the trousers or the outrageous stripy socks, I did manage to get my mother to purchase three different styles of tartan jumpers for me!

I used to get the belt quite a lot at school, mostly deserved, sometimes not. It was a thick leather tawse with two tongues, and now and then a teacher would demonstrate how powerful both he and the belt were by whipping it out of his drawer, flinging it over his shoulder, then turning chalk sticks into dust with a sudden mighty whack on the desk in front of him. Several teachers at Banff Academy had a fierce reputation for the level of pain they could inflict on your bare hand while others, mostly female teachers who did not have a strong belting arm nor the inclination to hurt another human being, were never taken seriously. I even felt that certain teachers had an almost sadistic streak regarding the frequency and lame excuse that they needed for using the belt as a means of correction. The boys and girls of my generation were no angels but I had some teachers who would belt you for such cardinal sins as dropping a pencil or getting a question wrong! I even felt the agonising sting of the Rector's leather belt when my friend and I were summoned to his office after he saw us running about harmlessly in the playground on his return from his lunch break. The hideous crime? Stepping on the grass!

I would often sit apathetically at my desk with some kind of book in front of me, doodling away with a ruler or a compass, trying to keep the words of the teacher in focus. But concentration was always difficult when my mind was determined to find its own way into daydreams of the most tender eroticism, for like all young guys of my age, my hormones were out of whack. I craved freedom, absolute irresponsibility, and the right to be going elsewhere in pursuit of a new experience. I always felt I could learn nothing from text books!

Looking back, we were a fascinating concoction of swots, dunces, loners, dreamers, Romeos, braggers, victims, bullies, fibbers, introverts, extroverts and teacher's pets. By the time I was fifteen, I began to stay out longer at nights, spending countless hours loitering around the two fish and chip shops in Portsoy. I was too young to drink in the town's pubs and felt I had no alternative but to wander the streets at night to try and kill the boredom. All my spare money was spent on the pinball machines or topping up the jukeboxes for my favourite music. There was a group of us who did little wrong but who were a bit rudderless in terms of where we could see ourselves going in life.

It was very much at a time when Punk Rock music was coming into prominence in the UK. I never really took to this type of music, although one of my friends became firmly entrenched in its ideology. Punk Rock bands eschewed the perceived excesses of mainstream 1970s rock music. They created fast, hard-edged music; typically with short songs, stripped-down instrumentation, and mainly political, anti-establishment lyrics – often expressing youthful rebellion. They were characterised by their distinctive clothing styles, short cropped hair, and a variety of anti-authoritarian ideologies. I felt a bit miffed that the unwashed, anarchic and spiky punk hairstyle was termed as "Mohican" when I thought it more akin to the 'Huron' tribe, as displayed by the evil Magua!

As a family, we were fortunate to travel all over the British Isles and invariably this meant spending a few days visiting my mother's family in Blyth. This once prosperous town of the early 20th century had been in sharp decline for many years as the core industries, like coal mining, shipbuilding and fishing, had largely vanished. Despite this, I always felt a great buzz of anticipation when I could finally see the four massive chimneys of Blyth power station that signified that we were almost at the end of our arduous six-hour drive. I was fascinated by the stark contrast between the identical red brick Georgian gable-to-gable terraced houses in Blyth and the post World War II semi-detached council houses of Portsoy. The hustle and bustle of the Blyth open-air market was something I had never experienced before. I loved feeling part of the normal daily life as I wandered past the diverse array of stalls – selling anything from clothing to electrical gadgets, and from fruit and vegetables to jewellery – while listening to the jocular daily banter in thick Geordie accents. Coming from a passive, secluded town in the far North-East of Scotland it was a real culture shock to see metal grids on shop windows and graffiti on the walls. Wheels and hubcaps were frequently stolen off parked cars, particularly in the area where my mother's sister, Irene, and her family lived. Mum's younger sister, Eleanor, and her family also lived in Blyth and every other year we stayed with them. Irene and my mother could have passed for twins, if you ever saw them Together – both had fiery red hair, but Irene was smaller and slimmer. Irene's husband, my uncle Tony, was an imposing dark-haired well-built man who reminded me of a gangster from the movies. He didn't say much but what he did say never needed to be repeated. On one occasion, he gave my father a weak cannabis joint to try but after a couple of draws of the "funny fag" my father decided to revert back to his trusted legal nicotine rush.

My cousin, Tony Junior, was only a few months younger than I was but he made me look like a shrinking violet in terms of the trouble he would get into. Already at a young age, Tony was feared amongst his peers. He possessed incredible strength and I sometimes struggled to beat him at arm wrestling, even when I used both of my hands against his weakest hand. He frequently went to the Silver City amusement arcade in Whitley Bay with his best friend, Raymond 'Dinger' Bell, where he would astonish and antagonise Hells Angel bikers and night-club bouncers – ten to fifteen years his senior – by registering higher scores on the boxing machines. While I was always up for a game of football, Tony was more interested in playing around with air-rifles, machetes and knives. While on one of his holidays with us in Portsoy, he was a like a boy possessed when he found out that my dad owned an air-rifle. I can hear him still. 'Uncle Bill ... Uncle Bill! When am I getting a go of your air rifle?' Once, when we visited Blyth, I asked my Auntie Irene where Tony was and she told me he was at the playing field, just a two-minute walk from the house. I went over there, expecting to see him playing football but instead he was throwing a javelin impressive distances across the field. After greeting each other I asked – realising that a light spear was not an item easily purchased in your average sports shop – 'Where did you get that thing?'

In his cool, measured Geordie accent Tony replied, 'I am good at throwing it and I wanted one, so I got one ...'

I was impressed by Tony's tough-guy image and the self-assurance that he portrayed, even at such a young age. Although we were similar in height Tony was more muscular. He had a slick 'Adam Faith' hairstyle, while mine was also shoulder-length but more comparable to comedian Jasper Carrot's coarse-textured mop. We were almost identical in that we both had piercing, deep- sunken eyes, which gave us an unfortunate 'menacing' look. Tony's threatening look was no turn off as far as the opposite sex was concerned, for he always seemed to have a steady girlfriend. I was also drawn to the fact that Tony did his 'own thing' – even though, like myself, that 'own thing' was quite often the wrong thing – and he did not seem to have the need to be part of a gang, choosing instead to hang about with his mates who were all regular mild-mannered lads from the same housing estate. We both seemed to 'live on the edge' as natural born risk-takers, although the repercussions of our individual actions normally had different consequences in terms of severity of punishment. My more harmless edge was often triggered by restlessness, impulsiveness and recklessness, while Tony's sharper edge was led by his boldness, lawlessness and rebelliousness.

The transitional period between decades was always going to be highly charged with an excitement of things to come and of an era coming to an end. The decade of 1970s had its final burst of energy with the emergence of 'New Wave' music, which for me was a more sane and rational alternative to Punk. Simmering beneath the deliberate crudeness, realism and rage of Punk was the sleek, brightly-coloured, cosmetic, futuristic fantasy world of New Wave in which the dress code was tight-fitting suits and skinny ties. It was now time for me to create a new 'cool' look for myself. I jettisoned my platform shoes and bought blacked-up Doctor

Martin boots. My flared trousers were retired in favour of drainpipe jeans and I proudly displayed a metal comb in my back pocket. My hair was drastically shortened, styled with the aid of copious amounts of my dad's 'Brylcreem'. I even had myself stinking of Brut aftershave although I was yet to have my first real shave! Then a band came along that gripped my imagination: The Boomtown Rats. I didn't view them as Punk, or even New Wave, but rather like 'Progressive Rock' and I loved the way they combined melodic flair with intelligent and sometimes very witty lyrics. They may have come across as a brash bunch of ill-natured deviants snarling rock anthems, but I was attracted to lead singer Bob Geldof's magnetic personality – yes, this was the same Bob Geldof who, several years later, was to mobilise the whole pop music industry to the plight of starving children in Ethiopia after watching a harrowing documentary. The song 'Rat Trap', which reached number one in the pop charts, was a bit of a cult song for my mates and myself, for it came at a time of our lives when we could identify with the lyrics, in which our working-class hero of the song claims that he's 'Gonna get out of school, work in some factory to work all the hours God gave him to get himself a little easy money', making it sound glamorous – even something to actually look forward to! My favourite Rats' song was 'Joey's on the street again', telling the story of a loner, a romantic rebel to be idolised by someone like me, but never one you could get close to. Any time something crazy happens he gets the blame, whether he was responsible or not. He marries, has kids, finds a job but still he gets into brushes with the law. The authorities don't let him have any peace as he attempts to walk the straight and narrow. When I look back on it, he seemed like a heroic, romantic character – the classic, archetypal rebel in the James Dean mould. Joey's fate was left up to the listener's imagination – It was up me to decide whether Joey was a rebel to be admired or just another low-life chump, chewed up and spat out by both law-abiding society and the underground world. Maybe he couldn't handle either lifestyle. It was a subtle reminder that Joey's life really served as a warning for me to steer clear of trouble and strife before I was seriously tempted and would end up like him or the 'Billy' character in Geldof's 'Rat Trap', at a fragile time of my life, when my youthful impressionable philosophy could well have been: Where would the glamour be if we didn't live fast and die young? My obsession with The Boomtown Rats was relatively short-lived, lasting only a few months either side of my fifteenth birthday.

I had never really excelled at school and my only ambition was to leave as soon as possible to start making some money straight away. Football was still very much central to all that was happening in my life, but I was totally taken by surprise one day in my Navigation class: 'I don't like that sort of thing. It has nothing to do with football,' declared Mr Allan, my teacher, in a very authoritarian way, as he pointed to the two metal badges that I had clipped on to my school jersey.

I was taken aback. They were only a couple of harmless badges, and this was Banff, so what was the problem? Mr Allan was, of course, correct. They had nothing to do with football. But it was to be many years later before I fully understood why he had reacted that way. What I had purchased the night before at a Rangers v Juventus European Cup game in Glasgow as a £1.20 innocent-looking keepsake had hit a raw nerve with this teacher, who had been brought up in the atmosphere of sectarian rivalry that existed between Catholics and Protestants in the west coast of Scotland. I had taken a day off school to go to my first big European match with my mother's cousin, Sandy, and a couple of his friends. I was amongst 80 000 supporters who watched Rangers pull off a monumental 2-0 victory against the champions of Italy. "No Surrender 1690" and "Billy Boys" were the two badges that caught my eye as I made my way to the match. Even at the age of 15 I knew that I was a 'Proddie', although I scarcely thought about or believed in God.

At a time when I was in my last year at school and easily influenced by anything anti-authoritarian, I identified strongly with the biggest chart hit of 1979, Pink Floyd's 'Another brick in the wall', which was a direct frontal attack on the education system. Typically, and playing right into the hands of someone who never enjoyed secondary school, this anti-establishment hit had massed choirs of kids hauntingly singing, 'We don't need no education, we don't need no thought control.' It was a protest song for me and many of my generation but, on reflection, a slightly unfair generalisation of the school system of that time, which also included many decent, competent, hard working teachers. School seemed to be only about academic intelligence and kids who were intellectually bright were encouraged to aim for university, but there was little emphasis on developing the social and emotional skills that would be just as important in later life for us all – whether we were academically gifted or not. There is a popular well-worn saying, 'Your school days are the best years of your life' but where that came from I will never know, although it would be fair to say that the education system never failed me. It was more that I never gave it my best shot.

At that stage of my life I had absolutely no interest in religion or in going to Church. All my friends came from secular backgrounds and I actually did not know anyone who attended Church. Also, if any of our circle had been seen going to Church they would have felt the brunt of endless ridicule and sarcasm – and I would have been very much at the forefront of giving it out. For me and my peer group, anyone who professed to be a Christian was automatically declaring themselves to be a soft, saccharine Mummy's boy. I feel that school tended to confuse the issue regarding God and whether or not He existed, for on one hand we would pray the Lord's Prayer during the morning assembly, and on the other hand we would be studying Biology books, charting Darwin's evolutionary beliefs, where there were pictures showing the process of apes evolving into man. Were they promoting a new 'sit on the fence' theology called 'Evolation', I Wonder!

My parents had always impressed upon us the value of having a good work ethic and as soon as I was old enough I went out to seek seasonal employment, like picking raspberries during the summer and picking potatoes, in our "tattie holidays", in the month of October.

The raspberry picking was relatively easy as you could do most of your work standing up. I never made much money at the rasps, for by the time I had eaten as many of them as I possibly could, I was too full up to do much work!

Conversely, the hard graft of being crouched forward for long periods as we picked up loose "tatties" was not something that I ever enjoyed.

It was a real test of human endurance. We worked in pairs and it was the muckiest job imaginable. What really motivated me to keep going was the comparatively decent money that the farmer was willing to pay – as much as £7 a day – and the thought of a nice hot bath when I got home. Sometimes the only respite we got was when a large stone was caught in the farmer's digger causing it to break down.

Needless to say, we never cleared any big stones from our stance when the tractor was approaching us!

I had no real sense of ambition when I prepared to leave school at sixteen. I had taken Navigation and Nautical Studies as I felt I was destined to go to sea. The fishing industry was thriving and lucrative in the '70s and early '80s and most of the boys from Macduff and Gardenstown were leaving to take up berths with their fathers or other family members.

By the time I left school I had taken my father's advice and decided to take up a trade. After a few failed attempts to find an apprenticeship as a plumber or a joiner I was offered a job with a local painter and decorator. I remember the excitement of running the short distance to my house with my first pay packet. The amount was printed on the front of the small brown envelope: £20.66. I would give £5 to my mother, as agreed with her, for my digs. (My father believed I was giving her a £10 note but we thought that what he didn't know wouldn't bother him).

I was only sixteen but I had no problem getting served in most of the pubs, so I was off to Banff the following evening and headed for the Marquee. These massive tents were popular round about that period; dances were held there, with local live bands often playing, and they were notorious for lawlessness, flirtatious displays of sexuality, drunkenness, and mass brawling – but perhaps that was part of their seductive and glamorous appeal!

That first night, however, I didn't even make it to the Marquee. Instead, I was taken home by the police after they picked me up, lying on the street, paralytic with drink. Apparently, full of reckless bravado, I had accepted the challenge to drink a half bottle of vodka in twenty minutes.

I was charged with the bizarrely named offence 'Drunk and Incapable' and was fined £5. I promised my parents that I would behave myself and cut out the binge drinking, which I did – for a week or two.

Having a job meant that I had some money to spend but it soon burnt a hole in my pocket. My mates and I were always conniving methods to get to Rangers matches – so desperate were we to follow our beloved team.

On one occasion Gary and I even ended up travelling down to Glasgow in a Celtic supporters' bus from nearby Buckie, and I vaguely remember concealing my true loyalty by stuffing my Rangers scarf inside my jacket.

It was a midweek game and, just to make things a bit more disadvantageous, we bought tickets for the Celtic end of the ground. Naturally, we kept a low profile, as we were the only Rangers supporters on the bus. Although we did not know anyone else, we did not feel any sense of hostility or danger as the bus drove us down the A9 to Glasgow.

Rangers won the game 1-0 and we were content to sit quietly, maintaining our low profile, on the return journey.

The disappointed Celtic supporters soon went through their repertoire of Irish rebel songs. Perhaps the fact that we did not join in was a give-away – and this was emphasised in a revolting manner as I started receiving a large amount of spit on the back of my head from the man sitting directly behind me. Gary, sitting on the seat next to me, began receiving the same disgusting treatment at regular intervals. So scared were we, that we just endured this for the remainder of the journey. It came as a massive relief when we were picked up by our taxi in Buckie for the trip back to Portsoy.

This was our harsh introduction to the world of religious hatred and sectarianism.

At the age of seventeen, it would have been fair to say that I was hardly a leading fashion icon. With ginger shoulder-length hair, permed at the back, an earring, and dressed resplendently in a bleached denim jacket with the sleeves ripped off, I cut a fearless sight – or so I thought at the time. There I was, proudly showing off my Rangers badges on the front of my jacket and heavy rock badges on the back; reflecting the two great passions in my life.

I regularly travelled the 400 mile round trip to Glasgow with a group of friends to watch my team. Rangers were a struggling club in the early 1980s when Aberdeen and Dundee United came to the fore in Scottish and European football. Crowds had dwindled down to around 15 000 or less for most matches, and the vast open spaces of Ibrox stadium would often create an eerie, ghost-like atmosphere as the team failed to lift itself above the level of mediocrity.

We usually drove to matches by car but occasionally we went in an organised bus, always making sure we had our supply of alcohol, or "cairy-oot", that we smuggled on board for the long journey ahead. It was easy to conceal vodka by pouring it into a Coca Cola bottle before we boarded the bus.

Pitch invasions became fairly commonplace at Rangers matches in the late 1970s and Gary and I had attended matches where such invasions had taken place, most notably at Ayr and Aberdeen. However, everything that we had previously witnessed seemed tame compared with the events that unfolded at the end of the Scottish cup final between Rangers and Celtic in 1980.

Games between these two biggest clubs in Scotland were characterised by sectarian singing from both sets of fans, which occasionally spilled over into off-field violence.

After watching our team being defeated 1-0, I returned, disappointed, to the bus. The game itself had been relatively trouble-free, played in a good sporting spirit and with no real serious disputes. When we switched on the radio, however, we were shocked to hear of a Rangers' 'charge up the park'.

The game was over ...

What could the commentator mean?

We heard rumblings about some sort of 'invasion', but it wasn't until we arrived back home and saw the images from Hampden being beamed across national television that we realised the full extent of what we had narrowly missed.

I watched in amazement at the ridiculous sight of hundreds of long-haired, alcohol-fuelled youths, wearing tank tops, flares, platform shoes, and with scarves tied round their wrists, re-enacting their own mini version of the 'Battle of the Boyne' on the Hampden pitch. In place of King William of Orange on a white horse there was the incredible sight of several policemen on horseback, batons in hand, charging through the mayhem while glass bottles and every conceivable missile imaginable were being hurled through the hate-filled air with righteous venom.

When the dust had settled there were no fewer than 210 arrests.

I wondered what would have happened if I hadn't had to catch my bus and therefore had stayed longer. Would I have ended up on the pitch? As I preferred to keep well away from any physical confrontation, I would like to think that I wouldn't have joined the invasion. Yet, I can't deny that it would also have been easy for me to have become caught up in the hatred, camaraderie, fanaticism, and that tribal sense of belonging.

I never really understood what Catholics believed or what Protestants held fast to. I didn't know the historical background, for I hadn't been brought up in a segregated school system. I didn't actually hate any Catholics – save for a couple of hours on a Saturday – but It seemed acceptable to transform myself into a foul-mouthed bigot to fit in with the masses, secure in the knowledge that I could just jump into a car or on a bus and four hours later I would be back to my peaceful, unruffled surroundings in the North-East of Scotland.

Around this time there had been a TV documentary highlighting Rangers' policy of signing only Protestant players, which was heavily criticised for being sectarian. This was also at a time when the often volatile situation in the west of Scotland was even further cranked up with IRA hunger strikes in Northern Ireland.

While touring Ireland on a camping holiday in the early 1970s, my parents had innocently purchased an LP record called 'Irish Rebel Songs', which they would have viewed as being Irish folk music. The record was played constantly in our old wooden radiogram, especially when my father came home from the pub. Over the years, I got to know the words of songs like 'The Merry Ploughboy' and 'Kevin Barry', but I was never aware that these were seen as pro-IRA ballads. It was therefore a bit ironic that in the volatile atmosphere of an 'Old Firm' game many of the songs the Celtic fans were singing were more familiar to me than those of my own supporters.

By this time, I was no longer interested in going on holidays with my folks, who usually went to the continent with their good friends, Bill and Brenda Dawson. They had purchased a trailer tent and would travel round Germany, Belgium and Holland. Keith was still going with them and he was allowed to take a friend with him for company,

Sidestepping parental guidance, which I viewed as a hindrance, I chose to spend all of my time in the company of my mates, and a trip to Bavaria in Germany, organised by the youth club of a neighbouring town, was my first experience of a foreign holiday. After an arduous two-day bus journey, and an alcohol-fuelled ferry trip sandwiched in the middle to break the monotony, we ended up at our destination: Teuschnitz, a small town in Bavaria, approximately 70km from Nuremberg.

Gary and some other friends were there with me and we had a great time because all the young German men were away on National Service leaving us with what seemed like the pick of the young Fräuleins.

This was my idea of Utopia!

Most of the girls could speak excellent English, so there was no language barrier. The only down side of the trip was having to live on what appeared to be their staple diet, of either noodle soup or cold meat and cheese, for the whole fortnight.

Although we went on organised trips during the day, the real highlight for me was having the freedom to go to the local pubs in the evenings, and I took a real liking for peach schnapps, which came in a small glass and, as was the German custom, had to be knocked back in one.

Gary had managed to pull a girl who was a dead-ringer for the singer Kim Wilde – at that time a familiar face in the British pop scene. I must admit, I was a bit envious of him but to my utter amazement her cousin Carmen asked me out.

Wow!

Carmen was always in our company but was so attractive that I dared not waste my time asking her out. She was dark, slim, and carried such an aura of self-assurance that I had convinced myself she was altogether inaccessible.

Being teetotal, she had unfortunately seen me drunk several times, and had also been present the previous evening when I'd had one peach schnapps too many and ended up vomiting over the table we were all sitting at. This embarrassing spectacle made it all the more implausible that I interested her in the slightest. Carmen was a year older than I, drove a silver Mercedes and worked as a foreign correspondent.

I was in dreamland. But the holiday was almost over.

We would meet up and talk for ages in her car.

'You seem a bit nervous Colin,' she remarked in a genuinely concerned kind of way. 'Are you afraid to kiss me?'

'Erm ... n ... n ... no. I just like you so much that I don't want to do anything silly,' I replied awkwardly.

We decided to keep in touch, and we did for a few months. I could hardly get her out of my mind. Ironically, writing wasn't really my thing, so I failed to keep up the correspondence.

Gary and I returned the following year with a new mix of people. Predictably, Carmen came to the forefront of my mind again. I prayed that she was single and still interested in me.

On our first night in Teuschnitz, we entered the pub we used to frequent with renewed excitement and anticipation. However, something had changed that was not supposed to be part of the script ... There were loads of young German males mingling with the females. Then it dawned on us: They had come back from doing their National Service.

I soon felt deflated and broken-hearted when Carmen introduced me to her boyfriend.

'Why did you stop writing to me, Colin?' she asked.

Although far removed from the tragic drama of Bizet's opera, I had been well and truly jilted by the beautiful Carmen.

THE GREAT VAN ROBBERY

As part of my Painting & Decorating apprenticeship I had to attend college block release in Aberdeen, training for my City & Guilds certificate, so I used to stay in digs in the Northfield area of Aberdeen for several weeks at a stretch. This was my first time away from my parents' house for any length of time and it opened up a whole new world to me.

I remember the first day my father drove me to Aberdeen in the car. I was apprehensive and although it was only 55 miles away from my home-town of Portsoy, it was so different. It filled me with excitement and trepidation. I saw the huge skyscrapers, the massive roundabouts and busy roads. People were milling around on the streets, and I did not know any of them!

This seemed a million miles from Portsoy with its population of only 1800. At home I knew almost everybody – many by name and all by sight. And everyone else knew me, where I lived, and who my parents and brother were. Nevertheless, I felt comfortable almost immediately in my new lodgings where my landlady and her husband made me feel very welcome.

Out-with college hours I seldom ventured out in the evenings, choosing instead to save the little money I had to go to Pittodrie stadium to watch Aberdeen play. As I loved football in general, I was never overly concerned who they were playing against but I did make a special effort to see the famous George Best perform when he was playing for Hibernian.

My other great passion was hard rock music and I found that I was able to hear some great bands play at the Capitol, in the centre of the city. My favourite was Black Sabbath. I became obsessively drawn to their image and their song lyrics. Sabbath perpetuated an image of escapism and disorder to me. Their vicious sound of heavy rock with its enervating, lamenting vocal solos both shocked and excited me.

They all had dark shoulder-length hair, wore huge crosses, and dressed completely in black, their faded t-shirts bearing a violent cartoon-type graphic on the front. They usually had a scowl on their faces - or at least a look designed to keep old ladies and conservative Church leaders at arm's length - and possessed an attitude that could only be described as very rebellious.

I listened to their LPs for hours on end and my favourite track was 'Under the Sun'. This track had their trademark doom and gloom message, albeit in a less oppressive way than usual, as it chugged along at a steady pace and occasionally broke into an amped-up acceleration which made my heart pump a bit faster.

I never saw 'Under the Sun' as a blatant attack on God, but rather as an attack on religious hypocrites who kept inferring the band were evil and demonic and going to Hell. Hence the line in the song where lead singer Ozzy Osbourne declares they want no 'Jesus freaks' telling them what it's all about. And in another verse they are just as adamant that they don't want a preacher telling them about the God in the sky or where they are going when they die.

Their stance, like mine, was probably borne of frustration and rebellion against what I considered the self-righteous element of society, ready to judge others.

In truth, I was often blind to the fact that I myself could be judgemental when it suited me!

At college I would literally starve myself at lunchtime so that I could scrape enough cash together to purchase a vinyl record from 'One Up', an independent music store at Rosemount, a brisk ten minute walk from the college, which had a stash of second-hand LPs and cassette tapes, as well as posters and signed memorabilia. 'One Up' was designed for music-enthusiasts but not music aristocrats, which was just as well because I certainly had a poor self-image.

I could pick up records for as little as 50p. So what, if they were a bit scratched? After all, I was a young baby-boomer, regarding myself as a die-hard music lover, and I just lapped up the crackling sounds that came from my bog-standard record-player, even if now and then I had the inconvenience of picking off the fluff that had gathered on the needle as it rolled along the grooves of the worn vinyl.

My first real post-Carmen crush was on the girl who lived in the house next door to my digs in Northfield, and she was also very much the girl-next-door type. She would often be on the same bus when I was on my way back from college.

Although she was my age, she appeared a lot more confident and was quite at ease with people. I felt so in awe of her presence that I was afraid to talk much to her in case my stammer would become apparent, as it usually did when I was worried or excited.

I remember her telling me about having been to the cinema to watch *Kramer v Kramer*, starring Dustin Hoffman, and that I should have been there too because it was a great film. I hadn't had a girlfriend before and really wanted to ask her out but I could never pluck up the courage. I reasoned that as long as I didn't ask her out I would avoid the potential rejection and still retain the fuzzy feeling of anticipation, even though I was mentally torturing myself in the process.

And I was always struggling for money in those days; most of my wages went on paying for my digs. I went home every weekend and used to save the last fifty pence of my wages to take a bus from the centre of Aberdeen the three and a half miles to Dyce, from where I thumbed a lift the remaining fifty miles home.

Sometimes I would land lucky and get a lift almost all the way to Portsoy, but on other occasions it would take me as long as four hours and half a dozen lifts to reach home.

I enjoyed the diversity of skills that we were learning at Aberdeen Technical College, such as sign-writing, rag-rolling, and creating marble effects, which were techniques that we didn't experience in a day-to-day job situation.

In my small class of thirteen boys I was in the majority for once: I was one of five Colins! Within a short while I became good mates with one of the other Colins, who came from a similar rural background as I did and lived in the small coastal town of Rosehearty.

One day, Colin and I had a bizarre experience, which ended up with dire consequences for both of us. As we were returning from our lunch hour, we saw a delivery van pulling away from a large electrical store near the college. Suddenly, a big brown box, marked 'Stereo system' fell out of the lorry's open back door, landing in front of us in the middle of George Street. We shouted to the driver, who was now speeding away unaware of what had happened. Being decent and fairly honest guys, we thought we would do a 'Good Samaritan' turn and took the box back round the corner to the electrical store, only to find it had closed for lunch. As we had to be back at College and didn't want to leave the box in the street, we trailed it up the stairs to our fourth floor classroom. We told our teacher what had happened and he suggested that we return it during our afternoon break. Once again we found the shop closed, so we took the box back up the four flights of stairs, and by this time our classmates were displaying an interest in it.

I have always been a bit naïve and easily led. Two boys from Aberdeen, who seemed a lot more streetwise and self-assured than we were, suggested that we would be able to 'make a few quid from selling it', with very little risk. It was Friday and they said it would be easy to 'move it on' over the weekend.

I turned the matter over in my conscience. My distorted reasoning said that as we'd twice unsuccessfully attempted to return the stereo, the shop probably didn't want it back. So we agreed to sell it and split the proceeds. The boys from Aberdeen left with the box and I returned to Portsoy, where I didn't give it a great deal of thought over the weekend.

Monday morning just seemed like any other start of the week. However, my heart started beating rapidly and my mind working overtime when I spotted a police car sitting outside the college entrance. Two stern-looking policemen met me at the top of the stairs, and before I knew it four of us were being whisked away to the police station in the squad car. I was so nervous that I chattered away incessantly, as if I had just taken a verbal laxative.

In no time at all, we were arrested, fingerprinted and photographed.

Colin and I were given the rather remarkable charge of 'Theft by Finding'– this now added to my existing police record of 'Drunk and Incapable'. (It seemed entirely possible that I was well on the way to collecting the most unusual list of police charges in history!) The boys from Aberdeen received a more serious charge, which felt fair to us.

I was in the depths of despair.

I could handle the charge and the fine but I couldn't handle the shame that this would cause to my parents. My mum, especially, had always drummed into my head, from an early age, 'Colin, your character's all you've got.' Those words, and the charge of 'Theft by Finding' kept going round and round in my head. The word theft meant I was a thief and therefore of poor character.

I particularly feared what my father would say when he found out. My parents had been able to live with my earlier misdemeanours but this charge questioned my honesty and integrity, so that made it much more serious than any other situation I had got myself into.

The next four days seemed interminable. After college I found myself aimlessly walking the streets of Aberdeen trying to come to terms with what I'd done and its implications. I had always been a worrier but now I felt at my lowest ebb.

I began to contemplate a plethora of colossal and irrational scenarios in my mind as I started to blow the incident out of all reasonable sense of proportion.

Would I lose my job? Would my name be all over the newspapers?

Could I ever be trusted with anything again?

Friday night eventually arrived and it was time to face the music. I decided to just go straight into the house and blurt the whole thing out to my parents to quickly get it over and done with. I threw open the back door, raced through the kitchen into the living room and flung my bag down on the settee, before launching straight into the story, without giving my parents any chance to say a word. Panicking, out of breath, and with my arms waving frantically I kept repeating, 'I tried to put it back. I tried to put it back. I tried twice to put it back ... Honest!'

My mother and father were sitting on either side of the fire. It was like a game of ping-pong as I looked desperately from one to the other to see who was having the worse reaction. Finally my mother exclaimed, 'Oh Colin ... What now?'

I turned to my father, expecting something much worse, but he just smiled and told my mother, 'But, Margaret, calm down. He's telling the truth; he tried to put it back. He's just been very unlucky. He's always been easily led.' He then defused the situation by joking: 'Why didn't you just bring the damn thing back to Portsoy?'

My mother retorted, 'What're you laughing at? It's not funny, Bill.'

Once everything had calmed down again I felt a massive sense of relief at the way my parents, especially my father, had accepted my mistake.

Colin and I received a much appreciated, if somewhat unexpected level of support when Mr Gordon, Head of the Painting and Decorating Department, wrote a letter to the Procurator Fiscal suggesting that the crime was out of character for us and that we had been influenced by others. We were penalised with a £50 fine for our part in 'The Great Van Robbery' and thankfully the misadventure did not make the print media or the local Grampian news.

However, the incident would cast doubt on my honesty with another situation that arose a few months later.
A decorating tool had gone missing from our College class and our teacher was in no mood to let it go: 'We are not leaving college today until someone owns up. The police will be involved if need be.'
This was met with a tense silence.

He continued, 'Someone here knows where it is and I am not letting it go.'

Still no one came forward.

Then came his last throw of the dice: 'Well, in an incident like this the finger of suspicion will always be pointed at people who have been involved in this type of thing before.'

I was stunned! Livid! My heart sank. I could barely believe what he had implied.

Des, who was a good friend and ally, came up to me and could see I was shaken by what had been said. 'I thought he was bang out of order. We all know what happened with the stereo incident. I would do something about it if I were you.'

That was all the reassurance I needed to go up to my teacher when he was standing by himself, working at the window, and with my customary unsubtle approach I told him, 'I couldn't believe what you said just now. You were imply ... '

Before I could complete my sentence, he lifted his eyes from what he was doing and said with a softness and calmness, 'Colin, I know it had nothing to do with you. I know exactly who it was, but I have no proof.'

LIVING FOR THE WEEKEND – DEBTS, DAMES AND DRUNKENNESS

My life soon settled into a familiar pattern, with football, promiscuity and heavy weekend drinking the focus in my increasingly chaotic life. This was the time when dances in the local Town Halls were being replaced by the exciting new world of Discos and late drinking licences.

Our "Local" in these days was the Park Hotel, a curiously shaped and vividly white building very much typical of the architecture of the 1960s. It was there that I became familiar with heavy gambling in the shape of 'card schools' in the lounge area of the hotel.

The fishing industry was at its peak in the early eighties and a take-home pay of £300-£400 per trip a substantial sum of money back then, was common for many of the crew of the seine-net boats. These men often frequented the pubs where we drank. Even younger fishermen who were on half share and quarter share would often be earning up to five times more than my take-home pay from my job as a second year apprentice.

Games would start with low stakes but within a short time 'fivers' and 'tenners' would be thrown into the empty ashtray holding the money, which accumulated into amounts ranging from £20 to £200. For the more conservative and cautious, who played with a limited budget, a small win or a small loss was allowed for, but for a teenage maverick like me, it had to be either excessive loss or extraordinary gain.

The excitement, uncertainty, and the buzz of winning played right into the hands of my impulsive and reckless nature and I could lose or gain in almost equal measure over a relatively short space of time. Most of all, I loved the way gambling shut off my thoughts and numbed my feelings to anything in the outside world.

I was seduced into the habit by something which most gamblers experience – beginners' luck. On the first occasion when I played 'three card brag' I almost doubled my take-home pay of £35 in an hour and a half. It didn't take me long to figure out that this was an easier and more exciting way of gaining money than working forty hours a week doing a mundane painting job.

Predictably, my luck changed and I began to lose, leading me to borrow money from my close friends. In what seemed no time at all I had accumulated debts of almost £150.

It became very easy for me to lose control of my money when gambling excessively. As the money started running out it became very tempting to gamble even more money in the hope of a big win in order to clear my debts. More often than not it led to even more debts and more desperate gambling.

After a few months, a point had been reached where there seemed to be no way back and, in all honesty, I became afraid to face up to my debts, so I just continued to gamble.

However, things came to a head one Friday night on my way home from work.

Without even going home to get changed, I went directly to the Boyne Hotel where a card school was in full flow in the lounge bar. So desperate was I to claw back some of my debt that I opened my pay-packet and joined in.

True to recent form, I continued my losing streak and gambled away my week's wages in little more than half an hour. Dejected, and in a state of helplessness, I picked up my piece bag and made my way home with nothing but a few coins in loose change in my pocket.

Feeling a great deal of anger and frustration at my self-inflicted predicament, I crossed the town square, stopping only to carry out the senseless and inexplicable act of punching a hole in one of the Salvation Army Hall windows.

I was now facing a dilemma. How would I explain to my mother, at no later than 6 o'clock on a Friday night, where my week's pay had gone? Never one to be secretive or esoteric about anything troubling me, but also being acutely aware of the distress it would cause my mother, I decided I would tell her half the story – that I had lost all my pay in a one-off gambling session – adding the white lie of a fall on my way up the road to 'explain' how I had cut my hand.

To my surprise, she was remarkably calm and assured as she gave me some tried and trusted words of wisdom regarding my character and how I was old enough to be accountable for my silly and often selfish actions. My father was coming home soon and I knew that if he ever found out about what I had done, his way of handling would have been in direct contrast to my mother's.

When I had reassurances that she wouldn't tell my father, I crept pathetically through to my bedroom to ponder the gravity of the situation I had got myself into.

Lying on top of my bed with the light on, staring aimlessly at the ceiling and considering my seemingly helpless predicament, I heard the door open quietly as my mother entered the room. In a low measured manner she shoved a £20 note into my hand and said gently, 'Colin, if you promise me that you will stop gambling I will write off this week's digs money as well.'

Tears welled up in my eyes as I replied with a lump in my throat, 'Okay, Mum, I won't gamble again.'

I had caused my mother grief and I felt it was time to show that I could keep my word.

The following day came and it was back to the Boyne Hotel to meet up with my mates to plan the night ahead. Walking down Cullen Street from my house meant that I had to pass the Salvation Army Hall in the corner of the Square. It was ironic that the Salvation Army officer was out measuring up the broken window for a new pane of glass. Shamefaced, I just carried on walking past.

A thought flashed through my mind, 'Will I tell him it was me?' But cowardice won in the end, as I convinced myself that owning up would just make the situation worse.

In the months that followed, I cleared my debts. A tough lesson was learned thanks to the grace and understanding shown by a loving mother.

I never did play cards for money again and have never had the inclination to do so either.

My gambling career may have come to an abrupt end but my drinking and womanising were beginning to flourish ... My alarm clock went off – it kept perfect time on Sunday mornings. It was the sound of the church bells ringing at 10.30 a.m. telling me it was time to get up, get changed, and get to the pub for 11 a.m. My house was located a short distance from the Kirk, and even with the front door closed I could still hear the chimes in my back bedroom.

During my late teens and early twenties, Sunday mornings always followed a familiar pattern. After a late Saturday night the predictable hangover followed. While I was attempting to piece together the events of the previous night, my father was playing that same old corny audio tape: Rod Stewart's 'Sailing', 'Cider Drinker' by the Wurzels, and Pussycat singing the seventies ballad, 'Mississippi', were blasting out of the music centre, bidding me to join the land of the living. 'When will he ever put on something different?' I used to moan to myself as I lay in my bed with a thumping headache.

I would open my eyes and give a sigh of relief as I slowly scanned our blue, red and white bedroom walls with all the posters and paraphernalia of Rangers Football Club that adorned them. Relief, in the sense that I had made it back home safely despite the fact that more often than not I could barely recall coming home.

I remember waking up one morning and thinking how grotesquely out of place a poster of a loyalist paramilitary group was, in their full combat gear, complete with balaclavas and rifles. It had pride of place in the middle of the team groups, match programmes and pennants. These posters, along with other 'Loyalist' merchandise, such as cassette tapes, badges, and banners, were purchased by Keith and myself outside the various football grounds where we had been to see Rangers play.

The smell of fried bacon would waft through from the kitchen.

Sunday was a special day, even for this non-religious family, so a cooked breakfast was on the menu – and tradition decreed that my father did the cooking for my mother, who was having a well-deserved long lie.

I took the short-cut to the Park Hotel, down the Doctor's lane. Sometimes, if I was early, I met people going to the Church. What a sentence – having to sit on rock-hard pews for an hour and a half singing boring old hymns. I could listen for hours to hard rock bands like Black Sabbath and Deep Purple, sprawled out in a chair in the comfort of my own house. To me that was real music!

The women going to Church were immaculately dressed. They wore colourful and stylish hats and seemed to live in a different world from me. To me, their realm was boring, predictable and bland, and although mine was far from perfect no one could ever call it dull.

I loosely believed in God, but I could do that without having to go to Church.

That was my typical Sunday morning for many years throughout my late teens and twenties. There was absolutely nothing to attract me to Church during these years. I perceived it to be a middle class institution, and thought of most churchgoers as being self-righteous and social climbers.

When I did have to face the ordeal of Church it was usually to attend a marriage service. Weddings frequently took place on a Saturday afternoon. Sitting, as always, near the rear of the Church, I would do anything rather than concentrate on the minister's word for the newly-weds. Suffering from impatience and irritability I mumbled my way through the tedium of old hymns and drawn-out prayers.

My mind wandered; my main thoughts being the Rangers football match and what the score was. I also pondered the drinking session I would take part in at the evening reception. To pass the time, I once counted all the bald heads in the Church and when that was done I calculated all the different colours on the stained glass windows.

In spite of my feelings of apathy and disdain towards the

Church, one issue always preyed on my mind – death! I knew it wasn't final. It was hard to explain but I had never feared the physical pain of dying, though I did fear the consequences.

I would often see posters outside meeting halls and places of worship proclaiming things like 'Jesus Saves', and 'Jesus is Lord', as I went past in the service bus, yet not at any time did I wonder what it all meant. Heaven to me was a place you went to if you had done more good than bad in your life.

I considered that I was a borderline case.

I had this imaginary scale of one to ten in my head. One was for pure evil and that may have been someone like Adolf Hitler, and ten was for the epitome of goodness, which may have been Mother Teresa. On a scale like that I should sneak in at possibly five or six and, besides, I had enough time in the rest of my life for more good deeds to ensure my place in Heaven.

The existence of God was never really at the forefront of my mind but, as I was quite regularly in a crisis due to my reckless weekend behaviour, I would often find myself lying in my bed praying to Him to get me out of whatever predicament I had got myself into. Despite these existential conundrums life rolled on.

Work-wise, I had just completed a three-year apprenticeship and I was kept on by my employer for another six months until, due to lack of work at a difficult time of year, I was paid off. Fortunately, my father was in charge of a new housing development in Insch, near Aberdeen, and was able to take me on as a general labourer. I found it exciting to be doing something entirely different and enjoyed the experience, although it did mean a longer working day with more travelling involved.

It also gave me a greater respect for my father.

Working with him at close quarters gave me an appreciation of the job he did and the pressure he was often under. He would have a completion date to adhere to, and he was responsible for the wellbeing of approximately twenty men. I saw my father as quiet and almost introverted but, in his own way, I felt he was well liked and respected among the squad of men of which he was in charge.

However, that was never going to become a long-term career

for me because the company, an Edinburgh-based firm, went into liquidation a few months later. So, following a chance meeting in Aberdeen with a former college friend, it was time to return to my trade.

This friend had recently started working offshore and prompted me to apply for the job he had vacated with a Dyce-based company called Aberdec. I was successful in my application and was taken on – initially on a six-week trial – and I moved into digs with two lads I knew from Portsoy, who rented an attic flat in Beechgrove Avenue.

I settled reasonably well into my new job and the other painters made me feel welcome. The trial period wasn't mentioned by my boss as I entered my seventh week so I assumed he was pleased with my work. I was never too concerned about finding or holding on to employment for I knew I was a conscientious and diligent worker.

The job was not a particularly high earner even though this was the beginning of the oil boom in Aberdeen. My wages were certainly not a reflection of the city's newly found affluence; my take-home pay was a modest basic wage of £73 – a drop of more than £35 from what I had been earning as a labourer. This did not cause me a great deal of concern. I was just relieved to return to my trade in a settled job.

My workmates liked a drink and I never needed much persuasion to go along with them. It was quite usual, when working near the city centre, to have two or three pints of beer at lunchtime, topped up with a couple more after our day's work – especially if we were working late. More than once I went on a pub-crawl on a Friday night with one of my workmates without even bothering to go home and change out of my working clothes.

Money may have been tight after I had paid for my digs but I always made sure I had enough for my Friday and Saturday nights out.

Whenever I returned to Portsoy for the weekend I played football for the Park Hotel in the pub league. The games were played on a Sunday morning and after Saturday night my team-mates and I were never in pristine physical condition when we kicked off at 10.30 am. It was not uncommon to see one of them vomiting at the side of the pitch during the match.

When we played away from home we were always invited by the home team for soup and sandwiches at the pub they represented. Quite often we ended up having a drinking session, which carried on in to the early evening.

I was just existing through the week and living for the weekend, whether that meant city nightclubs or pubs back home, as I searched for that elusive young lady who was going to change my life forever.

Initially I went home most weekends but if I was working on a Saturday morning I stayed in Aberdeen. I would always describe myself as a 'home bird' and although I didn't dislike living in Aberdeen I never felt as relaxed and comfortable as I did back home where I had my friends and family around me.

My only friends in Aberdeen were my workmates. Most of them were married so I often went out by myself at weekends. Alcohol made me less inhibited, somewhat rash and, on reflection, generally foolish – although I convinced myself I was always more compos mentis than some of the social group I hung about with.

Despite my indifference towards anything religious I developed a soft spot for the Salvation Army, or the "Sally Annie" as we affectionately called them – perhaps not least because of my conscience regarding an outstanding glazing bill. When they came round the pubs on a Saturday night I made sure I gave them a good donation. Sometimes, when I had really overdone the drinking, I woke up the next morning to find a copy of their venerable paper the *The War Cry* stuffed in my jacket pocket. I liked Mr Wullie Morrison, the Salvation Army officer based in Portsoy at the time, and I respected the fact that he would always take time to stop and talk to me and my mates as were making our way home for our tea after our customary Saturday afternoon drinking session.

Becoming more sophisticated in my food preferences, I progressed from the Vesta Curries in a box, which had been the height of exoticism in the 1970s, to the 'Authentic Real Deal' as Indian restaurants and Take Aways seemed to spring up all over the UK.

I had my first ever "Indian experience" when visiting my family in Blyth, and I fondly recall being instantly drawn to the rich, woody blend of raw spiced aromas that wafted down the street after I breezed out of a town-centre pub during a night out with my cousin David. I had always been a bit suspicious of cooked food from the Asian continent, but then again, I was quite tipsy and in a ravenous mood where anything spicy with lumps of meat would have tasted delectable.

I can safely say that a serious chilli-addiction was birthed that evening as I slobbered greedily over my foil tray, demonically devouring my lamb biryani with a plastic fork.

It was while living in Beechgrove Avenue that I had 'a brush with religion' in the shape of a downstairs lodger who sometimes cornered me to talk about God. This young man, just a few years older than I was, had apparently been "saved" after his life had sunk to rock bottom, due to his involvement with drugs while at university, and was eager to share 'The Good News'.

I sometimes heard hymns being played in his room as I made my way upstairs to our flat but I always made a mad dash whenever I went past his room in case he came out and cornered me on the stairway. Occasionally, when he knew I was in the flat by myself, he came up and made an excuse to see me; usually asking to use our fridge. Standing menacingly at the living-room door he would start asking me searching questions about God, which made me feel most uncomfortable. I was never relaxed with him and actually felt intimidated, although that was probably more to do with my imagination than a true reflection of his character – in fact, I found most religious folk a bit creepy.

After a few minutes, and a few curt one-word answers from me, what felt like a cross-examination was over, and I felt relieved when he left after giving me a couple of tracts. This boring, repetitive, religious propaganda would always receive a swift derogatory glance before being tossed into the nearest bin.

After 18 months in Beechgrove the landlady decided to sell the house, which meant I had to find alternative digs. Fortunately, another two older lads I knew from Portsoy invited me to share their flat in Torry. This was a great move for me because Torry, almost out-with Aberdeen, was like a town in itself, with a better community spirit, and I felt more at home there.

One evening I went along with one of my flatmates to a pub called 'The 19th Hole'. There was a Country and Western band playing and the pub was jam-packed with people. We managed to get ourselves a drink before noticing a couple of seats next to some girls in the far corner of the bar.

I spotted that one of the girls was wearing a watch and I leaned over the table to ask her the time. Quick as a flash she stuck out her arm and showed me the face of her watch, which had no hands. She was only wearing it for show! This appealed to my cruel sense of humour so much that I ended up creased in fits of laughter, much to the annoyance of her friends, who were sitting next to her but did not see the funny side of things.

I lived quite happily in Torry for several months before leaving Aberdec to work with another Aberdeen-based company who were advertising for painters and decorators. This suited me, for my father and my brother were also employed by them, carrying out work at Mintlaw, near Fraserburgh, and commuting every day. It was time to go back home again to the more familiar and comfortable surroundings.

However, that sense of stability and security was soon to be challenged in the most unforeseen of scenarios.

A SHOCK DIAGNOSIS

It was a bolt out of the blue ... The year was 1986 and my mother was diagnosed with breast cancer. However, concerned as I was about my mother's condition, I never really feared the worst. Yes, I knew cancer was serious, and I appreciated the implications of surgery and the trauma Mum would suffer of having to lose a breast. I also understood that she would have to undergo painful chemotherapy treatment, but my mother was young and in my ignorance I thought that breast cancer was a form of the disease without fatal consequences.

At this time my life was continuously following the same predictable path. A girlfriend would have me relatively settled for a few months, then would come the split up, followed by a return to the single life of nightclubs, drunken late-night parties and heavy weekend drinking.

Wrapped up in an egotistical, hazardous, rampant weekend lifestyle, as well as working long hours developing my decorating business, I did not stop to consider the seriousness of my mother's illness.

However, my father seemed different – more mellowed perhaps; more sentimental and reflective about life. I would often come in on a Friday or Saturday night and find him still sitting up late having a drink. He would talk to me about his own mother. I had not heard him mention anything about her before, but now he kept telling me that he had never really appreciated her the way he should have when she was alive. He told me on several occasions, 'Appreciate your mother, Colin. I wish I had appreciated mine.'

I would inevitably say, 'I do, Dad,' and then make a lame excuse to go to bed so as not to feel guilty. My conscience was being pricked; I knew that I too had never really appreciated my mother in the way that I should have, even as I grew into adulthood.

Things were looking better as Mum went into remission; her hair started to grow again and she put on weight. As far as I was concerned, my mother was back to normal and everything was going to be all right again.

I know that the effects of the surgery and chemotherapy took a massive toll on her, both physically and mentally, yet she handled everything in the brave and courageous way that characterised her. Hope was short-lived, however, for the cancer returned.

Even then I didn't grasp the severity of the situation – not until one day, when I was working on the main street in Portsoy and my mother passed in the passenger seat of her cousin Alison's car. She looked so poorly that it shocked me to the core. Alison gave me a 'toot' of the horn and my mother seemed to struggle to find the strength to raise her hand to give me a wave.

A petrifying thought overwhelmed me at that moment, a sudden realisation of something that I had always feared in the back of my mind. I returned to my van and sat transfixed – just trying to come to terms with the stark fact that I would be losing my Mum. Although Keith and I were still living in the family home we didn't discuss our mother's illness. Our four-year age difference meant that we had a separate group of friends and even though we shared the same interests in football and hard rock music, we were not particularly close.

Mum was becoming increasingly bedridden and I began to spend more time speaking to her as she lay in bed. I had always been close to my mother and I felt guilty that she'd had to put up with so much trouble and strife from me, especially in my teenage years.

I kept encouraging her and telling her that she was going to get better, but I think she realised what was happening. I don't know if she had a strong faith but she didn't seem to fear death.

It was a Saturday morning and I was working at the Station Hotel located in the centre of town.

'Do you want me to co-drive you to your work?' said my father, before I had a chance to ask him. I had started my own business, but I still had not passed my driving test. Nothing seemed to follow any logical pattern in my life. My father was really eager to talk to me. He was overly pleasant, but I could see that he was fidgety and ill at ease.

A sick feeling came over me while driving the short distance. We were only a few hundred yards down the road when he told me to pull into the side as he had something to tell me. I had barely time to turn the engine off when he blurted it out tearfully:

'Colin, your mother's dying. She only has a few weeks to live.'

Then, instantly he changed the conversation by making a painful reference to the death of his own mother, at a similar age: 'The doctor said my mother was okay ... That there was nothing wrong with her.'

I composed myself and drew a deep lungful of air. Suddenly, an unexpected calmness came over me as I looked him in the eye. My voice quivered with emotion. 'I've been bracing myself for that and I can handle it. But will you promise me that you won't now go the same way with drink?'

Sobbing into his handkerchief he replied, 'Don't worry about me. I'll be okay.' Then he added, 'I never thought that your mother would go before me. I know I haven't been good to myself with the drink and the cigarettes. I wish I had been taken away before her. Honestly I do.'

'It doesn't work like that,' I replied, displaying an unexpected surge of rational reasoning. 'We're only suffering what other families suffer all the time. It's tough, but we just have to get on with life.'

These were strong words from me and perhaps they came across as insensitive but it was almost as if I had accepted the inevitability of my mother's death and had to be strong for him. My attention had now switched to helping him cope.

'Do you want me to drive?' he asked.

'No, I'll be fine,' I replied.

And I was fine – for the five or ten minutes it took me to get upstairs and into the empty bedroom where I was working.

With not a soul in sight I cried and cried – so much so, that I felt I was never going to stop ...

I suddenly realised that our roles had changed: I was now looking after my father. But I was stronger than I thought and Dad was weaker than I ever imagined. I had been under the impression that my father was the strong one of the family. I was wrong: it always was my mother.

Dad needed help and support. Quite frankly, I feared him drinking himself to death. If my mother was going to die it was going to be painful, but how could I handle losing my father as well? In little less than a week my mother had passed away at the age of forty-seven.

Actually, it came as a sense of relief when she died. The cancer had taken a cruel toll on her and many readers will know the anguish and sense of helplessness that comes from watching a close family member go through the trauma of physical suffering. Knowing that the pain in the end can only be controlled by heavy sedation is a harrowing and heartbreaking experience.

In spite of the painful loss of my mother there was a feeling of acceptance of what was an inexorable death. I had felt for other people, and especially for two of my best friends, Gary and Johnny, who had been through a similar experience. I could now fully empathise with them and their loss.

On the day of the funeral, Harold, my mother's brother, took me aside in my house.

'You really need to be strong for your father. It's a massive loss for you and Keith but it's even harder for him.'

I appreciated what he said but it was something of which I was already acutely aware.

After the funeral I wanted to give my father something to look forward to so I suggested that he should visit his sister Mima in Australia for Christmas. I told him that if he were to book a flight,

Keith and I would each pay half of the cost.

This seemed to renew a spark of life in him. I knew Christmas would be a bad time for my father, and that his drinking would probably have escalated, but he was going to a warm place, to a totally different environment, and I felt that would do him good.

He came back from Australia looking renewed and full of vigour. He told me that he hadn't had much to drink, and judging by the photos he had taken I had no reason to disbelieve him.

A FRAGMENTED FAMILY

In some ways I felt I never really went through the natural grieving process after my mother's death, simply because all my concerns and worries were now directed towards my distraught and despairing father. There was no doubt that he was devastated and in need of support from Keith and me.

I can vividly recall an incident, just a few weeks after Mum died, while I was driving through Macduff, when I saw him leaning against the metal railings at the harbour, gazing desolately over the sea. He didn't noticed me as I drove past, but I felt compelled to stop and park my van a bit further on. However, as I indicated to draw in I felt there was nothing I could possibly say to him, so I just drove on, clearing the lump from my throat.

He was very much alone with his grief.

Whenever I looked into his eyes I could see the overwhelming sense of sadness and loss, but I knew that my father was a deep, complex and sensitive man, and that it was going to be a difficult struggle.

That struggle would have been bad enough under normal circumstances but he had a serious drink problem and was also a heavy smoker. He had not been good to his body over the years and it was now beginning to take its toll.

During the previous few years, my father's life pattern had mainly consisted of working, weekend drinking, watching TV and his yearly holiday abroad with my mum and Bill and Brenda Dawson. He had never shown any interest in getting involved with any of the local clubs or organisations.

It had been a few years since he had lost his boat down at the new harbour during a storm. His outboard engine was subsequently stolen from the adjacent old harbour, thereby curtailing any seafaring opportunities.

Without ever having been a keen gardener he had always kept the garden in decent shape but as his drinking became more regular my father seemed to lose the motivation for that as well.

Relations were quite strained between the three of us after my mother's death. She had been the glue that cemented the family together and with her no longer there, things predictably became fragmented between us.

I recall waking up at 7.30 one Saturday morning to start work and looking out the window to find my van gone. I quizzed my father, who was always up at the crack of dawn, and he informed me that Keith had taken it to drive a girl home who had stayed at the house overnight.

I was livid! My van was not insured for Keith, but more importantly ... he had not asked my permission. I was raging, pacing the living room floor, and with every passing minute seeming like an hour, I decided that I was going to teach my brother a lesson as soon as he came home. Keith had probably not been away for more than 20 minutes but the damage had already been done ... I was going to clobber him.

My father was trying to calm me down, but I was having none if it. I was fuming. So, when Keith returned I waited until he opened the living room door then, cursing and swearing, I lunged at him, swinging my fist but only connecting with his head rather than his face. After a brief scuffle I was left with a staved hand that I could barely move for days while, ironically, Keith came out of it relatively unscathed apart from a few scratches and a torn jersey.

When the dust had settled I felt bad enough about the incident but seeing my father in tears made me feel even worse. I just seemed to be tense all the time and in constant turmoil.

In May 1989, I was best man for Gary who was getting married to his long-term girlfriend, Olwen. The wedding reception was held in Elgin Town Hall and I knew that I would have to give a speech.

Naturally, I was flattered at being asked but the thought of speaking in public filled me with apprehension and dread so I made sure that I had a few shots of vodka and orange, before we went to Elgin, to give me the Dutch courage required for being thrust into the limelight.

When it was my turn to speak I was amazingly calm and relaxed, and I felt I handled things well enough, even adding some humour to get chuckles of laughter from the guests.

The day after the wedding I was in the front garden when my father approached me to tell me how proud of me he was at the way my speech had gone. I was taken so much by surprise that I felt the tears well up in my eyes. He had given me so little praise and encouragement throughout my life that a simple comment like that had almost reduced me to tears.

I was finding it increasingly difficult to hold things together – with my Painting business flourishing I was working long hours for six days a week. It was not as if my father was ever abusive when he was drinking but it broke my heart to see him living a life of desperation and despondency.

What I had thought was just natural grief, tinged with self-pity, was now manifesting itself as deep depression. He was becoming more tearful and negative about the future. It was as if at the age of 52 he felt that without my mother his life was not worth living. Sometimes he was working away from home for weeks on end, which gave me some respite, because it meant that I could get some level of normality back into my life, which had been engulfed with his morbidity and negativity.

Keith seemed to have a closer bond with him and could handle his heavy drinking better than I could. I was more intense and irritable and had been concerned about my father's level of drinking since my mid teens. Perhaps Keith was as well, but we had never discussed it.

In some ways there was a certain amount of hypocrisy in my taking issue with the level of his drinking, for I was still very much a weekend binge drinker when I was not in a stable relationship. However, I reasoned that I was just a social drinker who could take it or leave it, while my father was an everyday comfort drinker, who increasingly needed alcohol to numb painful memories and to help him sleep.

When I tackled my dad about his drinking his reply was often narcissistic. He would turn things round by saying that the more I mentioned his drinking the worse he would get. In a sense it became obvious that he was transferring his guilt on to me. This only added to the feeling of hopelessness, for I was trapped somewhere in a hole between the devil and the deep blue sea.

When I suggested that he went on holiday to have a bit of a break, my father asked me where he should go, because he had never been to any hot destinations in Europe. I mentioned Yugoslavia, for I had been there with my good friend Mango several years before and had found the climate really warm. It was also cheap to eat out there.

I was pleased that my father was receptive to the idea. He duly booked a fortnight's holiday and off he went. As was the case when he had returned from Australia, he looked fitter and healthier than before he had left.

'Colin, I've got something to tell you,' he said rather tentatively as we talked about his holiday. 'I've met someone on holiday who is now my friend.'

'That's fine,' I replied, after a few moments' thought.

'She has invited me down to visit her and her family.'

'Fair enough, just go for it,' I said, to his obvious surprise. I think my father thought I would have been angry about any future relationship he could have, due to the close bond I'd had with my mother, but nothing was further from the truth; I knew that he needed a sense of purpose in his life, and meeting someone else would maybe stabilise him and give him renewed hope and direction.

He travelled down to see her, and Marion came up to Portsoy to visit. I liked her. She was a tall, attractive lady – well presented and well mannered. Although Marion was different in many ways from my mother, she and my dad got on well. Being teetotal and a non-smoker, Marion seemed remarkably tolerant of my father's excesses.

Despite the fact that he now had Marion in his life, my father's natural grief and perhaps a certain level of self-pity had steadily developed into what I could clearly see as a deep depression. He was still managing to hold down his job, but seemed increasingly detached from the world.

With hindsight, it looked as if he was gradually withdrawing from life itself. At this stage, my father was on medication from the doctor for depression, yet he continued drinking heavily. Often, I would draw up to the house after my day's work and sit in my van for a few minutes to brace myself before I entered the house. It was soul-destroying, seeing him trapped in such a dense, black cloud.

I found it difficult at times to see any light at the end of the tunnel for him.

Things came to head when I received a phone call from the police telling me that he had been charged with drink driving on his way down to Yorkshire to visit Marion. Although I was obviously concerned for his mental and physical well-being, I was furious about the fact that his irresponsible action could well have caused a fatality on the road.

If I thought that things could not get much worse, then I was badly mistaken. My father told me on numerous occasions that he just wanted to die and that he had nothing left to live for. When I pointed out that surely Keith and I were worth living for, he would say that we would be all right, because we were young and had our whole lives in front of us. I believe his self esteem was at such a low ebb that he felt his very existence was a burden to not just us, but everybody else close to him. At this point I was in the house with him all the time, because Keith was now living in Aberdeen.

I vividly recall the Sunday that one of my father's friends had driven him home from the Boyne Hotel, and told me that I should get the doctor to him as he looked in a bad way. Dad had gone into the house and had barricaded himself into the bedroom, and would not let me in to speak to him. Fearing he was attempting to take his own life, I ran round to Dr Taylor's in a state of panic and begged him to do something.

Dr Taylor, who was as much a family friend as GP, hurriedly

signed a form that would admit my father to Cornhill hospital, a local psychiatric facility, that very afternoon. I told him my dad was back drinking and in a state of total disarray, and Dr Taylor told me something that came as a revelation to me. He said, 'Colin, your dad does not get depressed because he drinks, he drinks because he is depressed.' This simple reasoning by an experienced GP stunned me somewhat, for I had always been under the impression that drinking was the root of my father's problems, not depression.

He was still in a daze when I returned to the house, but was only too willing to let me take him into Aberdeen for the help he needed. It was almost as if, in his apathetic and totally lethargic state, he would have been willing to go anywhere.

Driving my father into Aberdeen was a strange experience. He became almost childlike as he spoke to me about things that he had never discussed before. It was a weird, sad, but unforgettable experience.

During the journey he talked incessantly about girlfriends I'd had and which ones he really liked, and also about his own childhood experiences. He described the beautiful scenery round about us. He spoke of the burden he felt for Keith and me. Everything had suddenly become so effortless to talk about; almost as if he was detached from reality and at peace with himself.

I could not help feeling intense sympathy for my dad as I left him in the hospital. He looked such a sad and pathetic figure, shuffling wearily along the floor with the nurse who was taking him to his ward. Walking back to my van, I felt I was abandoning him. With the door closed I wept uncontrollably, pleading with God to help me – but more importantly, to help my father ...

I visited him several times during his three-week stay and I was encouraged by his steady improvement. His speech was slow and I noticed that his handwriting was untidy, due to the shake in his hand, but he looked fit and well with normal colour returning to his face, which was always an unhealthy scarlet red, brought on by his high blood pressure and heavy drinking.

When my father came out of hospital, I worried that he would relapse again but, to his credit, he stayed off the drink for the best part of a year. It was almost as if I felt it was my personal responsibility to have him fit and well. His health improved dramatically – so much so that he was able to return to his work again. I feel that his developing relationship with Marion had given my father a greater sense of purpose, and it was the best I had seen him for many years.

It was around this time that the 'religious guy' from the downstairs flat in Aberdeen fleetingly entered into my life again. I had gone to 'Tuttie Fruitties', a recently opened café bar in Buckie, with a girlfriend. On entering the bar I glanced upstairs to see a somewhat sad solitary figure sitting dejectedly at a table, staring into a pint glass, clearly the worse for wear through drink.

At that moment a cynical and unsympathetic thought went through my mind: 'Where is your God at now mate.' Then, as I was standing at the bar sipping my first drink, I noticed him slip quietly out of the door, and suddenly I lost myself for a few seconds.

His presence had made me feel uneasy in an odd sort of way. With some semblance of normality back in my life, I achieved a childhood dream by going to the 1990 World Cup in Italy to watch Scotland play. With a group of friends I travelled by bus to our base in the South of France for the three matches against Sweden, Costa Rica and Brazil.

Although the organisation of the trip was shambolic, it was a marvellous, unforgettable experience. We stayed in a town called Antibes, halfway between Nice and Cannes. Antibes had stunning mediaeval streets, lots of pedestrianised sections, as well as an impressive marina full of stunning yachts owned by as many billionaires as millionaires.

I recall going on an organised trip to Monaco, getting off the bus, then paying almost £3 for a can of coke from a vending machine – just to remind me how really expensive this one-square-mile income-tax-free principality was.

We walked down a steep winding pathway to the harbour. As I marvelled at the many super-yachts in the marina I was desperately hoping to get a glimpse of someone rich and famous, simply relaxing aboard their own vessel. We then made our way along to the Grand Casino where we were allowed into the front entrance free of charge. We could see through to the gaming rooms, which were spectacular, with stained glass windows. There were paintings and sculptures dotted around everywhere.

The front part of the casino was obviously destined for the low budget plebs – like me, when I was addicted to the buzz of gambling. There were numerous slot machines on which you could easily spend your limited cash supply in the hope of winning some back. I remember feeling very relieved that my gambling days were well and truly behind me.

During a train journey to Nice we stopped at a place called Juan Les Pins, which was immortalised in the sixties song 'Where do you go to my lovely?' by Peter Sarstedt.

On another occasion in France, my mate Graham Hutcheson was looking for me and he had asked someone in our party if they had seen me. The guy asked what I looked like, and when Graham described me he thought for a few seconds and replied, 'Is that the boy that looks as if he is in a bad mood all the time?' I did see the funny side of the observation, commenting that I was happy enough but had never got round to notifying my face.

In fact, with Gary married and out of circulation, Graham had become my closest friend. So close were we as mates that we could hardly be separated by a cigarette paper.

It was now two years since my mother's death and my relationship with my father was the best it had ever been. I felt that he had a greater respect for me and appreciated me more, possibly because I had grown up a lot and was now working hard at developing my own business.

My dad's whole demeanour changed, and he suddenly took pride in the house and the garden again. Deep down I was proud of him. Having been a binge drinker myself, I did not underestimate how difficult it must have been for him to apply total abstinence. Just to have a father sober and in reasonable health was something that millions of sons around the world would take for granted, but for me it was unusual and something I appreciated and cherished so much.

However, another bombshell was about to drop when my father went to visit the doctor to see about his high blood pressure that had troubled him for years. The doctor had informed him that the arteries in his legs were clogging up due to his years of heavy smoking and if he did not stop soon he would have to have his legs amputated.

Dad looked shocked and shaken when Marion told me this in the kitchen one afternoon. Now he had another battle on his hands. Despite his problems, I felt that Marion gave him a level of constancy in his life; a stability that he probably found impossible to live without.

He began to talk openly and frankly with me about his drinking and smoking, and he was determined to conquer his drinking first, before tackling what he viewed to be the lesser of the two evils, which he acknowledged was his smoking.

BLYTH REVISITED

Later in the year, my focus was back on club football and a trip to Yugoslavia to watch Rangers play Red Star Belgrade. Yugoslavia was still a federation of half a dozen ethnic republics welded together under the iron-fisted rule of the Communist dictator, General Tito.

Some of my friends had travelled to Bucharest three years earlier, near the end of megalomaniac dictator Nicolae Ceausescu's oppressive reign. Stories of long queues outside near-empty shops, money launderers patrolling the near deserted dimly-lit streets, and almost inedible food, had me concerned that Belgrade would be somewhat similar.

Because of this preconception, I had half expected to see Communist grey and dull, trailers, institutional postwar architecture, and visible abject poverty with peasants selling meagre rations of fruit and vegetables at the side of the road to make ends meet.

It was nothing like I had anticipated. Belgrade turned out to be a fascinating giant hotchpotch of architectural chaos, spanning from the Habsburg empire, to post-modern Yugoslavia and almost everything in between. On top of this, there were many parks, impressive monuments, museums, cafés, restaurants, pubs and shops.

So unsure was I about what to expect temperature-wise in this Balkan city that on my friends' advice I took a pair of shorts with me, even though it was actually near sub-zero temperatures once we got there.

As much as I loved the football and the camaraderie between my fellow supporters, I was very much enchanted by the assorted European cities and their contrasting and diverse cultures. On the eve of the game we had our customary drinking session in our hotel, which brought me in contact with a fellow Rangers supporter called Vince who came from, of all places ... Blyth!

Naturally, the thread of conversation led to whether Vince knew any of my family who lived there. When I mentioned the name of Tony Cole, I saw a definite look of astonishment and shock on his face ...

'I don't know him personally, but I know of him,' he tentatively replied. 'He's a hardy b ...... him.'

I had not been in touch with Tony for many years and had only heard snippets about how he was doing from my correspondence with his mum, but I knew his life had gone down an unlawful path and that he had spent time in jail.

My friend from Portsoy, Jimmy Marnoch, was my regular room mate on these overseas football trips and later that evening, looking serious and tense, he approached me with a troubled look on his face. 'I just heard something from Vince about your cousin Tony. Listen to this ... '

The story goes that Tony had come out of a nightclub and was being 'goaded' by a guy who was driving around in the apparent safety of his car. However, not at all fazed by the metal protection between him and his antagonist, Tony sprinted across the road, leaped onto the bonnet of the moving car, and with frightening Bruce Willis style audacity and efficiency booted in the windscreen and pulled the unfortunate dupe out, to give him a violent beating.

Phew ... I just shrugged my shoulders ... What was I supposed to say?

But even with a bellyful of drink, I was taken aback. OK, the story was third hand and had possibly grown 'arms and legs' during the flight from Tyneside to the soon to be new capital of Serbia, but surely this wasn't the kind of thing that someone would make up. Was it? And besides, knowing the adolescent Tony, my gut reaction was that there would be a strong element of truth about the story. To be honest, my feelings were quite mixed; in part, admiration at Tony's breathtakingly audacious stunt, but also revulsion at such a savage and outrageous assault – whether he had been strongly provoked or not.

As destiny would have it, a few months later I was in Blyth for the first time in almost 10 years.

I travelled down with Jimmy and Graham to stay with my Aunt Eleanor for a weekend and I had invited my father to come with us; he was still in regular contact with my mother's two sisters and I felt he would welcome the break.

My cousin David was married with a family and had settled down, but what Tony was doing in his life was anyone's guess – even though I knew he was also married to his long-term girlfriend, Jane, and that they had a young daughter called Emma.

In those days I was the proud wearer of a brand-new royal blue Rangers shell suit, similar in style to the turquoise one worn by ex BBC sports pundit David Ike, who had proclaimed himself to be the Son of God whereby he became the definitive symbol of his New Age conspiracy theories.

After Graham, Jimmy and I had spent the whole of Saturday on a drinks 'bender' in Newcastle, we met up with Tony on the Sunday afternoon. Naturally, like myself, he had changed a lot in appearance with the passage of time. The long blonde locks were gone and his hair was now cropped short and balding on top. I was surprised at how amiable and non-threatening he looked. Only the tattoos on his neck, gave a tell-tale sign of his fierce reputation. He seemed smaller than I had imagined, for I had a vision of him having developed the physique of 'Desperate Dan' as drawn by a 'Dandy' comic cartoonist.

Tony invited us back to his house, which was situated in what I felt was a more presentable looking part of Blyth. Typically, I wasted no time in quizzing him about the tale that had made its way to Belgrade. His measured response seemed to have a rueful tinge, slightly mischievous even, as he mumbled something about not believing everything I hear in a strange country.

We had not long seated ourselves on the settee in his living room, when there was a knock at the door and the next we knew a skinny skinhead guy in his twenties appeared and emptied the contents of a black bin bag on the floor in the middle of the living room. Naïvely, I asked Tony where all the trendy casual clothes had come from. His trademark laid-back response was a wry smile and a shake of the head!

I immediately spotted two designer t-shirts and bought them for the grand total of £5. Tragically though, when we arrived back home my brand-new shell suit, that I had worn with such pride over the whole weekend, had turned a pale lilac in the washing machine after it had been washed at the wrong temperature ...

I returned to Blyth a few months later, this time for the wedding of Eleanor, who was getting remarried after being widowed when she lost my uncle Dick a few years earlier. My father and I were both kitted out with kilts. As I had no steady girlfriend at the time, Eleanor allowed me to invite Graham along instead. Keith was supposed to be there as well but there was some confusion regarding his pick up time in Aberdeen and he never made it, much to the displeasure of my father, who characteristically laboured to blame me for the mix-up.

My father stayed with Eleanor, while Graham and I had been invited to stay the weekend with Tony and Jane. What we did not know, however, was that Tony was out on bail on a very serious charge – an attempted murder charge, to be precise.

The charge was in connection with the alleged shooting of a notorious hard man in the Middlesborough area, and as part of Tony's bail conditions, he had to appear at the police station every night at 10 p.m. because a curfew had been placed on him, not allowing him to leave his house after 11p.m. As was to be expected with such a grim setting, the atmosphere in the house was strained and tense. Jane, who was understandably at her wit's end, looked constantly drained and gaunt with dark shadows visible under her eyes as she chain-smoked cigarettes in between drinking copious amounts of strong coffee. She knew full well that with Tony's criminal record, if the charge were to stick, he would be looking at a long stretch behind bars, which would mean the inevitable break-up of the family unit.

Obviously, with all that was going on, the last thing that Jane needed was two pleasure seekers from Scotland, down for a boozy weekend, staying at her house. However, despite this dark cloud of uncertainty that was hanging over their lives, Graham and I were determined not to let the atmosphere of unease and disquiet spoil our weekend.

Tony had turned to smoking cannabis after coming to the conclusion that alcohol was making him aggressive and violent. Cannabis, he reasoned, lengthened his fuse and pacified his aggressive nature; making him more calm and relaxed.

Predictably, on the Friday night we ended up in the local night club where I could not believe how freely available all types of drugs were. It seemed that everyone I came in contact with was on something or selling something that you could snort, swallow or smoke. I had never witnessed anything like it.

The drug problem was reputed to be so serious in Blyth around that time that one stall holder was asked to leave the market for selling hukka pipes, which are decorative ornaments commonly used for smoking cannabis.

Being a non smoker, drugs were never really my thing, and any time I had tried smoking cannabis I had only felt dizzy and a bit sick. But this was Blyth and it was difficult to avoid the temptation of narcotics. The next I knew, I was having a few draws of 'skunk', an ultra-potent form of marijuana that was being freely passed around outside the nightclub. Even that was not enough to satisfy my craving for the ultimate buzz, for I even took a snort of a peculiar yellow vapour, commonly known as 'poppers'. I felt the effects within seconds and it lasted for one to two minutes.

My next hazy recollection is of being invited back to some stranger's house for a party. When I arrived, there was no alcohol to be seen and I realised that I was at some sort of gathering in a dimly-lit drugs den. About 25 people were there, mostly teenagers and people in their twenties. Even in a sozzled and fixated state I felt ill at ease.

At long last it was time to head back to Tony's.

Whether Graham was there with me or not, I honestly can't remember.

After attending the marriage ceremony for Eleanor and Ray on the Saturday, Tony asked Graham and me if we fancied going to Newcastle later in the evening. An associate of his had been married that same day, and when we pointed out that we did not know the groom, Tony said he had cleared everything and we were welcome if we were with him and Jane.

A short while later, we tentatively followed Tony and Jane into the club where the reception was being held, where we were immediately introduced to the man mountain of a groom who gave me such a firm handshake with his massive shovel-like hand that I thought he had cracked a few bones. I dreaded him giving me a hospitable pat on the shoulder and ending up with a dislocated shoulder blade!

All the drinks were free and, needless to say, Graham and I took full advantage of our host's generosity. We only stayed about three quarters of an hour, so that we still had time to go to the nightclub which was open into the early hours of the morning.

Following another bout of drinking, I returned to Tony's house with a girl I had picked up at the night club. Heavily inebriated and fumbling about in my pockets for a key, I could find none, so I had no alternative but to knock at the door, not only wakening Tony but Jane and Emma as well. Jane answered the door with a face like thunder, giving my female companion a distrustful glance before letting us in.

In the morning, I woke up with a thumping headache and a dryness in my throat – the unpleasant legacy of smoking whatever I had been smoking. I was relieved and not too surprised to find that my lady friend was gone.

Graham and I both decided that although our weekend had been excessive, even by our standards, the best remedy for a hangover would be to top up with more drink later on in the day. Tony and Jane were very much into the 'Rave' music scene which had Disc Jockeys playing modern dance music with the accompaniment of laser light shows, projected images, and sometimes artificial fog. Tony and Jane took Graham and me to a rave in Blyth on the Sunday night, and although the music was not really my scene, after consuming a few drinks I began to quite like the rhythm.

Afterwards, we went back to Tony's house where if I'd had an ounce of sense I would have gone to bed to sleep off the excesses of the previous 48 hours. However, the familiar impulsive nature that has blemished my character all my life meant that I ended up smoking some more of the super strength skunk.

At first I felt fine, almost mellow, but as I smoked more I began to feel anxious and started speaking gibberish in between silly fits of giggling. Then all of a sudden my eyes were tingling and everything started to blur. The drug seemed to unlock some sort of paranoia in my head. I suddenly felt that everyone was speaking about me, and that Tony's Alsatian dog, sitting harmlessly on the carpet, was going to attack me.

Without doubt, I was experiencing one of the most scary moments of my life. I can only remember Tony saying, 'Don't give him any more of that stuff. He's had enough.'

I'd had more than enough!

In no time at all I was feeling a terrifying combination of paranoia, fear and anxiety. Psychosis set in, and I felt as if I was having a panic attack. At one point, I was simply too frightened to get out of my chair. I was well and truly stoned.

I eventually managed to stand up, and walked unsteadily upstairs to the bedroom, hoping that a lie-down would make me feel better ... but I was badly mistaken.

I was experiencing what is known within the dope smoking fraternity as 'a whiter' – white being the appropriate word to use to describe my ghost-like pallor. I felt I had to get to sleep, but my hell was just beginning. I sat bolt upright in bed, took a deep breath, and a cold sweat washed over me. I told myself I was okay and settled down again, but about two or three minutes later, I experienced the same feelings again. After once more telling myself I was okay, I tried to go back to sleep.

I spent the next four or five hours wide awake as panic swept through me every time I was drifting off. The more panic attacks I had, the more I panicked, and the worse they got. I found myself staring into pure darkness, convincing myself that I would never see morning again.

I was truly terrified.

I have never been so relieved to see morning arriving – to hear birds chirping, to open the curtains and look outside at the normality of parked cars and neighbouring gardens with trees.

Why on earth had I smoked a skunk joint that rendered me comatose for several hours? Was I expecting to float six feet off the ground for a couple of hours just to feel really good? Did I think this was going to be my Holy Grail? I kept asking myself these questions.

We were leaving early, and Tony seemed almost apologetic about the whole weekend.

'Jane's not annoyed at you Colin ... It's me, and the attempted murder charge that's the problem. She's at her wit's end.'

I bore Tony no ill will. The skunk smoking had been my own choice, my harsh lesson, I concluded.

I'm a drinker – he was a smoker. It was as plain as that, as far as I was concerned.

There was a certain sense of irony in the fact that my father appeared to be in finer rational and physical condition than I was, as he sat in the front of the car, conversing with Graham, on our way home to Scotland. I just sat remorsefully in the back while paranoia made way for a strong sense of unhappiness and isolation. This intensity, a mild form of depersonalisation mixed with wistful feelings of estrangement, ebbed and flowed in me throughout the six hour journey.

A strange nostalgic, sad feeling overwhelmed me when I recalled the many innocent happy days that I had experienced in Blyth and nearby Whitley Bay. It felt like only yesterday when, seemingly without a care in the world, I embraced the spirit of childhood as I ambled along lively streets, play parks and vast areas of derelict ground. I was soon lost in my own thoughts while reminiscing about the swing boats and donkey rides at the Spanish City fairground, and I recalled the song 'Tunnel of Love', by Dire Straights, with the line: 'Like the Spanish City to me, when we were kids ... ', which recounted their own childhood memories.

On such journeys, I was only a mere tourist in Blyth. But things had changed over the years, and I should have known better. Nowadays, drugs seemed to be everywhere and so were dealers, and that deadly combination was pushing crime rates higher and higher. A disturbing sense of menace had settled on the town and I realised I did not fit in. I was very much out of my depth. In reality, I was still struggling to move on from harmless youthful adventures, and my desire for all that was familiar to remain unspoiled.

It was alarming how easily I had allowed myself to be sucked into a soulless drug culture that had opened my eyes to the brutally stark reality that the idealistic perspective I used to have of my mother's birthplace had been shattered.

Without doubt, my brief experience of the darker side of Blyth had given a slightly distorted image of this once proud pit village with a struggling business community of declining industries, which inevitably manifests itself in low aspiration among its population as the town appeared to be descending into complete deprivation

I could handle the regular hangovers and occasional blackouts, but the panic attacks and paranoia were something that I never wanted to experience again.

Although I had started to develop my business and had sampled a piece of most things, I had not lived what many would have considered a sheltered life. I realised that I was far from street-wise in the manner that Tony obviously was, but I did not envy his life style in the slightest.

I did wonder how different his life may have turned out if he had been brought up in the relatively crime-free corner of North-East Scotland. And, of course, there was also the reverse thought of how different things may have been for me if I had grown up in Blyth.

Even though Tony had undoubtedly brought much of his troubles on himself, I still had an element of sympathy for him. After all, he was my cousin, and I believed he was acutely aware of the stress and worry he had caused his family, but he seemed to be trapped in a vicious circle of transgression as his life had slid into disarray and crime. His family regularly faced trauma and readjustment and needed support to cope and to rebuild their lives. There was little sympathy for families going through this experience, with the popular opinion being that the perpetrator should have thought of the effect his crime would have on his family before committing the offence.

I really could not see myself returning to Blyth in haste. I felt a strong sense of security in my own little world in which, although far from virtuous and unsullied, I felt in control. But I knew full well that I had to protect myself from my own rash and impulsive nature.

In late 1991, and with my father's life now seemingly stable and alcohol free, I felt that the time was right to move out of what had been my family home for 25 years, and I purchased a house in Schoolhendry Street, overlooking both the new and old harbours in the opposite side of the town. I felt confident that I could leave my father on his own to develop his relationship with Marion, secure in the knowledge that I was only half a mile away if he ever needed me. I still lived in Park Crescent for a few months, while I was renovating and redecorating my new house, and appreciated the help that my father gave me in fitting my new kitchen and assisting me with the alterations as I looked forward to a new chapter in my life.

For the first time in years, I felt I was moving in the right direction.

Then, in March of the following year, my life was thrown into a state of turmoil again as my father and Marion decided to go their separate ways. I was deeply disappointed. They seemed so compatible and content in each other's company, having been through so much together in the previous couple of years.

I never took sides or delved into the reasons for the split, but I was just completely shocked and saddened by their decision. I genuinely liked Marion and admired the loyalty she showed to my father during the most difficult period of his life.

My obvious concern was that this latest setback would bring back the drinking and deep depression. One evening, when I came home from work, my dad spoke to me about his fear of living by himself and his need for me to visit him every day. I saw real fear and uncertainty in his eyes and I reassured him that doing that was no problem, but at 28 I had made a commitment to move out and live on my own and I had to see it through.

I gave my father the opportunity to get involved with my painting and decorating business to keep him active during what I knew would be a difficult time for him. He seemed fine for the subsequent weeks following the split. He gave me a hand with the work I was doing for a film crew who were making a television advert for a drinks company, which was a pastiche of the old Scottish film *Whisky Galore*. Some of the filming was done at the nearby Whitehills community hall and I was asked to do some work at short notice. So I kitted him up with a white boiler suit and we worked well together to get the contract completed in a tight time schedule.

At the beginning of May, I noticed my father was back drinking again. He did not need to speak or stagger; I recognised those all too familiar glazed, bulbous eyes. I never knew whether to be angry or sympathetic when he was like this, and quite often I was a bit of both.

His sister Alice came to visit him with my uncle Bill and they were deeply concerned about his wellbeing. Typically of such a warm-hearted family-orientated soul, Alice urged him to come down to Larbert, near Falkirk, where they lived, for an extended break, but drained of all motivation and barely able to function, he chose to stay at home.

I always felt so responsible for him and when he relapsed it provoked a sense of guilt in me, along with an overwhelming sense of helplessness. There was always tension between us when he was back drinking. I couldn't help feeling that way, even though I knew how hard he had battled over the previous four years.

I felt demoralised once again. Where would we go from here?

Within a month I had an appalling answer to that question.

THE AFTERMATH

In the long hours and days that followed my father's suicide I could only respond with numbness. I was lost in a sea of confusion and bewilderment, but the outpouring of support from friends and relatives allowed me to plough through the early days of shock. This was interspersed with the occasional flash of unexplainable anger that lurked beneath the surface.

Such were the inevitable feelings of guilt, shame, anger, hurt, and even abandonment that it was difficult for me to show natural grief. As a steady flow of close friends and family members visited me, I found myself detached from the reality and enormity of what had happened. This could best have been described as the calm in the eye of a storm. It was as if the unfolding events were happening to some other person.

On the morning of the funeral I went to my front door to pick up the milk that was delivered daily. As I bent down to pick up the glass bottle, it slipped out of my hand, shattering the glass and spilling the milk all over the doorstep and pavement. At this trivial mishap I instantly burst into a flood of tears. It seemed that whatever little strength I had left evaporated at that precise moment.

Although it was very touching and comforting to receive vast amounts of sympathy cards and personal messages, I knew that when the dust had settled I would be very much alone with my confusion and unwanted legacy. I would have to face up to life as a victim of suicide with that certain degree of stigma, shame, anger and guilt attached to it.

I realised that it would be almost impossible to return to a normal life.

A short while after my father's death, Keith and I had to go to register the death. We were sitting directly opposite the registrar as he was filling in the form. About halfway down, we came to the question 'cause of death', which had already been filled in as 'hanging'. He hesitated a while before muttering, 'I don't like that word there.' For what seemed like an eternity – but in reality was only about 15-20 seconds – he pondered over another word or phrase to use, causing me to focus on the horrific event that had occurred only days before and that was still so graphically fresh in my mind.

With the churning in my stomach getting worse by the second, I almost grabbed the document from him to rip it to shreds. The registrar's genuine attempt to be sensitive had had an adverse effect on me. I just wanted this horrendous ordeal to be over.

On the whole, the many good people in the small coastal town of Portsoy were supportive and comforting after my father's death, although, perhaps predictably, the odd small town gossip, looking for a small piece of sensationalism, managed to distort certain facts somewhat.

I soon concluded that sitting about the house obsessively going over recent events was the worst thing I could do, so instead I started to hit the night-life scene in Banff.

On my first real venture out, I found myself drinking with a couple of friends at the bar when I was approached by a girl I knew who had obviously been drinking heavily.

'Coco! Coco! Is the story that's doing the rounds about your father true?'

Immediately, the red mist descended, and I fired back aggressively, 'Doing the rounds? What do you mean, doing the f ... ... rounds? Would it be f...... . well doing the rounds if he had died of a stroke or a heart attack?' before angrily storming off to the bar downstairs.

One of the hardest things I had to deal with was the realisation that the person who had given me life had decided to renounce his own. When I was a child growing up, my father was my hero and my parents were invincible; in some ways they seemed almost infallible. However, as adolescence and adulthood beckoned, their weaknesses and vulnerabilities became blatantly obvious.

The hopelessness of my feelings was magnified when I came to terms with the reality that despite living in the same house as my dad for most of my life, I did not know him well enough to anticipate what he was capable of.

Even though my father had a recent history of mental illness and the fact that I had already thwarted one previous suicide attempt, I was totally unprepared for the horrendous shock and devastating impact of losing him in this way. It felt a bit like losing a filling in your tooth after eating something chewy: you keep putting your tongue in the empty space, but there's nothing there except a jagged edge.

The first challenge Keith and I had to face was the torturous ambiguity that suicide left on our lives, which prevented natural or definite closure and didn't allow us appropriate mourning.

In the first six months following my father's suicide I was consumed with replaying every last detail of the days, months and even years leading up to his death. I analysed everything he had said and every syllable I had uttered in the most minute detail. The 'whys', 'what ifs', 'should haves' and 'could haves' were always on my mind. I felt an intense feeling of isolation and dislocation from all that had been familiar. I would find myself reflecting on the previous six years with almost a sense of disbelief as I struggled to make any sense of all that had happened.

I could not help but focus on the painful years since my mum had first been diagnosed with cancer. All the false dawns of hope had made the final outcome so cruel. Not even the fact that I was free of all the worry and stress made me feel any better. I had been so proud of my father when I was a kid but now I was deeply ashamed of what he had done, and I didn't know anyone who had been through a similar experience that I could talk to.

I was in the unenviable position of having to ponder the tragic contrast of a mother who fought so hard to preserve life and a father who could not face it. Deep down, I knew there was a certain inevitability about my father's self-destruction, but that was of little comfort to me.

Sometimes, I would perceive my dad as selfish and irresponsible, only thinking about himself. In taking his own life in the manner that he had done, he must have known that his own son was likely to be the first person to find him. But then another thought would enter my head to contradict that. Maybe, in his final moments, with a tortured mind of hopelessness and low self worth, he saw himself as an embarrassment and a burden to Keith and myself, and that taking his life seemed his only option. The repercussions of that final act may never have entered his head.

It did not take my brother and me very much discussion to agree to sell the house in Park Crescent. Although it had been part of so much of our lives, too many sad events had happened for us there to even contemplate holding on to it. In fact, I could barely bring myself to even drive past the house that had been my home for 25 years.

About two months after my father's death, a representative from the local Church called round to my house to visit me. She was very sympathetic and understanding but there was never any inclination on my part to go to the Church or to find any kind of solace in God. It also never entered my mind to seek any level of counselling, choosing instead to bury myself in a heavy workload to keep my mind occupied and tire me out physically so that I could get some decent sleep at night. Basically, I felt it was my own predicament and entirely up to me to get over it.

Before that fateful day in 1992, suicide was just another word to me and never a prominent one in my mind. For me, it was something that very occasionally happened to other people, perhaps rock stars, famous people, and the odd unknown, but certainly not to a normal ordinary working class family. From that day on, suicide seemed to become a permanent fixture in my mind.

Two years before, I had heard on the early evening news that Del Shannon, a famous singer and song writer from the 1960s, had taken his own life. This had shocked and saddened me. I just loved his hit singles such as 'Runaway' and 'Keep Searching'. I had always played these hits on pub jukeboxes. His unique untrained voice and piercing falsetto would send shivers down my spine every time I listened to it. Yet, he was someone unknown from across the Atlantic, and it was difficult to relate too strongly to a famous person I had never met.

Because of the nature of my father's death and the stigma attached to it, I felt the silence on the subject a bit unsettling. It somehow added to the weirdness of my loss and the fear that I would always be alone with it. But it didn't take me long to figure out that the instinct to preserve life is much stronger than dealing with the issue of death, especially one that is intentional. Suicide may well have been the end result of my father's personal struggle, but it was just the beginning of mine.

I had heard on several occasions that 'Death is Final!' but to a survivor like me that sounded like a sick joke. Although our relationship was frequently uncomfortable, even somewhat antagonistic, the hurt and sadness really kicked in when I imagined the name of Bill Murray being brought up in conversation, whereby his last desperate act in life became the immediate focus of attention and people appeared to totally forget about the fulfilling and decent life my father had led for the best part of 50 years.

I recall answering the phone late one evening to be greeted by one of my father's cousins. He was obviously deeply affected by what had happened. Although he barely knew me he just wanted to talk and relay a few stories about going to Sandend, or "Sanine" as it was better known locally, to visit my dad and his brothers and sisters when he was a young lad.

It dawned on me that night how many other people had been traumatised by my father's death. I felt for Taffy, my neighbour, and his son Billy who had both gone into the house on that fateful day. This reality confirmed that the shock waves that reverberated in the wake of my dad's death – not only because of his death but also because of the brutal way he had ended his life – would have been felt as far away as Australia, where his sister Mima and all her family lived.

Football had always been something I could fall back on, whatever the circumstances, and I felt that travelling to matches to watch Rangers play was as good a therapy as anything. This gave me a sense of belonging; a camaraderie between follow supporters sharing the same passion. Rangers had qualified for the Champions League and I had discussed with some friends to go to as many games as possible.

In late 1992 and early 1993, as well as watching all the home games I flew to Copenhagen, to Bochum in Germany, and also managed to fit in a drink-fuelled car and ferry trip to Brugge, in Belgium. The excitement and anticipation of a successful European run helped to take my mind off my father's suicide – for a while at least.

Late one evening, in Germany, as Gary and I were returning to our hotel, we noticed some kind of fracas outside a night club on the opposite side of the road. We did little more than glance over to see what was happening but suddenly we were being confronted then chased by what appeared to be a deranged maniac.

Thankfully, our hotel was nearby and we made a quick sprint to what we thought would be a place of safety. How wrong we were! The mad man came right into our hotel shouting abuse in a language we did not understand a word of. Instinctively, in a state of blind panic, we both jumped over the reception counter to the astonishment of the receptionist who had been calmly doing her job. We subsequently ran into an office and barricaded ourselves in, while we waited for the police to arrive to sedate this clearly disturbed individual.

In Copenhagen, I quite characteristically hopped onto a train going in the wrong direction, much to the dismay and amusement of my two friends who were in stitches, standing on the platform watching and waving as the carriage doors closed and the train pulled away from the station. Fortunately, the train only went a few miles further down the track before we reached the next station. I just sat there, doing a bit of people watching while enjoying a couple of beers before taking the next train back to Copenhagen.

In Brugge, Keith and I decided to go out for a late drink, but the only licensed premises that we could find open was a small pub up a narrow side street. When we sauntered in, we found ourselves in the company of around a dozen Scottish sports journalists who were there to report on the match. The only recognisable face was that of TV commentator Archie MacPherson. We found it ironic that the most famous person among them was the only person willing to come up to the bar, offer us a drink and have a chin-wag.

The start of the following season saw me in Sofia, Bulgaria, with a group of friends. Once again the trip could not pass without incident. With just a minute to go, Levski Sofia scored a wonder goal from 35 yards to send Rangers out of the European Cup. If that hammer blow was not enough, the Bulgarian police inexplicably turned on the Rangers fans behind the goal.

I know that some football supporters are no angels but this terrifying, attack was totally unjustified. Just in front of where I was standing, several fans were getting mercilessly clobbered by the thuggish baton-wielding Bulgarian police for no reason other than that they originated from another country. We had to flee from hundreds of frenzied baying Bulgarian supporters and get on our bus to travel back to our hotel. There, we were then warned not to leave the hotel for our own safety, and we were left wondering what would have happened if the Bulgarians had actually lost the match.

Keith phoned me on the first anniversary of our dad's death. The call came out of the blue. We had not grown any closer during the previous year but it was obvious that he was struggling with things as well. We had never shared problems and concerns so I think we both found it difficult to speak about him.

A few months later, I was shocked and stunned by the terrible news that the mother of two of my best friends was missing. I was aware that she had recently been suffering from depression, and in an ironic twist of fate I remember one of the brothers confiding in me, shortly after my father's death, that he could never handle such a traumatic experience.

When their mother was never traced, I could feel a deep sense of empathy for my mates and their father. I reasoned that at least Keith and I had a sense of finality to our loss, regardless of how violent and brutal it had been. However, that seemed insufficient consolation as from time to time I would suddenly be confronted with it again.

I was having a night out in Aberdeen when I was introduced to a guy. When I told him my name and where I came from he asked, 'Are you any relation to Bill Murray, the site agent who worked with R B Farquhar?' When I replied that he was my father, he said, 'I used to work with him down beside Glasgow.' He went on, 'How is he doing anyway?'...

I just seemed to clam up. I hesitated for a couple of seconds, then replied nervously, deliberately avoiding eye contact, 'He's doing okay', after which he responded, 'Tell him that Stuarty from Huntly is asking for him.' Sheepishly, I mumbled I would.

I simply didn't have the heart to tell him the truth and give him a shock that he wasn't prepared for.

Eventually, the raw intensity began to fade. The tragedy of the suicide no longer dominated my days and nights and I learned to live with the traumatic events that had left a stain on my life forever. I really had no option. I don't know if 'coming to terms with it' or 'time heals all wounds' were phrases that could justifiably have described how I felt, but definitely time taught me understanding, which helped to alleviate some of the pain.

One thing that had never changed was my weekend drinking. Although by now I had more or less restricted my excesses to a Saturday evening, I would often invite friends back to the house after the pubs had closed. There was loud music, laughter and drunkenness but there was never any trouble, and no complaints from the neighbours.

Jim and Helen Merson were a lovely elderly Brethren couple who lived directly opposite me in Schoolhendry Street and Jim would always shove some tracts through my letter box. Out of healthy respect I would browse through them, make no sense of any of the old fashioned biblical text, and end up discarding them.

I remember receiving a Christmas card from Helen with an added comment:
'You are a very nice and quiet neighbour,' and a thought instantly sprung to mind: 'You don't know the half of it, Helen!'

On one occasion I recall coming home drunk to an empty house at two in the morning, rummaging through an old tabloid newspaper looking for a tarot reader to phone – such was my need to find direction or purpose to my life.

My lifestyle had changed very little in more than 15 years since I had left school. I had settled into what I perceived to be a normal lifestyle, but if that was normal then my life was far from fulfilled.

ARE YOU A MILLIONAIRE YET?

Never before had I been approached about any other business ideas or concepts, when in the autumn of 1995 my good friend and neighbour, Michael Minty, invited me to his house to view a business presentation. Minty (as he was known) had become involved in some kind of American direct selling idea and I was intrigued by what it entailed.

Minty and I had known each other for many years and I knew him well enough to realise that he wouldn't get involved in anything corrupt, unethical or immoral. I also knew that he would methodically research any financial project before committing himself. Although I had always been open minded and receptive to new ideas, I had never really imagined doing anything in business outside of my trade.

I remember sitting in Minty's living room with one other "prospect" when a sharply dressed man wearing a suit entered with a white board and easel. This chap looked familiar and it soon dawned on me that he was none other than Keith Baxter who ran a plumbing and heating business in nearby Macduff. Ironically, our paths had crossed just a few weeks earlier when we were both working for the same customer on a house just outside Banff.

This all felt a bit weird, but he soon began his slick and persuasive presentation and even though I struggled to grasp the mechanics and dynamics of the business plan, I was immediately drawn to Keith's enthusiasm and passion for what he so obviously believed in, and I was impressed by the fact that the corporate supplier had over two million distributors and operated in more than 60 different countries.

Having been given an information pack home with me, consisting of two audio tapes and several booklets, I sat up to 2 a.m. immersed in the text and listening to the tapes. One of the tapes was a question and answer session presented by Valerie Singleton, a respected national television presenter, and this seemed to add credibility to what was being offered. I instantly became really excited about the possibilities.

So much so that I could barely sleep that night.

The following evening, with almost childlike enthusiasm, I called Minty and asked him when I could get started. Little did I know at that point how much impact that decision would have. To be honest, I probably would have considered an idea that involved selling sand to the Arabs, such was my desire to find new direction in my life.

I had reached the stage where I had a very poor self image, carrying all the mental baggage of broken relationships, reckless lifestyle – and, above all, the guilt and shame of my father's death. My life pattern had become stale and predictable. It was one-dimensional, and it would be fair to say that I was shabby inside and out. I had been papering over the cracks ...

I certainly needed restructuring, remodelling, expanding and – if you'll excuse the cheesiness of this – a fresh coat of paint!

In retrospect, I needed to change my way of thinking, because my life had been a reflection of my limited reasoning, but this gave me renewed hope and purpose. This limited philosophy, which had penetrated my life, was explained by the following analogy from a business leader at one of the early seminars I attended:

'There was an experiment where a scientist raised some baby fish in a small glass tank, which was inside a larger tank that held adult fish. The little fish in the smaller tank could see the fish in the larger tank, but because of the glass barrier could not swim out. Once the small fish had grown up, the researcher removed the glass walls of the small tank so that they could swim out. But instead they stopped at the exact place that used to be their walls. The habit and memory of the edge of their world was more real to them than the freedom that was possible now that the glass had been removed.'

Like these fish, I had been accustomed to swimming in restricted surroundings, convinced that this was the only way to survive. I had obviously become a product of my environment.

My Painting and Decorating business was ticking over reasonably well and I appreciated all the good customers I had, but some of the work was often mundane and predictable compared with the excitement of sponsoring people and setting up new clients.

Network Marketing had originated in North America in the late 1950s. Products were moved directly from manufacturers to consumers, avoiding any need for advertising and bypassing the normal retail channel (and costs). As they bought into their own home-based business venture they were self-employed, and not agents or employed sales people working for a specific company. No stock was required and the start-up cost was less than £100.

Using the franchise method of duplication similar to certain popular fast food chains and coffee shop franchises, distributors (as they were termed at the time) could sponsor anyone into the business, giving them access to the same products and services for the same cost as they received them. They in turn had the same freedom to sponsor other people.

A small income could be made to supplement the wages of their full time job or, as in the case of some of the high level leaders, a passive residual income could be attained that was several times more that the average salary which was promoted, rightly or wrongly, as financial freedom.

I loved being part of a supportive team system where there was a positive atmosphere of encouragement and appreciation, and where everyone was pleased about the success of other people. This was a far cry from the conventional business climate that I was familiar with whereby I had experienced no help or support. On the contrary, I had been faced with a certain amount of bad feeling and even contempt from one or two other local decorators when I first started out in business, as they perhaps viewed me as a serious threat to their livelihoods.

Such was my level of commitment that everything else in my life was pushed to one side as I became fully focused on becoming successful. There is no doubt that I made countless mistakes in my over-eagerness to convert others to this whole new way of thinking, which regrettably meant that I was neglecting some of the people I was closest to in my life.

The training system also introduced me to new books and audio tapes. Reading books soon became a regular part of my daily pattern. After years of reading football magazines, true crime novels and tabloid newspapers, the introduction to positive mental attitude books and Christian inspirational books came as a revelation, to say the least.

Most of these books were not about selling or Network Marketing ... they were about me! I hadn't realised I had so many insecurities and distorted thinking patterns.

The Magic of Thinking Big, by David Schwartz, was the first self-help book I ever read and as I applied some of its principles to my daily life, I began to feel more confident and self-assured. Schwartz convinced me that there was no need for me to have an outstanding intellect or prodigious natural ability to become successful.

I began to grasp that true success was not simply the accumulation of money or material possession, but that it came in the form of reaching certain goals, which would lead to psychological, emotional and spiritual self-fulfilment. These were intangible commodities of which I had never previously been aware. Spiritual fulfilment was still very much a grey area for me. I assumed that meant a relationship with God, but I was still not sure that He existed.

Over a period of time I became drawn to John Maxwell, Norman Vincent Peale and Robert Schuller, who wrote more Christian-based than secular self-help books. I became an avid reader, often having three or four books on the go at the same time, but if I found one I really liked I would read it from start to finish in less than a week.

I did, however, find it difficult to stay awake while reading, primarily due to an exhausting day's work. Gradually, though, I began to find it easier, and while settling myself with a book in the bath, I would sometimes read for as much a two hours at a time, for I had mastered the skill of adding more hot water by turning on the tap with my left toe, while at the same time letting water out by adjusting the plug with my right toe – without interrupting the flow of my reading!

Before long I realised that we live in a society that seems to find fault with and criticises anything that it doesn't understand, and Network Marketing, with its high turnover of distributors, was an easy target for such critics. Some people were eager to relay horror stories to me regarding other people's experiences, although they had no first-hand knowledge or participation of these experiences themselves.

Around the same period, a pyramid-selling scheme called 'The Golden Circle' came to prominence. People I knew, who had rejected my legitimate business proposal, were only too willing to invest hundreds of pounds into an endless chain with no end product or service where each new level of participant had less chance of recruiting others, and with a greater prospect of losing large amounts of money.

I regularly hosted cosmetic evenings at my house, attended by a group of ladies I'd invited. A business associate would come along to take care of the colour consultancy analysis and sales. I was delighted on one occasion when I had a one-off cosmetic sale of just under £200 from one client. There was also a three week period in which I was selling a manual carpet shampoo applicator practically every day.

One of my most bizarre sales was to an Indian waiter who purchased an expensive underwater camera. Michael Minty and I set up several Indian restaurants as commercial clients. When one restaurant owner seemed to be dodging to pay a bill, I decided to negotiate an agreement with one of his staff. That deal was, that I would receive a free Indian carry-out every Friday night until the debt was cleared!

It was also exciting when my business expanded into various parts of the UK.

One day, as I was standing waiting to get served at my local bank, I was greeted with, 'Are you a millionaire yet?' in a somewhat smug and sarcastic manner by a lady as she entered. Never usually short of a quick reply I was taken aback. I had never mentioned becoming a millionaire to anyone, and had she known my true motives for doing something different with my life, she might not have been so eager to put me down. I had never begrudged anyone anything they had ever achieved, nor envied anyone who was better off financially than me, so I was profoundly pained by such a put-down.

I had gradually developed into an unyielding, strong-willed, if at times insensitive, person as I had grown into adulthood, and had seldom been the type to follow the beat of someone else's drum. I began to realise that adversity, treated the right way, could make me stronger, and I used that to my advantage. I suppose, in a perverse kind of way I welcomed the ridicule and criticism, for I would use that as a way of motivating myself.

I had a reasonable sponsoring rate and had no difficulty retailing the products, which I also used myself and therefore could comfortably recommend to other people. I was certainly no smooth, polished or sophisticated salesman, but my natural enthusiasm, and belief in my product, meant that exceeding my monthly retail target was a relatively simple task.

As part of the training system, I went to major seminars in Birmingham's National Indoor Arena three times a year where we were privileged to hear about high achievers from all different areas of life.

From the world of sport, I heard the likes of Alan Hansen, Sally Gunnell and Matthew Pincent. Former news presenter Martyn Lewis, mountaineer Chris Bonnington, and Falklands veteran Simon Weston were just some of the speakers that I was fortunate to listen to and learn from. It was such a privilege to personally meet Simon and have a brief conversation with him. On June 8, 1982, he was with other members of his regiment on the ship the RFA Sir Galahad in Bluff Cove, just off the Falkland Islands, when it was bombed and set on fire by enemy Skyhawk fighters. The ship was carrying ammunition, including phosphoric bombs, and thousands of gallons of diesel and petrol. Twenty-two out of his platoon of thirty men were killed.

Simon Weston survived with 49% burns, following which his face was barely recognisable. He then endured years of reconstruction surgery, including over 75 major operations or surgical procedures, whereby skin from his shoulders was used to make eyelids, and skin from his buttocks to form a new nose. He suffered psychological trauma, drinking heavily and even becoming suicidal, and admitted that his behaviour during this time had been 'terrible'.

Simon credited his mother with helping him to overcome this. In particular her act of reuniting him with his old regiment, who refused to mollycoddle him, forced him to face up to the harsh realities and to be positive about everything including his future. The circumstances surrounding the attack on the Sir Galahad that day at Fitzroy have been the subject of much controversy, but he has never been unduly interested in the apportioning of blame.

With his downbeat modesty and good humour, he set such a supreme example of how to take whatever setbacks life has in store for you. Unlike most brave soldiers, Simon Weston's real heroism did not begin until his army days were done. It would be totally understandable if he still suffers some disturbing and painful memories of his comrades who perished in the bombing of the Sir Galahad battleship.

I was learning such excellent personal and business teachings from the book and audio cassette programme that my confidence improved considerably, and my Decorating Business went from strength to strength. When I joined, I had been so driven by success and had seen this as an easy way of making money, but in the process of the struggle I had become less interested in the financial rewards and more drawn towards learning new skills and techniques. The retailing and sponsoring almost became secondary motivating factors.

What really gave me much pride and satisfaction was witnessing positive changes in some of the people I had introduced to the business. Graham, my best mate, developed so much confidence and interactive and social skills that it helped to make starting up his own Plumbing Business a natural progression in his life.

Even after four years of relentless toil and just moderate success, I would not hear one bad word spoken about the training system or the marketing plan. I tended to see everything as flawless, and although there were the inevitable personality clashes with dealing with so many different people within the network, we all had the right to choose who we worked closely with. I think it would be fair to suggest that I still viewed the whole concept with rose-tinted glasses ...

One day, after several years of experience, Michael Minty approached me wearing his unique dead-pan expression.

'I think there's something about you on the current tape of the week' – in reference to the audio tape we received weekly through the training programme. Instantaneously, I was quite excited, for I had been active in building the business and felt that my commitment was being recognised. Minty hesitated a moment before saying, 'I don't think it sounds very good for you,' continuing pensively, 'It's not the same story that you told me.' He was referring to the meeting I had with my business support team leader, in a nearby town.

I listened anxiously to the tape in question, and as I heard a distorted account of events being relayed I immediately felt a sick churning sensation in my stomach. I was devastated! I felt so betrayed. I wasn't at all prepared for such a gut-wrenching surprise;

a classic ambush that came without a hint of warning. I could barely take in what I was hearing. My business adviser's account of what had transpired had the thin shell of the truth but was most definitely contorted for the purpose of telling a more engrossing and amusing story at my expense.

This man that I had respected and admired for the way he and his wife had overcome great adversity to build a large network of people. I had been working closely with him for four years and could not for the life of me understand why he had decided to convert from mentor to tormentor. He had not mentioned anyone by name but I was in no doubt as to who it was he was putting down in such a patronising and insensitive manner.

The audio tapes were being distributed to thousands of people all over the UK and I knew that what they were hearing had been fabricated, even though they would have been oblivious as to who the fall guy was. It also perplexed me to think what the actual motive could be for recording such an inaccurate version of events, considering that my business mentor had a vested interest in helping me succeed and would have been aware that I would be listening to the audio tape.

In the pursuing days and weeks I went through a great deal of soul searching. I was naturally hurt and downcast by what had happened but I was still determined not to let the actions of one man lead me to turn my back on the many people with whom I had developed a strong bond.

I genuinely felt that for all my obvious shortcomings I was a loyal and trusting person but perhaps I had been too naïve in the blind trust I had placed in someone else whom I had perceived to be an almost flawless business advisor. After making my feelings known I received an apology of sorts. I soon got over it and became active again, but the trust was lost and could never be properly restored.

FROM GAMRIE TO AMSTERDAM

Although my small painting business had over a ten year period taken me as far afield as Aberdeen, Inverness and Edinburgh, I had never actually worked in the village of Gardenstown, just 18 miles east of Portsoy. Very few people used the official name of Gardenstown, named after its 18th century founder James Garden, when referring to the village, choosing instead to use the Parish name of Gamrie. In fact, I don't recall ever having been there in my entire life. I really never had any reason to visit this unique and unusual village. So when I received a phone call from a lady called Isobel Nicol, on the recommendation of her daughter who I had previously worked for in Buckie, I was willing to take the step into the unknown.

I was so out of touch with what was going on in Gardenstown that I was shocked and saddened to hear that William Jack, a young man I had been friendly with at school, had tragically died in a car crash several years previously.

Stephen West, a native of Gardenstown who had done a large percentage of the decorating work there, had retired and there was a need for someone else to fill the void. In a short time, just less than half my workload began to come from the village and its surrounding area.

I had been friendly with some of the men who lived there when I was at school but I had never seen any of them since then. Practically all the Gamrie boys in my year at school took Navigation and Nautical, and I clearly remember a few of them sitting in a row behind me in class wearing their distinctive 'Fair Isle' jerseys which were synonymous with the fishing fraternity at that time. Gamrie was dominated by the surnames of Watt, West and Wiseman, with a liberal sprinkling of Jacks, Ritchies and Nicols. Michael Ritchie, my business associate in Network Marketing, also lived there and we became good friends, enjoying nights out as well as Business training experience.

The village, uniquely positioned, clinging to a steep hillside above Gamrie Bay, was visibly split into three tiers – the old original village near to the sea, the second tier of the newer council housing schemes, built after the Second World War, and making up the third tier were the newest houses in the form of detached bungalows, furthest up the hill, as you enter the village. I found that Gamrie had a certain quirkiness about it as I came across names for things that I had never heard before. Seemingly, 'baltics' were wellington boots and a 'helio' was a thermos flask!

The top tier was considered by incomers and locals alike as the prosperous part of the village. 'Now, we don't have as much money as the folk that stay up the brae,' was the psychological or even subtly manipulative bargaining tool occasionally used by some of the old village residents when they asked me to quote for decorating work. I didn't mind them saying that – it was a good attempt – but ultimately it wasn't going to make any difference to my basic hourly rate or my even-handed method of doing business.

'You need to be saved, ma loon,' (you need to find salvation, son) was a statement I heard on more than one occasion, uttered by some of the older folks of Gamrie, as my white Renault Kangoo van started to become a familiar sight around the village, due to the amount of work I was doing there. I can't say that I ever gave the remark a great deal of thought but it was just part of the overall Christian influence that was entering my life. My basic understanding of being "saved" was that you believed in God and went regularly to Church.

This all seemed in stark contrast to my own home town where people who attended Church seemed few and far between. I remember there had been a form of mini revival in Portsoy, a few years previously, when a small group of people I knew reasonably well became Christians within a relatively short space of time. Within the town they were generally viewed in terms of being 'into religion' or 'Churchy' folk.

I soon knew who attended all the various places of worship in Gamrie. Although I was aware that there had been high profile splits and breakaways between the denominations, it made absolutely no difference to how I viewed them as painting customers. The vast majority were respectable, clean-living people, and even with my limited understanding of the Bible it was easy to figure out that they all worshipped the same God.

It became apparent that there had been a good deal of hurt and bad feeling involved with these bitter splits when one person described the Church that they had served in for many years as 'the devil's hoose'. This did little to change my long-held negative perception of the Church and I remember feeling that all this infighting would be enough to push away anyone searching for God in their life.

I had been reading about the life of Abraham Lincoln, and that shortly before the end of the Civil War he famously observed how ironic it was that both sides read the same Bible and prayed to the same God.

How relevant that statement still was, almost 150 years later as I, an outsider with no religious upbringing, looked upon the situation in this small fishing community.

It soon became common place for me to give thanks before enjoying a cup of tea and a selection of scrumptious home bakes with my customers, but this never made me feel uncomfortable or uneasy at all, for I respected their faith as well as their generosity. It was something that I had only experienced occasionally in local fishing villages, like Findochty and Sandend, where the Brethren influence was strong.

No one seemed more committed to their faith than Mary Johnston, an elderly spinster well into her eighties, who had been postmistress at the local Post Office for many years before her retirement. Mary's whole life seemed to revolve around her relationship with God, and, if nothing else, I could only admire her for her strong faith and scriptural knowledge.

With such a fundamentalist Christian slant in many of the books I was reading, perhaps subconsciously I was becoming more willing to talk openly about God and whether He really existed or not. We would often have discussions about 'religion' and although I was practically illiterate as far as my biblical knowledge went, I was never short of an opinion. Some of the literature was written in the 1940s and 50s and I recall on one instance when one of our business leaders was asked by one of his distributors if these books were still relevant in today's society, only to be told that life principles are timeless and if the scriptures, written 2000 years ago, are still being read by millions worldwide, then surely a book written half a century ago was as well. I also recollect quite clearly Michael Minty, complete with his usual dead-pan facial expression, once commenting: 'I wouldn't be surprised if we get the Bible through the training system some day.'

On another occasion, when I was painting the exterior windows of the Kirk, I jokingly suggested to Steven West, who was giving me a hand by holding my ladder for the highest windows, that I would come down to the Church on Sunday to finish painting them. Steven was not long in letting me know that if I did that it would be the last job I ever did in Gamrie.

I did not mind painting Churches and meeting halls but I never considered attending any of them on a Sunday.

My partner Linda and I would normally go for a drive on a Sunday and one of our magical mystery tours took us to the remains of St. Johns Churchyard, situated on a hill just above the village. I had become fascinated with old Churchyards and if we came across one I just had to stop and have a look round it. Linda and I had a standing joke about my 'ghoulish' new-found hobby but I was genuinely fascinated by the history of old churches and the lettering on old gravestones.

It was the dawn of a new millennium and I was sprawled lazily over Linda's settee, sleeping off the excesses of the previous 24 hours, when I was wakened by a knock at the door. As Linda answered I could hear faint voices but the accent was unfamiliar. Then all of a sudden it registered: That's Tony! And the next thing I knew, my cousin, to whom I had barely given a thought for many years, swaggered with self-assurance into the living room, closely followed by a dark-haired female whom I did not recognise.

After I had got over the shock of this unexpected visit, it took a while before I realised that this carefree, giggling woman was Jane – such was the dramatic change, not only in her appearance but also her demeanour, since the last time I had seen her, almost ten years earlier.

A visibly calm and relaxed Tony told us that they had decided on the spur of the moment to travel up to a nearby seaside town where Jane's relatives came from, and then decided to pay me an unanticipated visit. He assured me that he had been trouble-free for years and that the attempted murder charge was dropped after the alleged victim had been stabbed to death.

That evening, the four of us went to one of the local pubs for a drink. It was then that I noticed the registration of his red Ford Escort Convertible ... GBH! Obviously the new leaf had not been completely turned over yet!

Tony and Jane stayed with me that night and after Jane went to bed Tony and I talked into the early hours about the previous few years. Tony began to share some experiences of his time in Durham jail and that he used to ask for a top floor cell so that he could get an improved view of the spectacularly lit-up Durham Cathedral at night. He also told me that he used to volunteer to do the Bible reading at the early morning services of the prison Church!

Tony's surprising curiosity and enthusiasm for historical artefacts and ruins meant that I took him and Jane to visit the ruined Boyne and Findlater castles near Portsoy the following day. I could hardly believe that this was the same tormented couple I had last met in Blyth all those years ago.

My life at this point was fairly settled and I had been going out with Linda for the best part of three years. Keith was working in Holland, fitting false suspended ceilings, and he invited me over for few days to visit him. Linda suggested I should go, as Keith and I did not see all that much of each other, so I quickly made plans to fly to Amsterdam, stay a night, then travel by train to Gilze Rijen, a town situated between Breda and Tilburg, the following afternoon.

Keith had suggested that I should not bother pre-booking a hotel in Amsterdam because it would be just as easy getting fixed up once I was over there. On his advice I arrived at Schiphol Airport and after collecting my holdall from baggage reclaim, I made my way to the main terminal building where I was able to book a night's accommodation from the list of available hotels that lit up on a computerised map of the city. I felt it was important that I was staying near the main Central Station so that I could easily find my bearings. After making the short train journey I quickly set off to my hotel, which by my reckoning was only a short walk from Central Station.

It was early evening and darkness was starting to come down, so I was looking forward to getting checked into my hotel and finding somewhere to eat. I had almost reached the hotel when 'out of nowhere' appeared this black man in his late twenties or early thirties. Making eye contact with me, he asked in a soft whispering voice, 'Hey man do you want some Skunk? H? Charlie? Whizz? Ecstacy? LSD? Valium? Viagra?' I glanced back, just shook my head and walked on.

I wryly thought: Welcome to Amsterdam!

Having entered the hotel and checked in, the receptionist gave me a key and told me where my room was. I was directed to the top of a narrow steep stairway and my room was right up in the attic part of the building. I opened the door and was shocked by the dilapidated and dingy appearance of what could safely be termed as a hovel!

The woodwork, which I guessed had at one time been white, was all chipped and cracked and now a yellowy beige colour. The faded wallpaper was covered in graffiti. The ceiling paper was blistered and 'bagged' to such an extent that it was in danger of landing on a guest in the middle of the night. As I commented earlier, I had been in a few hencoops on my travels over the years, and I realised I wasn't paying top dollar for my stay here, but this was something else!

I had no intention of spending a minute more than necessary in my new surroundings so I decided to go for a walk, since I had lost my appetite by now. I gave myself a quick wash and a change of clothes before heading out.

In no time at all I realised that my hotel was inside the notorious Red Light District! Walking past a "Coffee Shop" I smelled the thick distinctive odour of cannabis smoke, but I didn't feel in any danger, just a bit taken aback, and I had definitely no inclination to smoke any funny fags after my Blyth experience!

After walking several thousand metres past various dubious-looking establishments, I eventually found a normal pub where there was a screening of a live English football match on Sky TV. I decided it looked safe enough to go in to watch the game and have a couple of pints of beer. I didn't really feel in the humour for excessive drinking but I felt comfortable with the atmosphere. I purchased a pint at the bar and bought another one at the start of the second half, which made my two pints spin out for a couple of hours thus enabling me to take in the entire game as well as the post-match analysis.

I pondered my next move. I was quite tired after a long day of travelling, but I felt an impulse to walk round this infamous Red Light District that I had heard so much about. Typically, I quickly dismissed the sensible option to return to the hotel as I began to rationalise my thinking. I had never been to Amsterdam before, and in any case, the Dutch shamelessly regard it as a tourist attraction. Surely it's all right to look but not touch? And would I ever be in Amsterdam again?

My mind was made up. I began walking in the raw, misty evening, and a steady drizzle descended as I meandered past the old buildings, leaning at odd angles and overlooking the tree-enshrouded canals.

However, the atmosphere had changed. What I had felt as non-threatening a few hours earlier was now manifesting itself into an uneasy spectacle as I noticed shadowy figures lurking in doorways, looking to sell a vast range of drugs. Pitiful and weird looking male characters, many of Turkish appearance, would shuffle along the street either staring menacingly at me or with their shifty eyes fixed firmly on the ground.

I was met by groups of boisterous foul-mouthed British males, presumably in Amsterdam for a stag night or 'lads weekend', and I passed sex clubs, peep shows and porn shops. Just in front of me two policemen were walking along quite nonchalantly – one laughing out loudly, seemingly without a care in the world and oblivious to everything around him. Bizarrely, no one gave them as much as a second glance.

Walking past an old Church, I recall thinking what a strange and inappropriate image it represented. It was probably the area that I found wholly inappropriate for a Church, for next I was waved at and enticed over by a succession of scantily dressed prostitutes who were standing or sitting behind large windows, hoping for trade ...

Something came over me, and all of a sudden I felt so sad for these girls. The immoral environment and seedy atmosphere that would no doubt have thrilled me in previous years was subtly challenging me, making me feel convicted. Something deep within me was telling me that this was not right.

Perhaps, partly because I was in the solitude of my own company – without Linda who I cared about and respected – but with a clear, sober mind, I felt that this whole vicinity epitomised evil and exploitation. The only desire I had at that very moment was to return to my dingy hotel room.

The following day, with my train journey not until late in the afternoon, I decided to spend a few hours exploring Amsterdam's unique urban scenery. I made my way down narrow cobbled streets that ran along the city's many picturesque canals, until, as if by accident, I came across a lengthy queue of people waiting to enter what appeared to me to be a plain-looking three-storey house.

Inquisitive to find out what was of interest, I approached a man at the rear of the queue. 'It's the house of Anne Frank,' he replied. The name was familiar and I remembered learning something about Anne Frank's diary when I was at school. Her story had been well documented in many books and films.

With plenty of time on my hands, I decided to take my place at the end of the queue. I soon found myself in the house, climbing the steep stairs that had changed little since 1945. I began to feel deeply moved in one of the rooms, when I noticed writing on the walls and some pictures that Anne had glued there. I read her father's first letter; a grim reminder of the horrors of that time and the persecution that the Jews suffered.

Several people were moved to tears and I myself was quite emotional. I felt connected with the time, the dangers, and the poignant reminder of the lives of these families. Everything was right there in front of my eyes: the windows that they would have risked to look out of and the places where the floor creaked; the secret entrance, concealed by the swinging bookcase – and finally Anne Frank's original diary, so immaculately preserved.

Who would have thought I could be so deeply affected by someone I had never known?

Once outside, I sat down on a bench alongside the canal, opposite the museum, gazing up at this powerful piece of history and attempted to comprehend the brutal discrimination of a race of people, questioning how Man could treat his fellow Man with such heinous acts.

Throughout my train journey later that afternoon, I reflected on the previous 24 hours and how I had unwittingly found myself entwined in places where such evil, exploitation and brutality had taken place. My memory drifted back to the scene in the film *Schindler's List*, in which we follow the plight of the little girl in the red jacket. The genius of director Steven Spielberg was so evident to me when he used colour against black and white to pick out this one child as a symbol of all the six million helpless victims exposed to such ruthless slaughter.

How could the Nazis kill someone so young and innocent? That was my overwhelming thought back then, but as I sat through the train journey the question that was constantly gnawing away at me was: If there is definitely a God, how could He allow such atrocities?

On the back of my Amsterdam experience, I felt drawn to study the work of Victor Frankl. I had come across some of his quotes in books I had read, but the title of his pioneering book, *Man's Search for Meaning,* had always intrigued me, and I purchased the book with great anticipation.

Dr. Frankl survived the war, and, partly because of his suffering, developed a revolutionary approach to psychotherapy called logotherapy. At the core of his theory was that man's primary motivational force is his search for meaning. Perhaps to find some sort of understanding of my father's choice to give up on life I became engrossed in his teachings, which I found neither negative nor anti-religious, and Frankl soon became a great influence in my life.

He was a humble medical student in Austria during the 1920s and became a disciple of Sigmund Freud, and later Alfred Ardler. Frankl eventually challenged their authoritarianism and was expelled from two schools.

In 1930, he earned a doctorate in medicine and was later in charge of a ward for the treatment of female suicide candidates at the General Hospital in Vienna. It is said that none of the patients took their own lives during his tenure. When the Nazis seized power in 1938, Dr. Frankl was put in charge of the neurological department of the Rothschild Hospital, the only Jewish hospital in the early Nazi years.

In 1942 Frankl was deported to concentration camp Theresienstadt, along with his wife and parents. Though assigned to ordinary labour until the last few weeks of the war, he never ceased trying to cure fellow prisoners from despondency and to prevent them from committing suicide.

During that time, Frankl endured years of unspeakable horror, including the extermination of most of his family in Nazi concentration camps. He believed that if there is a purpose to life at all there must be a purpose to suffering and dying, but suggested that we find that out for ourselves. He also taught that everything can be taken from a man, apart from one thing: the last of human freedoms – the ability to choose one's attitude towards any given set of circumstances.

Dr. Frankl's writings, about severe pain and unbelievable injustice to develop a pattern in order to find meaning in the often painful pathways at work, were a shining example to me. He frequently quoted Friedrich Nietzsche, the late 19th century German philosopher who, in one of his more lucid moments stated, 'He who has a why to live can bear almost any how' – a testimony of human endurance in the face of almost unbearable adversity, as long as the reason to live was strong enough.

Such was the powerful influence of this book on me that I read it from cover to cover over three sittings. Several years previously, I had read *Power of Positive Thinking*, by Norman Vincent Peale, but I felt that Victor Frankl took that concept to the next level.

I vividly recall sitting in my warm living room on a bitterly cold winter's evening with the wind howling outside, staring at a simple mug of tea with a great sense of appreciation after I had read a particularly harrowing piece of the book.

ONE MAN'S OPINION

For once I seemed to have stability in my life with the good solid relationship I had enjoyed with Linda for the best part of four years but, sadly, we decided to split up. We had gradually grown apart, and perhaps I was feeling restless.

We had been close. Linda had been my best friend, a loyal confidante and a good listener – well, she had to be when she was with me! Thankfully a strong friendship remained, despite the inevitable sadness that our romance was over.

Quite frankly, I had no desire to return to my previous social life of drinking every weekend in the local pubs and night clubs. Although I liked the company, I was loath to listen to the latest small talk in that wearisome, repetitive, predictable you-could-set-your-watch-by, 'I told you that would happen' type of environment that the local pub scene had become to me.

A change in my Saturday night routine was called for, and I managed that by going to Fraserburgh with my good friend, Michael Ritchie.

I found the vibrant, bustling quayside bars in stark contrast to the stale, predictable night life in my home town. I felt totally at ease just being another anonymous face on the pub circuit where I could mix freely with the Saturday-night revellers.

We normally booked into a guest house, then drove home late Sunday morning, when the effects of our previous evening excesses had worn off and only the customary hangover was left. My drinking may have subsided over the years but I was still prone to the occasional spectacular relapse.

Yes, indeed, for several months it suited me fine until I came to the realisation that I was back in the same old rut ... A different neck of the woods it may have been, but doing what I had done all through my late teens and twenties was tiresome and inescapable, and gave me no lasting fulfilment or contentment.

Late in the year 2000 a split occurred within the IBS (International Business Systems) training system.

There had been rumours of a big fall out between some of the business leaders and, for whatever reason, the major Conferences, held every four months in Birmingham, were suddenly switched to Cardiff. I still never missed one, but it would be fair to say that a great deal of my early drive and enthusiasm had gone.

Although I was still driven by self-improvement and continuous learning I was coming to the conclusion that my primary motivating factor for remaining in Network Marketing was not the accumulation of money but promoting a cause or a concept I strongly believed in.

I really looked forward to an opportunity to recharge my batteries every four months, whereby I could have a break from the intensity of my hectic decorating business schedule and have a blast with some valued friends.

The monetary and material wealth that was clearly available to those who put in the time and effort did not greatly impress or motivate me any more. In reality, I just loved the positive atmosphere and the genuine people I was associating with.

The switch to Cardiff meant a longer journey for our group but I was quite excited about the change of venue. I had once heard Cardiff described rather unflatteringly as 'The Dour Maritime Capital of Wales', but if that were the case, somewhere along the line it had certainly transformed itself from a coal mining town to a cosmopolitan city that still proudly displayed its Welsh heritage.

Anchoring the city was the impressive Cardiff Castle, built upon Roman ruins that were later turned into a Norman stronghold.

Distinctive, charming and vibrant were the three adjectives that instantly come to mind when describing this fascinating city as I made my customary early morning saunter into the heart of town.

Cardiff was also an ideal opportunity for the single guys, like Graham Hutcheson, Michael Ritchie and myself, to experience the culture and nightlife of a different city. We found the weekend atmosphere in the city centre warm and non-threatening and we mixed easily with the Saturday-night revellers.

A sizeable group of us would meet up for a meal earlier in the evening, then move on to the packed bars and clubs, most of which had large video screens with Shirley Bassey and Tom Jones songs being perpetually played by the Disc Jockeys. Tom, the great showman, was singing with such passion that every time the classic melodic love song 'Delilah' was played practically every person in the jam-packed bar burst into deafening song during the chorus.

All this was so different from previous years, when we stayed in a town called Tamworth, situated about a twenty minutes drive from the National Exhibition Centre in Birmingham.

I was 'tickled pink' when I realised that Tamworth was once home to the Reliant Motor Company who produced the famous three-wheeled Reliant Robin. The most famous one was owned by the Trotter brothers, Del and Rodney, in the popular TV series, 'Only Fools and Horses'.

The "drinkers" would invariably end up in the disco next to our hotel until the early hours of the morning, as it had a late licence. It would not be too unkind to say that it was one of the grimmest and dingiest places I had ever set foot in – and that was saying something!

We were welcomed by a damp, mouldy smell as soon as we entered. Then we had to walk to the bar across a carpet that was so filthy that you felt your shoes sticking to the floor.

I usually shared a room with Graham, and on more than one occasion, following a particularly late night, one of our fellow distributors would have to phone to wake us up in the morning because we had to be at the NEC by 9.30 a.m.

Often hung-over and dehydrated, we would not have the stomach for a cooked breakfast, settling instead for a quick cup of tea and copious amounts of still water, secure in the knowledge that we could catch up on some lost sleep during the seminar by nodding off when there was a speaker who bored us.

The following February I attended the funeral service of Abbie McKenzie, the father of two good friends, Kenny and Bruce, at my local Church. Although it was such a sorrowful occasion, I felt myself really concentrating on understanding the content of the message being preached by the young minister, Iain Sutherland, who was new to the Parish.

For the first time in my life I found myself curiously receptive to what was being relayed from the pulpit. Iain's simple but appropriate message struck a chord with me. For once, I felt I was not listening to tedious religious rambling – I was listening to something I could understand and that made total sense, as well as the fact that it was being preached by a human being I could identify with.

Up until that point, my unflattering impression of most ministers was very much based on the dour, sombre, stereotypical 'Reverend I. M. Jolly' character, played hilariously well by the late Rikki Fulton at Hogmanay on television!

Several months later, I attended a major business seminar at the Cardiff Indoor Arena. I had my favourites among the speakers, but the man who challenged me on this occasion was not one of them – even though I could not help admiring the enthusiasm and conviction he brought to the speaker's platform.

I distinctively recall him saying something that baffled me, troubled me in a sense, and something I could not attach logical understanding to from my terrestrial perspective of life.

During one of his talks he boldly stated that God was the number one priority in his life – even more important to him than his wife and children.

This confused me somewhat, for I had thought that a man should always put his wife and children first. I mulled his statement over in my head several times during the following days but I still could not grasp his reasoning.

In the Autumn of 2001, I had decided to make a significant

investment in overseas property by purchasing a flat in the Spanish holiday island of Tenerife. It seemed a logical decision for me to make, based on how poorly pension funds were doing due to the mediocre performance of the stock market.

I had been flying regularly to Tenerife on holiday for a number of years, attracted to the warm winter climate that made me conscious of the all-year-round renting potential which in turn would create a passive residual income for me.

After spending endless hours on the Internet researching everything pertaining to the purchase of an apartment, such as availability, location, prices, and legal issues, I called my good friend, Stewart Masson, to ask for his advice. Stewart and his wife Moira had moved over there with their daughters, Karen and Shelley, a few years previously and were running a successful Scottish bar on the Island so, despite all the obvious potential pitfalls and stress of purchasing an overseas property, it was reassuring to know that they would be on hand for advice and guidance.

At short notice, I booked a flight from Aberdeen and boarded the Span Air plane with an incredible buzz of anticipation and adventure as I set off on my new business venture.

Following my arrival that evening, Stewart set up an appointment for me with an English estate agent in Los Christianos and drove me there early the next morning.

The owner of the British owned Estate Agency was not available, but another Englishman was there in his place. He immediately struck me as over-confident and self-important as he began questioning me at breakneck speed about my budget and the type of property I was looking for.

He came across as very much the stereotypical brash cockney. Perhaps he pre-judged me; seeing me as a potential time waster because of my milk bottle pale appearance and adding to that the fact that I am never the most relaxed or confident when I feel I am being interrogated rather than advised. Nevertheless, it was blatantly obvious to me that his manner was condescending and dismissive from the very start of our discussions.

After about ten minutes his boss arrived. He introduced

himself, sat on a chair alongside me and then, quite bizarrely, started whining about a sore tooth. It soon became evident that his 'side-kick' did not think I had the finances available to purchase an apartment and this was confirmed when, eventually, he nonchalantly leant back in his chair, pointed to six different fingers and told me to come back when my six numbers came up in the lottery!

I was taken aback, crushed in fact, and so lost for words that I did not know how to react. Meekly I slithered out of the building – a dejected man, belittled in the extreme, with my tail firmly between my legs.

Dreadfully downcast, I ambled down to the sea front to begin my long two-mile walk back to my base in Playa de las Americas. I was feeling so sorry for myself, wasting no time in getting into prime self-pity mode. I felt such a fool, and started to convince myself that I should have stayed at home; that I was out of my depth financially and that I should have invested my money elsewhere. In reality, I was having a monumental pity party where no one else had bothered to turn up!

Walking despondently along the sea front, wallowing in self pity and oblivious to the blazing sunshine in the azure midday sky, something began to stir inside me. A quote from Abraham Lincoln came to mind: 'No one can make you feel inferior without your consent.'

He was right. After all, it was only one person's opinion that had affected me so much. Why let that happen? I began to put things in proper perspective.

Gradually the tide turned. Another thought flashed through my mind: 'Go back and give the antagonist the full force of your vicious corrosive tongue' (which was now being used very sparingly but which was the disdainful potent weapon I could always fall back on whenever the need arose!)

Of course, this would not have changed the outcome of our meeting but it would at least have massaged my bruised ego and justified my 'don't suffer fools gladly – put people in their place' philosophy; the very philosophy that I was teaching people, whom I had sponsored into my Network Marketing business, to steer clear of.

Thankfully, the red mist lifted and rational thinking came back into play. I began to see things more clearly, feeling a powerful surge of tenacity and conviction.

I became solution-orientated.

All the finances were in place, and I had not come all this distance to waste my time or be treated with contempt by such a nauseating individual. As far as I was concerned, I might well have to live on nothing but bread and butter with watercress for the next ten years but I would be buying what I had flown to Tenerife for.

I arrived back at Stewart's pub around lunch time. Scotland were playing Croatia at football and the bar was filling up with people who wanted to watch the game on TV.

'How did you get on?' shouted Stewart from behind the bar.

'Waste of time, the guy wouldn't give me the time of day,' I yelled back.

'Never mind him, just go to someone else,' replied Stewart in his usual forthright manner.

That was all the reassurance and confirmation I needed. Watching football was the last thing on my mind as I spent the next 2-3 days tirelessly viewing several properties along the South Tenerife coastline.

Less than 60 days later I had purchased a one-bedroom apartment in the Torviscas area of Playa de las Americas.

Ironically, not one of the other three estate agents I had dealt with suggested that I didn't have the necessary funds in place, so thankfully a lottery win was never required.

Roughly three months later, I returned to live in my newly purchased apartment for the first time and I decided to invite an old friend, Myles Murray, to come over with me. Myles had recently separated from his wife and was understandably at a low ebb. I felt the break would do him a power of good.

However, having legal issues and renovation work to attend to, a week of our old customary heavy drinking was not the number one priority.

We talked a lot about things that had happened in our lives in a reflective and somewhat philosophical manner, and we even discussed the possibility of going to Church. Only a few short years previously such a radical suggestion would have been greeted by nothing but derision and contempt, showing us how much our thinking had evolved; perhaps also that we had matured and were now more open to change.

However, despite good health, loyal friends, no financial concerns, and an apartment in Tenerife, I still had a feeling of emptiness inside me. It was hard to describe. I wasn't desperately unhappy about anything in particular, and in many ways my life was going well, but I felt uneasy within myself.

Perhaps you could say I was 'happily discontented'!

WHO IS NICKY GUMBEL?

Once again, I was at a crossroads in my life and there was still that feeling of something missing; a void that I seemed unable to fill with anything that the world could offer. The books I had been reading during the past few years had been a great help to me in many areas of my life, but I was fast beginning to feel almost immune to what they were teaching me.

If there was one particular instance that led me to re-evaluate my life, it was an incident that occurred in Aberdeen about three months later.

I had gone out for a few drinks with Michael Ritchie but as the evening progressed, typically we had managed to get split up. It was bitterly cold and frosty when I left the city-centre in the small hours of Sunday morning. Although I had consumed some alcohol earlier on in the evening, I'd had only soft drinks since well before midnight because I did not want a hangover to hinder the long journey down to Blackburn, in Lancashire, where we were attending a Business seminar.

I felt fine, though freezing, as I came out of the nightclub at around 2 a.m. The short walk to the guest house took around five minutes but on approaching the entrance I glanced at my car and a foolish thought flashed through my mind: 'Why don't I take the car out for a run?'

I tried to dismiss this silly notion but the thought just kept on returning. Added to this, I felt remarkably alert and awake and it was as if I needed one final burst of excitement to complete what had been an enjoyable evening. Even this early in the morning, with daylight only a few short hours away, I did not want the evening to end. This was typical of me; getting up in the morning when I had been mixing and mingling with the opposite sex was always the last thing on my mind!

The next I knew, I was starting my car and off I went, feeling bright and alert, while I convinced myself that the two or three alcoholic drinks I had consumed early in the evening would have been out of my system.

My plan was to drive to Union street near the taxi ranks, look for any of the girls I had been talking to or dancing with that evening, and offer them a lift home.

No one needed to tell me that I should have been in my bed, but I felt totally powerless to stop myself.

I set off, driving as cannily and cautiously as I could towards Union Street. All of a sudden, while approaching a roundabout, the engine stalled. Glancing in my rear-view mirror, I noticed I was holding up a taxi behind, so I nervously tried to rev up my engine again. Next thing, an irate taxi driver leapt out of his cab at lightning speed and as I wound down my window he shouted into my face: 'What the heck are you playing at? Have you been drinking?'

In a blind panic and feeling unable to defend myself all I could muster was a mumbled, 'Sorry, mate ... '

'I should get the police,' he roared, eyes almost popping out of his head with rage, 'but just get the hell away from here before I do.'

My heart was beating frantically and I was not up for any backchat as I followed his clear, blunt instructions and drove my car the short journey back to my lodgings. As soon as I had parked the car, I made a mad dash for the entrance of the B&B without even daring to look behind me. I was in such a state of paranoia that I had almost convinced myself I was being tailed by the police.

I woke up in the morning with a knot in my stomach, but when I looked out of the window, my car was sitting perfectly parked outside the front entrance. However, my relief was overshadowed by the guilt I felt about having done something so thoughtless and irresponsible. It did not matter that I may have been under the legal limit, or that I thought that the taxi driver had over-reacted, but he had done me a favour. I did some soul-searching: What had prompted me to take an idiotic chance like that?

I began to feel that every now and then I had to self-destruct, powerless to prevent such acts of personal sabotage. It seemed that the selfish, instant buzz of immediate gratification was still leaving a dark stain on my life.

For a while this single incident constantly challenged me. I was ill at ease with myself once again. Although from the outside it may have looked like I was successful and content, something was still missing, but nothing I could really define, despite knowing the clear distinction between right and wrong.

I began to think more and more about the existence of God, but I had such negative memories of the Church that I couldn't see myself ever taking the plunge to attend a tedious Sunday morning service.

When I was working in Gardenstown, Mary Johnstone had given me a video about Jesus but, although I had left it on the shelf beside my TV, I had not yet got round to watching it. Because of my many conversations with Mary, I had now an open mind about the existence of Jesus. But a dead man coming back to life? In our sophisticated age, when myth had given way to science, how could I take such a claim seriously?

My experiences in Amsterdam had challenged me somewhat and my Aberdeen escapade had only reinforced the need for change. I realised that I had spent years chasing the pleasures of life – things that provided instant excitement – then dramatically changed track to focus on business success.

But still I was restless ...

In May 2002, I found myself doing a decorating job for a local couple, Neil and Liz Bowie. I knew them reasonably well, being of the same age as Liz, and I also knew that they were both heavily involved with the local Church in Portsoy. I felt this would be the ideal opportunity to ask about God, so one day, while working in the living room, I began asking Liz various questions about 'Church' and 'Religion'.

Liz seemed pleasantly surprised by this and answered any questions as best as she could, but suggested that I attended a forthcoming Alpha course which, she said, was an easy to understand introduction to the Christian Faith. She then gave me an invitation leaflet to take home with me.

I looked at the front cover of the little red booklet. There was a cartoon caricature of a man with the name Nicky Gumbel underneath it. In my ignorance, I just assumed this was the funny name given to the cartoon character. I had no objection to the invite – after all, I had tried just about everything else that life had to offer, so what did I have to lose?

Typically, I didn't bother to read the booklet but I did, however, leave it on my kitchen table so that I would not forget. I even mentioned to my friends, Francis and Maureen Watt, who owned the local decorating shop in Banff, that I intended going to an Alpha course. Being committed Christians they seemed genuinely pleased.

The only slight concern I had about this Alpha thing, was that it was going to be held in the upstairs lounge of the Boyne Hotel. I could see why the Church had wanted to use a less daunting venue for non Church goers, but this had been my local for many years, and a worrying thought entered my head:

What if someone recognised me going in?

On the evening of the course introduction I began feeling a bit uneasy. I wasn't so sure after all that this was a good idea. I wondered what I should wear. It was a Church organised thing, so should I dress accordingly? I raked through my wardrobe for a shirt that would be appropriate, dug out a pair of dress trousers – which were actually part of my business seminar suit – and checked myself in the mirror before I went, to make sure I had the right look of 'reverence' about me.

While walking the short distance to the Boyne Hotel, I felt my unease turning into real fear. Approaching the hotel with my heart pumping like mad I convinced myself that someone would see me going in and that I would be the talk of the town.

Sure enough, at the entrance I met someone I knew, and such was my hang-up about being seen at a religious meeting that after a brief exchange of pleasantries I just turned round to go home ... My bottle had gone!

No sooner had I started walking than the predictable self-condemnation started. That little voice in my head began to nag me: 'What on earth are you so scared of? So much for being a man of your word.'

I felt awful ... How could I be so weak ?

Back home, I just sat down and stared blankly at a wall for a while, pondering my next move. I decided I would phone Liz to apologise for not turning up and to promise her that I would definitely attend next week. I gave it a couple of hours before making the call. Liz wasn't home yet but her daughter Erin answered and I explained that I couldn't make the Alpha course and to let her mum know that I would definitely be there next week. Later that evening Liz called back and she could not have been nicer or more understanding. 'Absolutely no problem Colin. Don't worry about it. I will see you there next week.'

Later that week, when I was purchasing paint from Forbes Watt & Sons, Maureen asked me: 'How did you get on at Alpha?'

I hesitated for a second, then shrugged my shoulders before I answered, 'Ach, I backed out at the last minute. Couldn't go through with it. Don't know what came over me.'

Maureen asked, 'Well, would you like to come to our Alpha course? It starts next week.' I instantly warmed to her idea.
'Yes, I think I will,' I answered, because I saw a way of going through the course without anyone I knew finding out.

Francis and Maureen were members of the Riverside Christian Fellowship in Banff. However, because pride was still an issue, and just to make sure I maintained my low profile, I decided to park my car in a nearby side street so that no one could see it.

I believe Francis and Maureen were a bit surprised that I

actually did turn up for the first of 10 sessions. There was a group of about 16, including five or six Church leaders. Some of the people were familiar to me, but there was no one I knew really well.

We enjoyed a cooked meal and then watched an introductory video with the Title, 'Christianity: Boring, Untrue and Irrelevant?' This 45-minute video was presented by a smooth and convincing ex-barrister, Nicky Gumbel, who was now assistant pastor at Holy Trinity Church in Brompton, London. So he was a real person after all. My head was full of questions.

How could anyone in their right mind possibly believe these incredible Bible stories?

How could a loving God allow the cruelty and human suffering in such places as Auschwitz, Aberfan, and Cambodia?

I may have had reservations regarding Christianity but somehow I had always felt that God created me. To my mind, Man had not slithered out of the sea millions of years ago. Darwin's theory of evolution left me with even more unanswered questions.

Why do we appreciate beauty in art, music and poetry?

Why do we have a conscience and a sense of morals?

Why do we possess rational thought so superior to animals?

Where did the first life come from?

Surely, I reasoned, evolution required that non-living matter produced the first life form where there was no life before? But my simple observation of the world was that life could only originate from some form of life itself. I had never really bought into the widely held atheistic view that we were strictly a biological entity and that what brief life we enjoyed was restricted to a fragile and vulnerable body, aimlessly stumbling through a world plagued by war, famine and disease, as well as a multitude of other daily obstacles.

That would surely only have left the question of whether the world would self- destruct before our short and pointless life ground to a halt of its own accord, with our closest living relatives so pre-occupied with swinging from trees and munching bananas that they'd forget to mourn our passing.

I had also great difficulty believing that all species – from ostriches to octopuses and from hairy caterpillars to human beings – were a result of chance or the 'Big Bang', with all living things traced back to an original spark of life on our planet, millions of years ago.

Nicky Gumbel not only presented himself as a real person but also as a gifted speaker, able to integrate suitable and amusing stories within his talks.

I was half expecting to be 'Bible bashed' but was surprised to find out that I had the opportunity to voice my own scepticism and objections during the after-video discussion, where everything was relaxed, non-threatening and friendly.

I could never really differentiate between Church, Religion and Christianity. Nicky explained that Christianity is first and foremost about relationships, rather than rules. More about a person than a philosophy.

My brand-new basic understanding was that religion was about mankind trying to do different things to please God and earn His favour, whereas the essence of Christianity was summed up as being about the sinless life of Jesus Christ, leading to His death on the cross.

Church, I found out, was simply a body of people with a common belief in God.

This was all-absorbing stuff, but not overly challenging. However, Nicky really grabbed my attention when he suggested that other people's response to a Christian might be, 'It's great for you but it's not for me.'

This, he said, was not a logical position. He reasoned that if Christianity is true, it is of vital importance to every one of us. If it is not true, then Christians are deluded and it is not 'great for us' – in that case it is very sad, and the sooner we are put right the better.

I went home that night with lots of information swirling around in my mind but feeling that I should at least see out the whole ten week course.

The second week's video topic was, 'Who is Jesus?', and this one really opened my eyes to the truth. For the first time I was made aware of the accuracy of the Hebrew prophets, many centuries before the birth of Jesus, regarding His birth, life and death. The exactness and precision of these details confirmed both the truth of Bible prophesy and the existence of the inspiration behind it all.

I also heard that Paul the apostle recounted that Jesus appeared to more than 500 of His followers at one time, the majority of whom were still alive and could confirm what Paul had written. Many security precautions were taken with the trial, crucifixion, burial and entombment of Christ, as well as the sealing and guarding of His tomb.

This may all have been circumstantial, but for me it was powerful evidence that Jesus not only lived but had also risen from the dead.

In the space of a few days, my perception of Jesus had changed from just another biblical character to the lofty position of 'Saviour of the World' and 'Son of God'.

After that second video I had detailed discussions with the group and the conclusion was that I felt confident enough to do two things:

One: Park my car right in front the Harvest Centre!

Two: Attend a Church service in Banff.

I knew that the Riverside Church was viewed as a 'Charismatic Church' but was unsure what that really meant. I was naturally apprehensive as I entered the building to attend the morning service, but my fears were quickly dispelled when Christine Chinchen approached me and welcomed me to the Church.

Everything seemed so different from anything I had previously experienced. The individual seats were comfortable and padded. The decor was warm and inviting and a thick jade green carpet had been recently fitted.

The praise band were already playing, and an overhead projector was relaying the words of the songs on a large screen. I immediately felt relaxed and comfortable in what I could see was an affectionate, congenial, family atmosphere.

The praise band played worship songs for about 20 minutes

before the pastor arrived on stage to lead prayer. Instantly I was at ease and enjoyed the freedom of this different type of Church service – something I had never felt with the tediously predictable triple-decker hymn-prayer-sermon sandwich of Church services I had attended in the past.

The Alpha evenings were now something I looked forward to and although I probably had more to contribute than most, no one dominated the discussion and everyone was given the chance to air their views. I was not naïve enough to believe that Alpha was perfect or flawless, but I had the freedom and opportunity to dismiss or substantiate any of its teachings. I did this between sessions by checking things online as well as looking up scriptural references in an old white-covered Gideon's Bible that I had found lying about my house.

One of the later sessions was called, 'How do I resist evil?'

As someone who had continuously yielded to the temptations of the world, this was of great relevance to me. I always had an image of God as a bearded old man sitting on a cloud, wrathfully pointing at a sinner like me to admonish me for all I had done wrong and, on the other hand, I had the image of a devil with red horns and a winnowing fork in his hand, trudging through Dante's inferno.

I had my eyes opened when I heard that the ultimate aim of Satan is to destroy every human being and to put us on a path that leads to destruction. His main desire, according to Nicky Gumbel, was for failure to become a pattern in my life.

Now, this made perfect sense to me: If God was good, then the devil was evil. In each case the difference is just one letter but I could see that the power of God's Goodness could be seen in the Christian doctrine and that truth, reading the Bible, and listening to God's Word, was the only way to recognise that.

I began to understand why there is so much evil in the world. This was one of my biggest objections to ever accepting Christianity. The thrust of my argument was that the presence of evil disproves the power of a loving God. However, it was explained that God did not create evil but that sin entered the world through Adam's disobedience in the Garden of Eden. God did not create robots; He gave us a mind, free to think what it desires, thus giving humans the opportunity to make right and wrong choices.

God Himself had, in fact, the ultimate solution by sacrificing His Son, Jesus Christ, who defeated evil by dying for our sins on the cross.

One of the last videos asked the question: 'Who is the Holy Spirit?'

I struggled to understand the teaching that the Father, Son and Holy Spirit were all one person, and that God, Jesus and the Holy Spirit were indeed the 'Trinity' or 'Godhead' – that there was not a three-headed God, and that God was not just one person.

The course finished with what was called 'A Holy Spirit Day' when you could enjoy a day of fellowship with the Alpha group and have the opportunity to ask Jesus into your life as 'Lord and Saviour'.

Unfortunately, I had made arrangements to travel to Tenerife on that day, but it was good to take time out to get myself right with God. Although I believed that Jesus was all He claimed to be, I had issues I needed to confront before I could make such a life-changing commitment.

My difficulty still lay in believing that God could possibly love and accept me after the life I had led. Regularly attending Church, I reckoned, would help me chip away at some more of my rough edges before I was in a position to give my life to Jesus.

It was a struggle for me to read the Bible, for I found it daunting and a bit challenging, but I began to read inspiring stories of salvation and one of the first I read was *The Cross and the Switchblade*, which told the true story of a young pastor, David Wilkerson, who spent five years in New York ministering to disillusioned youngsters, encouraging them to turn away from drugs and gang violence. The main character in the book was Nicky Cruz, a young gang leader who was transformed by Wilkerson's ministry.

In *Run Baby Run*, Nicky Cruz writes the story of his life, including coming to New York, being the leader of a violent gang, then eventually meeting Wilkerson and becoming a Christian Evangelist.

These riveting books and narratives were an inspiration to me, even though I was not yet prepared to make the same commitment myself.

While regularly attending The Riverside Church, also called 'The Harvest Centre', I began to feel comfortable with the whole "Church experience".

It seemed to be a Church where everyone was accepted and where no one – despite their back-ground or their past – was condemned or judged.

The Christ-centred teaching was done with fun-filled enthusiasm and involved various activities. Services were always exciting and varied, with pastors and preachers coming over from various parts of the world.

I particularly remember a lady pastor from New Zealand who shared the parable of the wise old man, who said: 'Inside of me there are two dogs. A black dog and a white dog. The black dog is bad, the white dog is good. The black dog fights the white dog all day.'

When asked by his friend which one wins, the wise old man reflected for a moment then replied: 'The one I feed the most!'

Realising that attending Church was the right thing to do, I rarely missed a morning service.

Occasionally, I would go out on a Saturday night and drink a bit too much, but would still drag myself out of bed to go to Church the next morning. Feeling rough and dehydrated, I would excuse myself during the service and go downstairs to help myself to a couple of glasses of water from the chilled water-dispenser before returning to the service.

I was acutely aware of the fact that I wasn't saved, and I knew I would have to repent my sins and ask for forgiveness before I could become a Christian, but something was always holding me back. It was such a leap of faith, and I feared having to give up so much of what had been normal in my life.

After a few months of playing a game of 'Churchgoing', I began to feel restless and unfilled within myself again. The comfort zone that I had created for myself after Alpha wasn't making me feel cosy at all.

One thing I did know: I could never be half-hearted about anything I genuinely believed in, for I was always intensely committed to everything I set my mind on.

But how could I really commit to God if I was not saved?

I began attending the evening services at the Church in Portsoy, as well as the morning service in Banff. I knew most of the members of the praise band anyway and I found that the single service on a Sunday was not enough for me. During this "double whammy" I was constantly being challenged about my relationship with the Lord and I knew deep down that no amount of attending Church would give me forgiveness and eternal life.

A thought struck me: What would happen if I were to die suddenly – perhaps a heart attack or even an accident?

I rationalised that the Bible might be scaremongering but could I really afford to take that chance? Would the God I was worshipping with great passion on a Sunday willingly inflict such a harsh punishment on not just me but a great multitude of people who die every day? How could such a belief possibly tie in with the Bible's description of a God who was infinitely loving and merciful?

God, in fact, seemed to be a bit of a spoilsport for not allowing me to do the seemingly harmless things I enjoyed.

And then there was Hell!

Hell, was one of those topics that always made me feel uncomfortable. I had heard stories of Hell being a place of fire, demons, and endless torment. Throughout history many authors had written about it – 'Dante's Inferno', for example. Even Hollywood has made it the subject of many movies. But I found the doctrine of Hell confusing, to say the least.

Was it only a grave with no consciousness?

What about a place of correction and punishment that is not eternal? Or even an endless agonising burning in open fire?

Whatever it was, or wasn't, it was something to be avoided at all cost!

Once again, I seemed to be in a period of confusion, stuck firmly between a rock and a hard place. As the weeks and months passed by, the discomfort and uncertainty became stronger. I was becoming distressingly aware that there were no shortcuts or back doors to eternity.

Doing good works, and living a decent life was still going to leave me short of the mark ...

MY TRUE COLOURS

By now, the major IBS Conferences were held at Telford International Arena. This represented another exciting adventure as we were based in Ironbridge which, unbeknown to me, was a famous World heritage site. If our trips to Cardiff and Tamworth were dominated by contrasting nightlife, then this one was all about a unique industrial and natural environment with panoramic views and breathtaking scenery.

It was on one of these weekends away that I really felt at a spiritual crossroads.

On this particular Friday evening, we arrived in time for a wonderful Thai meal with some good friends and fellow distributors from the Liverpool area. I usually had an early night, while the others would go for a drink after their meal. This meant that as Saturday dawned bright and dry, I would be itching to go for a long walk around the area, which was once a hotbed of high technology and the centre of the Industrial Revolution.

The conference did not start until 12.30 p.m. so I had plenty of time for a rake around and it did not take me long to find one of the most breathtaking views I had ever seen.

I climbed more than 100 steps, which clung to the hillside, to make my way through a tunnel, eventually leading me into the churchyard of St Luke's Church where there was a bench waiting for me to rest on. From up there it felt like I was almost touching God Himself, as I looked over the rooftops and chimney pots to view the world's first Iron bridge, built by Abraham Darby ll.

Totally in awe of Darby's skill and ingenuity I just gazed at this remarkable bridge, with its arches majestically spanning the river Severn, that had enthralled tens of thousands of tourists who, like me, had walked to its highest point to glare into the depths of the water below.

Something made me feel that there was another place I should visit, somewhere nearby, and I found myself choosing a different direction, towards Coalbrookdale.

I walked for about 10 minutes, down steep steps and narrow lanes, then along Darby Road, where I came to another set of steps, leading to a Quaker Burial Ground. This rectangular piece of land was enclosed by a brick wall, lined with very modest grave stones. I knew nothing about Quakers or their faith, but I had a feeling that they were similar to Amish people in that simplicity was an important part of their life. I was touched that they seemed to have a humble outlook on life, their memorial stones being simple and low-lying. This gave me the impression that to them each person was of equal worth and respect.

I spent a good half hour walking undisturbed in this odd but peaceful place. I distinctively felt a spiritual presence. It was as if God was watching me, telling me to stop chasing worldly success and to appreciate simple, meaningful things instead.

Coming across the memorial stones of Abraham Darby, his wife and also his son, I noticed that the last burial had taken place in 1982. As I approached the iron gates on my way out, I found a plaque explaining that the ground had been given to the community by one of the Darby family.

Walking back to my hotel, I felt confused as to where my life was heading. For the first time ever I had no real motivation to go to the conference, wishing instead that I could spend the whole weekend visiting the various landmarks in the surrounding area.

There I was, 400 miles from home, with a group of good friends, yet it seemed that I always wanted to be alone so that I could reflect and contemplate. I was constantly searching for inner peace. The strange thing was that I never felt lonely from an earthly perspective.

Could there be such a self-contradictory being as 'an outgoing loner'?

Two hours later, wearing a business suit and carrying my briefcase, I had transformed myself into 'Mr Slick Businessman' and taken my seat in Telford Indoor Arena along with several thousand other distributors.

'Are you excited about your financial future?' came the now familiar opening leadership cry from stage. I felt flat, barely able to muster any kind of response, as a deafening yell of Y-E-S reverberated all around me.

I was beginning to see through all the hype and ballyhoo, recognising that the carrot that what was being dangled in front of my eyes was in part cleverly cloaked materialism, camouflaged in the subtle guise of success and accomplishment. To me this seemed detrimental and destructive to the pure Christian values I was being challenged to embrace.

This cleverly packaged 'American Dream' that I had bought into years previously, was appearing more like a mirage or a delusion to me, for I still had no idea where I was going or what I really wanted out of life.

Would another £1000-£2000 a month really make me any happier or any more fulfilled? Or would my real future involve God having an entirely different purpose for my life?

Being positive all the time was fine, if you knew where you were heading and what you were on earth for, but I just seemed to be in constant turmoil. What had excited and motivated me eight years before was having little effect on me now. I was always trying to find balance in my life, but in reality all I was doing was spinning plates.

Church, Tenerife, decorating business, socialising and business seminars – I was always busy, even productive. But my life was not fulfilling.

I felt like an octopus on roller skates: lots of movement but no real direction.

I had been so focused on making a living that I had seldom stopped to consider what I was actually living for. I was even being challenged about attending weekend business events which meant missing Church on a Sunday. I was frustrated with how I remained entrapped in a reflection of worldly standards and practices, regardless of the efforts of Christian friends and acquaintances to open my eyes to the standards of Christ Himself.

Like a chameleon, I was changing pigments in my personality to match the colour of my surroundings. More astonishing than any of these abilities was my capability to mirror the Godlessness of my fellow man, despite knowing that these characteristics often conflicted with examples set by Jesus.

I was now flying to Tenerife every four months and enjoyed the fact that I could stay in my own apartment. This particular time I had booked two flights for the end of August 2003, as I had been going out with a local girl. After a brief romance we had decided to go our separate ways, but she was still keen on flying to Tenerife with me.

However, while decorating my own bathroom one evening, I suddenly felt what I can only describe as a strong urge that I should go on my own. I immediately dismissed the notion but it kept coming back. The powerful prompting was clear and precise: 'Go to Tenerife alone.'

Was this a word from God? Or was it just my own preference, now that I realised the relationship was all but over? I kept telling myself I would sleep on it and make my mind up in the morning but back came the same recurring message: 'Sort it out tonight ...'

There was no audible voice but everything seemed so clear, so I finally made a phone call to the girl concerned. It was a bit late but I was convinced it was the right thing to do. I told her that I felt it was best that I just went alone as we did not have any real future.

That was tough.

I may have appeared insensitive, and certainly my call was ill-timed, but I was sure it was right.

Naturally, there was a tinge of sadness when I boarded my plane at Aberdeen to fly to the Canary Islands alone, but as I embarked on my journey a strange calmness and contentedness came over me as if to indicate that everything was going to work out fine.

I took my daily devotion booklet, *Word for Today* on board with me and I must have read about twenty daily readings without even bothering to meditate on the scripture at the top of each page.

Having arrived on Friday evening, I spent the whole of Saturday walking aimlessly for miles and miles, stopping every now and then for a cool drink or a light snack. It was now almost a year since I had begun the Alpha Course and I felt as unfulfilled and lost as ever.

On my first full day in Tenerife I wandered into the heart of Playa de las Americas to an area called 'Veronicas', where in the searing late afternoon sun I came across a street evangelist, wearing a Manchester United top, having a Bible-waving rant to passers-by. To be honest, I did not know whether to cringe with embarrassment or go up and shake his hand for having the guts to publicly proclaim what he strongly believed in.

During one of my previous stays, I had found a Church in Los Christianos called the 'South Tenerife Christian Fellowship' and it had suited me fine as it was an English-speaking service. I normally took a taxi over from Las Americas to have a nice leisurely two-mile walk along the seafront on my way back.

The morning service was traditional and the large congregation consisted of a core of residents, as well as holiday-makers from various countries around the world.

On this particular Sunday morning I took a seat near the rear of a large room. The service itself was pretty unmemorable, with no rousing sermon and the old hymns, although lively and uplifting, were mostly ones I had never heard before.

Usually I went out for a meal with Stewart and Moira on a Sunday evening, but for some odd reason I felt that I should return for the evening service instead. There was no real logical explanation for going back to Church at night, other than that I was constantly being challenged about the fact that I had not accepted Jesus as my Lord and Saviour, but I felt that by coming to Church I would eventually make the breakthrough.

The evening service was sparsely attended and the only thing of note was when Lee, one of the residential street pastors, became involved in a heated debate with the man leading the service, regarding the sanity and effectiveness of the 'whacky' street preacher I had encountered at Veronicas the previous afternoon. I liked Lee. He was a young lad I had bumped into a few times. He had a real passion for God and was definitely someone who 'wore his heart on his sleeve'.

At the end of the service I just wanted to sit and pray. Why? I don't really know. I sat still for a few minutes until a man who had been seated down at the front eventually noticed me and perched himself in the seat next to me. He introduced himself as Hugo Anson, an English pastor who had set up 'Grassroots', a Christian charity that did outreach work on the island. He was friendly and seemed genuinely interested in me as we discussed where I was with my life.

Eventually he asked: 'Have you given your life to the Lord?' I immediately felt uneasy; I did not particularly feel comfortable with any such straightforward challenging questions.

'Erm ... No ... Not yet,' I replied rather tentatively.

'Well, would you like to do it, right here just now?' I hesitated for a few seconds before giving a nod, along with a deep sigh of tense resignation. A serious deal with my Creator was about to be done.

Hugo then gently asked me to repeat the sinner's prayer after him ...

I immediately felt peace and contentment, like I had come home – not home in the sense of residence but home where my life was in alignment with God's Will. It was so real and felt so right. There was no visible outpouring of emotion, no 'Road to Damascus' experience – just a quiet, blessed assurance that this was where I was meant to be.

God, in His infinite mercy, had taken me to a land thousands of miles from home, in the presence of a Godly man whom I had never set eyes on before, to transfer His Son Jesus of Nazareth the eighteen inches from my head into my heart ... Truly astonishing!

That now familiar walk along the sea front to Playa las Americas that evening, with Jesus freshly planted in my heart, was quite simply an exhilarating experience. Watching the concerned faces of the people as they passed by, I longed to tell every single one of them that despite all that was going on in their lives, Jesus loved them.

I almost felt the Spirit of God hovering over the face of the whole earth, creating, stirring up, putting in order all that was undone, as I recalled what the New Testament said: 'If any person is in Christ, he or she, is a new Creation.'

As I lay on my apartment bed that evening, it dawned on me how helpless and unaccountable I had been all through my life and how small and weak I was in the enormity of God's universe. I knew that walking that line between the old life and the new was going to be difficult, and that I would stumble many times, but the incredible reality was that there had only been one life all along – and it had always belonged to God.

Walking around in the baking hot sun of Tenerife for the rest of my time there, I began to marvel at the thought of Jesus Christ of Nazareth working and walking among men and women, like I myself encountered groups of tourists.

Reading the small red Gideon's Bible, that I had been given at the Church on the evening of my deliverance, I marvelled at the life of Jesus and the stories of the beginning of His ministry.

The miracles He performed, like raising men from the dead; healing the sick; opening the eyes or the blind; delivering men, women and little children from oppression or demons; touching with His hand the withered arm of a man, which immediately sprung into full growth and life again ...

The tremendous words that came from His lips during The Sermon on the Mount and the parables beside the seashore – such mysterious, compelling and profound things He said.

I wondered at the crowds, hounding Him, following Him everywhere for days on end, insisting upon His ministry, so that the news spread like wildfire throughout the land of Israel: Here was a prophet risen in Israel again.

Men abandoned their livelihoods and their ordinary everyday activities in towns and villages to go and listen to what He had to say.

In my case, I didn't say a word about God to anybody. Not a word or gesture. This may have seemed like I had something to hide, or was embarrassed about my faith, but nothing could have been further from the truth. It was just that I wanted all my Christian friends in Portsoy, Banff and Gamrie, who had encouraged and supported me, to be the first to know.

Back home, I excitedly called round a handful of close Christian friends to tell them the good news.

The poor imitation of the stealth bomber that I had been a year before, when I used to go to great lengths to conceal my identity while attending Alpha, was a distant memory as I unashamedly proclaimed Jesus as my Lord and Saviour to all who wanted to know – and to a few more who could hardly have cared less!

None of my closest friends were Christians, so I wondered how they would react. All but one appeared respectful of my decision, although I imagine they were a bit disappointed, that the Coco they once knew as 'one of the boys' had turned all 'good living' and 'religious'.

I was now one of those same do-gooders that I too would have mocked throughout much of my youth, but I could live with that because it sounded an improvement on being a 'do-wronger' or even a 'do the same as everyone else-er'!

The one friend who derided my newfound faith, when he came down to my house to visit, went home that same evening still believing that he was a descendant of a peculiar-looking lanky balding ape, complete with a jutting jaw, barrel chest and bowed hairy legs. I was not going to convert him to Christianity and he knew he was wasting his time promoting his evolutionary beliefs to me.

I just felt sad that he had let two negative personal experiences with 'religion' play a significant part in closing his mind to even the possibility that God existed.

I soon began to realise that it takes more faith to be an atheist than it does to believe in Almighty God. When I looked at Creation and how the world is set on a perfectly positioned axis, it reinforced the existence of God to me. If it were one degree one way, the whole world would freeze. If it were to swing one degree the other way, we'd be burned to a cinder.

Not long after returning from Tenerife, I was invited to give my testimony in Gamrie Kirk. Paul Williams, who had become a good friend at Portsoy Church, was covering for Donald Martin, the minister, who was away for the weekend. Paul told me that two ladies had approached him in tears at the end of a service after he had told the congregation of my salvation. 'One of them said she had been praying for you for years,' Paul told me with excitement. How could I refuse to give my testimony if it was God's will, especially since my salvation had been the answer to many years of heartfelt prayer?

Apprehensive, but far from terrified, I travelled to Gardenstown with Paul the following Sunday, and his natural enthusiasm and encouragement were so comforting that it helped quell some of the anxiety I was beginning to feel. I had not written any notes, preferring instead to speak more naturally and spontaneously, thus reducing the risk of stammering, for I frequently struggled with any challenging word on paper.

My heart began to beat frantically when Paul introduced me and prayed over me. Nervously scanning the congregation, I noticed so many familiar faces.

Mary Johnstone was there; Benny and Isobel Nicol, my first decorating customers; Steven West, my painting predecessor, and Jessie Ritchie, the mother of my good friend, Michael.

However, the real blessing was when I noticed, near the front, three generations of my mother's family who had travelled down from Portknockie to support me.

God had reassured me that this was not public speaking. It was simply me, sharing my story of salvation; just a normal person speaking to normal people. As I opened my heart to a congregation that I had come to know so well, a calmness came over me. I received added strength when I saw a customer of mine – a modest, godly man – was deep in prayer as I began to talk.

Joyfully I shared the story of my toughest trials through the storms of life towards victory through Christ and the miracle of my salvation. I had barely paused to take breath but the words came freely and naturally as I was filled with the power of the Holy Spirit.

Several weeks later, I was back in Gardenstown again, this time in the village hall, to listen to the ministry of Thomas Martin. I went with Michael Watt, a friend who had been a great encouragement to me as I was procrastinating in my quest to find Jesus.

Thomas Martin, or Tommy as he was more commonly known, was brought up in difficult circumstances in a deeply divided town at the height of the troubles in Northern Ireland. He joined a Protestant paramilitary organisation, was arrested, charged, and sentenced to a lengthy prison term.

In the notorious Maze prison, the most unlikely of places, Tommy became a peaceful negotiator and trusted helper – all through the power of Almighty God.

Michael's mother, Elsie, had lent me Tommy's excellent biography *Out of the Maze*, written by Noel Davidson, recounting this thrilling story of transformation that gave me a much clearer insight regarding the bitterness and unmitigated hatred on both sides of the religious divide, and a far greater understanding.

After Tommy had preached that Sunday evening, I was delighted to be invited back to Michael's parents' house, along with several other believers, for a meal and a time of fellowship. The spread of food that had been prepared was befitting of a king's banquet and it was a splendid end to the evening.

Before I left to go home, Tommy went into the boot of his car and presented me with seven copies of his biography to share with anyone I felt would benefit from reading it. He had such an infectious, uplifting nature, and we wished each other all the best as we parted with a warm handshake. Little did we know that we would meet again – in fact, very soon we would meet again! When

I arrived home, I noticed that I had taken his jacket by mistake. So, back into my car I went to drive another fifty-minute round trip to return his jacket.

Roughly three months after I had given my life to the Lord I was baptised at the Harvest Centre in Banff. My parents had christened me as a baby and although I will always appreciate that, I wanted this baptism to be my decision – like something that Jesus had experienced in the presence of John the Baptist, at the beginning of His public ministry.

After the morning service, I went downstairs where the large baptismal tank filled with water was set in full view of my Christian brothers and sisters. Leisa Wiseman, another girl from the Church, was being baptised as well so it was a very special day for both of us.

To me, this baptism was the celebration and re-affirming of my faith, and I saw this as my second great spiritual experience. Baptism was my outward expression of the inward miracle. It was a visible, tangible, physical expression of what was happening, spiritually. It was a picture, to be seen by others, revealing what was happening within me.

My baptism was really not so much about what I was doing – it was about what the Holy Spirit was doing in me.

After giving a short testimony, I was led into the tank by Norman Hill, one of the Church leaders. I was immersed under water for a few seconds and Pastor Joe Ewen prophesied over me, giving me the powerful word that I was going to have influence in the lives of countless people through the power of God Almighty.

I felt deeply humbled by the enormous sense of responsibility that God had placed on my shoulders. This was my personal challenge, but one that I was determined to see come to fruition.

A DIFFERENT VIEW OF SUCCESS

It dawned on me that I had been spiritually blind for many years, and even as a new Christian I occasionally slipped back into that blindness. I had a natural tendency to go my own way, which was in a different direction from God's care and His path.

I found it especially difficult to hand my life over to Him because I'd had to make my own decisions for so long – I had really been on my own since the death of my mother and starting up my business – but I soon began to realise that the more I took my sinful tendencies to the light of God I could be healed by His grace and power.

For the most part of my life I had accepted my personal beliefs without argument. This is what I had unconsciously bought into from what others had told me about myself, and the world around me. Or perhaps I had a certain interpretation of a past experience and assumed that future events would have the same meaning.

In 1994, ex-ITN newsreader Martyn Lewis made the news headlines with two controversial and widely-debated speeches, calling for a shift in the agenda of TV news programmes to achieve a fairer balance between the good and the bad news, and to report and analyse achievement just as much as failure and disaster. I related strongly with what Martyn was suggesting but I I could not help feeling that his pleas would just fall on the deaf ears of our national media moguls as they pandered to our country's insatiable hunger for shocking stories and bad news.

Many of us cling to every heartbreaking clip, every shocking picture, and every sickening piece of news, forcing ourselves to sit through a second-by-second account of what happened. It often leaves us feeling sorrowful, disgusted, angry, or distressed, yet we keep watching.

We could have kept ourselves informed of such vicious conflicts and disasters, as well as acts of almost indefinable evil, through more non-descriptive news feeds. Instead, we choose the most graphic and explicit form that envelops us in all that horror.

Two years later, in a packed National Indoor Arena in Birmingham, I had the privilege of listening to Martyn Lewis' strong and compelling views on the 'success ethic'. It became clear to me that for many people the desire to achieve success is the primary driving force in their lives.

Widespread media attention normally follows when someone 'makes it big', resulting in immense public interest. Then, when that someone is perfectly perched on their man-made pedestal, there seems to be a secret force – or dare I say a satanic force – moving into operation in this country to pull that successful person down, often by way of private revelations, baggage from the past or even sensational 'exclusives' on obscure relatives.

This makes me wonder why success or accomplishment is so often envied and undervalued in Britain, while the USA and other countries appear to put it on a lofty position and keep it there for more than a few months.

I had heard business leaders, football players and rock stars described in such superlative terms as legends, icons, and even immortal, but over the passage of time I found out that they were flawed and vulnerable, just like the rest of us.

As I have expressed earlier in this book, I feel I have developed, both personally and economically, from the ethics and principles that I have learned during the time I was attending business seminars, and that is something I will be forever grateful for. However, I soon realised that a certain amount of alignment had to occur before I could be in unison with the pure teachings of the Holy Bible.

So, when I accepted Jesus as my Saviour I had to unravel some of the false beliefs and teachings that had been ingrained in me.

I had to accept that some of the business gurus I had been influenced by and authors of books I had read, had used a "Christianised veneer" to endorse a subtly mercantile or even materialistic lifestyle by proclaiming that 'God helps those who help themselves'.

One successful American distributor had even suggested from the business platform that Church-related activities may well be good and wholesome but they should not come before building the marketing business.

Even with my limited knowledge of Scripture I felt challenged by that, as I had never read anything that supported the theory that you needed to be totally financially free before you could begin to serve and follow Jesus. When Jesus instructed His disciples to 'Come follow me', He meant right then, and not only after all their possible material needs had been fulfilled.

The penny finally dropped and the commandment 'Come follow me' from God's only Son became more significant and consequential than 'Follow, Follow' from the football terraces, or 'Financial Freedom' from the business platform. I was finally ready to walk with my Maker.

Another business owner, from Ireland, shared that he had presented a business opportunity to a married couple who had the impertinence to ask for time to pray about whether this would be the right move for them. 'They wanted to pray about it ... yes ... pray about it!' he emphasised sarcastically. He pulled a face, presumably reflecting total astonishment, while mocking this committed Christian couple who needed to consult God about becoming involved in a business concept founded by two devoutly Christian men.

There was a much used Network Marketing catchphrase that suggested 'if it's to be ... then it's up to me', which created a 'duty' mentality, rather than the 'delight in Jesus' mentality that I felt I had to develop to truly experience God. This meant living a life that is centred round Him and His purposes, which would require a daily denial of self, as well as submission to God.

I had read many self-help books that promoted having perfect balance to your life. This was normally illustrated by a pie chart that split into six or seven equal categories, such as spiritual, further education, family, and health and fitness. To me, this teaching reduced God to a bit part in my life, even amounting to just an add-on, which was contrary to the teachings of the Bible.

Many of these books suggested ways to discover the purpose to my life. All of them were self-help books of a sort. They all approached the same challenge from a self-centred view-point. They all tended to have the same predictable steps to find life's purpose; cultivate your dreams, write down long and short term goals, be disciplined, believe in yourself, find a mentor, aim high. Never give up.

As our post-modern generation strives to 'find itself', we are offered all the trendy self-help methods and therapies of contemporary pop-psychology, self-enhancement and self-actualisation. These psychological agendas encourage us to 'psych' ourselves into thinking that we are more than we appear to be, by recognising our inherent untapped potential, solely by applying a 'positive mental attitude' and 'possibility thinking'.

Of course, these concepts are well-meaning and often lead to short spurts of success, but I soon figured out that short-term success and fulfilling my life's purpose were two entirely different outcomes.

I acquired a new belief system that pulled my focus away from myself and placed my sights solely on Christ, and therein lay my true freedom: I was no longer prepared be in bondage to my own shortcomings and fears because I had been so blissfully distracted from them by God.

One of the many things that challenged me for many years has been working out the true meaning of success and living a successful life. I found it difficult not to be influenced by this world of covetousness and cynicism around me, and to view success by the standards of society and the secular media.

I had allowed myself to be seduced by the comfort and convenience of Western culture. I had been overly concerned about my future security here on earth. Slowly, what could have been termed as 'The American Dream' was erased from my heart and replaced with a more powerful dream of fulfilling God's purpose. I had inadvertently become a model of industriousness, believing that what I accomplished between 8 a.m. and 8 p.m. made me valuable. Praise and encouragement became an adrenalin-induced high to keep me going.

As the years rolled by, however, the more business ventures and projects I embraced, the more I feared failure. Then, gradually, my creativity and drive began to fizzle out. Eventually, I became aware of the fact that regardless of how hard I toiled, I was no longer satisfied.

I openly admit that much of the delight and satisfaction of being in a loving long-term relationship was passing me by, but I still wouldn't let go. I would almost torture myself trying to justify my existence by overwork.

It was only when I was challenged to focus more on glorifying the Lord by getting His work into perspective, that Christ began healing what was, in fact, inner insecurity.

There is nothing wrong with enjoying all the material things of this world. They, too, are gifts from God. However, I must always remind myself that they are only temporal and cannot give real lasting happiness.

True purpose in life cannot be found in anything that rusts or rots. Jesus alone gives meaning to life. He alone can give eternal significance to our eternal works.

Sadly, some of the most selfish and egotistical people I have met have been wretched in spirit, even though they had amassed great wealth. They seemed to focus too much on making money, while at the same time resenting others who also became rich. Those people mistakenly believe that money can solve all their problems and will make them happy.

Many secular music videos I have viewed have tended to be about escape and illusion – the illusion of fame, wealth, beauty, glamour and fantasy.

The video of Johnny Cash singing Trent Reznor's song, 'Hurt', isn't about any of those things. It deals with a theme that is virtually unheard of in music videos today – reality! It is a painful montage of moving, dimly-lit images of a weathered Cash playing piano and guitar in his memorabilia-laden home, interspersed with glimpses of the flood-damaged 'House of Cash' museum, and archival footage of him as a young man.

At some stage Jesus appears, initially in an ordinary painting and later in a flickering re-creation of the Crucifixion at which a crowd – from an early Cash concert – cheers as nails are hammered in.

Johnny Cash's furrowed face is etched with emotion as he sings, like a rumbling volcano, about the harsh reality of death and the vanity of fame.

'What have I become?
My sweetest friend
Everyone I know goes away in the end
You could have it all ...
My empire of dirt.'

Cash's rendition of 'Hurt' strongly echoes the Book of Ecclesiastes. It's a song about a man who eventually realises why he was created.

He desires fame.

He craves wealth.

He tries everything under the sun, until he finally becomes aware of the value of living under the One who made the sun.

This video had a powerful impact on me, for I had lived under the sun for forty years before eventually coming to that same harsh conclusion as the Man in Black.

To me, Johnny Cash appears briefly and concisely as a modern day Solomon – both had lived the life of celebrity, enjoyed all that this world had to offer ... and seen through it.

And both decided to share their experiences and solemn conclusions as a warning to the rest of us.

I think Jesus talked so often about money because He knew how much of our lives revolved round the acquiring, stewardship and distribution of it.

Sadly, many people live their lives with the 'if only' philosophy: 'If only I had more money, a better job.'

Or: 'If only I could win the lottery.'

Lottery winners understandably jump for joy like there's no tomorrow. They invariably freak out, clenching their fists in victorious gleefulness. Every burden evaporates as the elated lucky 'winner' goes completely delirious.

Winning large sums of money can have a terrible effect on social relationships. There is almost always envy, so winners may lose their friends, or families are ripped apart. When you are not used to having money you can become vulnerable, and there are plenty of people out there who are willing to prey on that vulnerability.

Some of us tend to view a lottery winner, or a person who has inherited a large amount of money, differently from someone who has laboured many years to earn it. In our culture, many people appear to be under the illusion that if they had more money, all their troubles would be over.

We look upon success as the unholy trinity of money, material possessions and beauty. Those who have it are often treated with greater respect, even idolised, and those of us who don't, seem to be relegated to social insignificance.

Money can be our seductive mistress.

It is easy to follow Jesus in a spiritual way, yet our human nature makes it just as easy to follow the world's obsession with material wealth. Society rams a 'have it now' mentality down our throats. Advertisers persuade us to buy things straight away, often on the never-never, with scant regard for the problems of tomorrow. I have to frequently reassure myself that my time on earth is but a blink of an eye, compared with eternity.

A wise man once said: 'Every man needs two conversions, one of the heart and one of the wallet.'

Joseph (John) Merrick had a life story I still find tragically fascinating. I recollect watching the Academy Award-nominated film *The Elephant Man*, released in 1980, in which he was played by John Hurt.

This moving film, with its poignantly expressive style, horrifying morbidity and inexplicable absurdness, had the equal capacity to inspire laughter and produce the odd tear from this insensitive if somewhat emotional viewer.

A simple smile from another human being, or even a pleasant greeting (which is something that we all take for granted), would undoubtedly have been treated by this man as the highest form of complimentary conduct.

It was said by his biographer that beneath his exterior features there was a noble and gentle man who accepted his fate as coming from God.

I was touched by this poem, by Isaac Watts, that Joseph Merrick liked to end his letters with:

'Tis true my form is something odd, but blaming me is blaming God.
Could I create myself anew, I would not fail in pleasing you.
Was I so tall, could reach the pole,
or grasp the ocean with a span;
I would be measured by the soul.
The mind's the standard of the man.'

I can only conclude that God brought Joseph Merrick into this world to teach us that goodness, beauty and kindness lie deep beneath what we see on the surface, and also to remind us that this unequivocally sincere man's story is much more about tolerance and understanding moral importance than something only to be remembered as a historical freak show.

But the truth is, while our physical appearance may make an initial impression upon others, it is rapidly demoted to lesser significance as our true personality shines through. Sadly, some people I have encountered, who are quite attractive physically, are so obnoxious in attitude that people are loath to be around them for any amount of time.

Others, who look a bit plainer or ordinary, seem to have lots of friends because intelligent and respectable people are attracted to their charm, wit, compassion, or overall spiritual depth.

When a frumpy, middle-aged woman from West Lothian sang 'I Dreamed a Dream' from the musical 'Les Misérables' for a British talent show, in front of sceptical judges and an incredulous crowd, she did more than sing a song well. Susan Boyle reminded us all of the meaning of human grace by almost reinventing the true measure of beauty.

In a breathtaking performance that resonated powerfully among millions of viewers, Susan gave renewed hope to many of us who have severe doubts about ourselves, and showed us what can be achieved with a modest appearance and the courage to try.

I still find myself trying to get my head round the many contradictions regarding wealth and poverty, not only in the world but also in the Church. Two contradictory gospels seem to have been manufactured by man over the years – the prosperity gospel and the poverty gospel.

Both are unbalanced from a scriptural point of view.

On the other hand, the occasional sermon I have heard would make me feel so guilty about owning anything tangible that I almost felt like melting down a gold filling in my tooth and giving the proceeds to the poor, to make sure I was a good Christian!

As someone new to Christianity and still attending business seminars, I became confused by two extreme attitudes towards wealth. I was listening to some successful business leaders giving me the impression that any conceivable problem in life could be solved by hitting it over the head with a bag of money.

Prosperity theology is, I believe, a modern-day invention of our affluent western society. This self-centred mindset appears irreconcilable with divine revelation as expressed in the New Testament.

There is nothing wrong with being financially successful – at least, not if our life does not totally revolve around money; acquiring it, hoarding it, or using it to show off.

Of course there is a proper place in the life of the Christian for money, but it has to be functioning effectively, not only in our own lives but also in our duty to bless the lives of others. Money, given with a loving and merciful heart, can enrich lives in wonderful and necessary ways, such as providing food, shelter and transport; financing hospitals and education.

For many Christians the biggest obstacle to overcome isn't to try and understand what the Bible teaches about money; it is how to come to terms with the irrational fear, insecurity and guilt regarding wealth.

We are often petrified of not having enough, and we may even worry when we think we have too much! At times, I will generously and ungrudgingly write out a cheque for someone in need or for a worthy cause, but on isolated occasions I can become the ultimate 'tightwad', digging in my heels and protecting my loot as if my whole life depended on it.

There is often an inconsistent struggle within the heart of most of us as we deal with the whole thorny issue of money. We sometimes need to take a sobering reality check. Rather than comparing ourselves to our own peer group, so we can always claim comparative impoverishment, let us think of ourselves as affluent global citizens – looking at ourselves in relation to all of humanity.

When we own a licensed mode of transport we are among the world's well-heeled, and those of us who own a home are better off economically than 95% of people on this planet.

By stepping back and realistically analysing our lives for a few seconds, most of us would have to conclude that we are incredibly advantaged. Even accepting that many people do have to work hard to balance budgets, we must recognise the fact that we are still financially better off than the vast majority of people in this world. Jesus did not seem to possess financial wealth, or have a need for it. His chosen trade was carpentry, which probably would have earned Him a modest living, thus able to supply His needs. During His three years in full time ministry, Jesus may well have received financial support from specific followers, for He had no house that He could call His own and He stayed with various people while visiting different towns.

In the end, Jesus was the most successful man in all history in the sense that He has positively influenced billions of lives over two thousand years. He would not have needed to spend time reading our post-modern success manuals, but every person on earth could benefit from reading His.

I don't believe there is really such a thing as an overnight success – at least, not sustainable success without a struggle. Life is a constant challenge. We are all given a trial during our lifespan, and this includes uneven luck, ill-sorted health problems and unfair amounts of obstacles.

However, I do believe that success is a mindset – that it is more about managing my mood and mastering my motivations than anything else – and I realise that managing my mood requires discipline to control my impulses while I try to stay positive, regardless of what happens.

I have finally come to the conclusion that success is no more than the progressive realisation of a worthwhile cause.

John C. Maxwell, an internationally recognised leadership expert, speaker, Pastor, and author, who has trained more than one million leaders world-wide, wrote a powerful book called *Failing Forward*. This book acts as balm and tonic for those of us who are losing heart. It reassures us that failures do not reflect upon us as human beings, and that one failure, or even a life of non-accomplishment, does not necessarily imply that the 'loser' tag that we often pin on ourselves, or have pinned on us by others, will be our life's most important legacy.

Maxwell reminds us that failure and disappointment often indicate that we are experiencing challenging circumstances that can provide us with life-enhancing lessons – if we are willing to be taught, and have the courage to face them humbly, honestly, and courageously, without taking them too personally.

Both my customers and I can get things wrong, and in that case our relationship could be easily damaged. However, if we can both acknowledge and accept our mistakes and commit to doing better; if we can forgive each other, and refrain from carrying grudges that we keep on a mental score card, then we'll both prosper.

If my business fails a customer, I acknowledge the issue and sincerely endeavour not to not let it happen again. Only in very isolated cases, over more than twenty years, have my customers not accepted my apology and appreciated my effort to make good.

I have known several people who have succeeded temporarily through vision, courage and tenacity. But they crashed because of lack of character. They achieved success momentarily because everything else was right, but their character was flawed.

The simplicity of telling the truth is too often overlooked in business today. Honesty is the best policy in all decisions and actions. It's the foundation on which trust and integrity rest. I am comfortable with that, as I believe I handle all my business dealings with honesty and integrity. I realise that I will always make mistakes, but they will never be due to a lack of integrity.

In my mind, to be trustworthy a person has to trust themselves first and foremost, believing in others almost to the point of naïve optimism. The reason for their idealistic views of others is based on their sound character and how they view themselves. This is why you see people of dubious character or critical spirit who cannot trust others to be honest. They know themselves too well and assume that everyone is just like them.

Accountability is surely always about assuming responsibility, not passing the buck on to someone else. Unfortunately, we live in a time when even our national leaders seldom admit sin – although caught red-handed. And when people at every level of public life avoid accountability, rather than 'own up', they cover up.

What happened to companies like Enron, where morality collapsed and management behaviour became reprehensible? I don't believe their leaders set out to break the law, so how did they end up disgraced and in jail?

Many of these problems can probably be traced to a failure of ethical decision-making due to a craving for power and money.

Forty or fifty years ago, when the rich and famous erred in a manner that now seems virtually guiltless, they were criticised by clergy, the media and even their own fans. Robert Mitchum, the celebrated Hollywood actor, was once thrown into prison for taking cannabis and setting a bad example to those who idolised him. Nowadays he would get a pat on the back and receive even more lucrative film offers.

George Best was more than a sublimely talented footballer; more than the first truly modern superstar of the beautiful game. Long before his tragic premature death, Best had become the stuff of worldly folklore.

At the peak of his womanising and footballing prowess, he had no equal. After his all too brief football career had ended, George was particularly fond of relating the tale of the night porter who brought a bottle of champagne to his hotel room with his breakfast, only to see Best in bed with Mary Stavin, the current Miss World. Champagne and thousands of pounds in cash, won from a night's gambling, were strewn all over the duvet. Viewing such an extraordinary sumptuous sight, the bellboy had allegedly lamented: 'George, where did it all go wrong?'

This tale classically mirrors some of the scenarios we have all faced as we struggle with the bait of instant gratification in a world that lures us into its web and then threatens to entangle us forever. Best's basic life principle was stubborn non-conformity, with an air of invincibility and the knowledge that he was special being the wellspring of his football-playing genius. It was the source of the adulation, the envy and the censure that dominated his life.

It is claimed that George had a Christian sister who frequently witnessed to him. If so, it must have been incredibly soul-destroying for her to watch helplessly as her prodigal brother continued along his path of self-destruction.

George Best was well and truly blessed, but perhaps he sadly never really understood or appreciated the One who blessed him, or at least that is what I thought! However, I recently heard that while in hospital, George had come to accept Jesus as his Lord and Saviour during the very last weeks of his life - the result of the faithful witness of a Christian nurse.

More than 30 years after Best graced the world with his mercurial God-given talent, another waif-like, dark-haired football sensation was being exalted for his brilliance around the globe – but for reasons poles apart.

As a committed Christian, he reads his Bible daily.

He prays, and listens to Gospel music.

As a member of 'Christ's Athletes', 10 per cent of his monthly salary is transferred to the Church.

However, Kaka, the Brazilian football star, who plays for Real Madrid in Spain, seems far removed from the prima donna lifestyle of many other of today's sporting superstars.

In fact, Kaka appears to be a freakish rarity in the 'money crazy' modern game, as the epitome of an intelligent, diligent, loyal footballer staying true to the game and the God he loves.

At 18, he suffered a spinal fracture in a swimming pool accident. Doctors told him his career was over, and that he could face paralysis in his legs.

Instead, he made a full recovery.

Kaka's primary motivation in life has always been his faith and trust in God. If, then, it is the debt he owes to Jesus, rather than money or fame that motivates and inspires him, it would seem that he is living proof of what Jesus once said, that, although it is hard for the rich to enter the kingdom of God, 'nothing is impossible with God'. (Luke 18: 27 NLT)

Perhaps with the extravagantly gifted Kaka we are seeing God do just that – not only on the field of play but, more significantly, off it as well.

Understanding the true definition of success from the likes of Kaka helps shed some light on the widely held misconception that all highly successful individuals are covetous; that they always want more, even in the midst of abundance.

These critics do not seem to understand why prospering individuals move from one challenge to another, striving to become even more purified, and are prepared to take the calculated risks along the way. The most successful individuals who have ever lived have resisted the natural human tendency to make up their own laws in life.

Likewise, I feel that if I am going to reach my full potential I must avoid the flexible principles of present-day thinking that has permeated our society.

Sitting in my house one night, after a particularly tiresome day, I asked myself these searching questions:

Why did many of my hopes and dreams die in my early twenties?

Why did I lose the passion I had for life when I was at school?

Is it the fact that I was not an unquestioning daydreamer any more?

Is it because I, like many other people, became numbed by the disappointments I had suffered over the years?

Or was it simply the fact that when I returned home every night from work I was in most cases too tired to dream and dare?

Was I too scared to risk failure to even try writing a book, or doing something out-with the safety and security of the routine in my painting and decorating job?

In those days, I used to think that success was defined by:

Acquiring great wealth

Holding a high-level position in a career

Attaining good grades at school or university

Winning in sport.

I have learned that we may not possess an outstanding skill, extraordinary charisma, or devastatingly good looks, but if we were to add perseverance to strong faith, we are able to achieve great things.

It would be easy for me to depart this world with my real purpose here on earth unfulfilled. Graveyards of broken dreams come about when we let life's circumstances grind us down. We end up giving up, after having convinced ourselves that our ambitions could not be accomplished.

When I accept whatever talents God gives me, be it many or few, I believe that with due diligence I'd nurture them to bear fruit – the best fruit attainable – to glorify Him. This, in my humble opinion, is the only level of success worth attaining in this life.

By doing this, I can say with total conviction that being at peace with myself through serving my Creator is more important and rewarding than being enslaved to the worldly perception of success.

RENEWING MY MIND

When I was 20 going on 12, I was proud of the notoriety that came with my endless treasure trove of witty one-liners and filthy humour. I was comical – and boy did I know it! However, looking back, I acknowledge that I often trod the very fine line between dry wit and cruel sarcasm.

So what form of wit/sarcasm was my speciality?

Well, take your pick! I had the full array. Biting humour, carefully crafted cynicism, the roll of my eyes, a well-timed sigh or groan – not forgetting muttering under my breath.

Each manoeuvre was intended to embarrass, undermine or subtly redirect the conversation for my benefit. On reflection, the loudness and bluster of my personality was frequently just a pitiful façade concealing the real me.

Despite my mother and the odd compassionate teacher being real encouragers, I struggled with my pronounced stammer, which was something I was genuinely embarrassed about. To counteract this insecurity and stigma, I inadvertently became sarcastic and caustic with my tongue.

It was not until I became conscious of this stronghold in my life that I could begin the process of restoration. Now, many years later, as destiny would have it, I have come to the conclusion that sarcasm – or 'the lowest form of wit' as it is commonly termed – is only an unfortunate camouflage for insecurity and lack of confidence.

Wisecracking may be funny at times, but one-upmanship is belittling and emotionally draining, and something I intensely dislike.

I still endeavour not to respond to a barbed comment from someone who feels the need to show some kind of superiority or disapproval. Also, I know full well that I am not the best at thinking on my feet if I am suddenly and unexpectedly challenged about anything.

My old tendency was often to respond in a defensive or confrontational manner which may have meant that I won the argument but damaged the relationship, even though I instinctively tried to avoid people who grated on me, due to personality clashes or lack of understanding.

My natural reaction was to defend myself against what I considered falsity and unfairness, but when I eventually became aware of the fact that this was a fruitless way of dealing with things, I think I went too far the other way, turning into an apologetic pipsqueak, often taking the blame – whether it was my fault or not.

Now I try hard to say as little as possible, thus giving myself time to reflect, contemplate, or even pray, before I respond. I feel that God uses such experiences to challenge me and to teach me about my flawed nature.

When I humbly take note of what upsets me, God, in his mercy, can reveal certain weaknesses in my life that require spiritual transformation.

One of the characteristics I often see in the world today is ungraciousness; it appears that too few of us are truly humble.

I have listened to people talk for hours about themselves and their accomplishments, whereby they always play the hero or heroine of their own parables. It never seems to cross their minds to tell tales about the times when they were unsuccessful and fell flat on their faces.

I learned a simple truth of life in the early days of attending business seminars, when I found that some people who struggle with what could be termed as chronic non-accomplishment do so because they think of no one but themselves.

With their 'looking after number one' life philosophy, I'm sure that even the self-centred person, or someone who is egocentrically engrossed in their own importance, may have moments of generosity and charm, but mostly they seem to be unaware of the needs of others. They have no apparent interest in meeting people on the same level, which makes them constantly disheartening to anyone and everyone. I view humility as a quiet confidence without the need for insincerity.

Humility is being content to let others discover the layers of our talents without having to boast about them.

Humility is a lack of arrogance, not a lack of belligerence or resoluteness in the pursuit of achievement.

Humility is the opposite of lordliness – that excessive, arrogant pride that so often leads to the demise of both the little-known and the famous.

While I am prone to a little whine myself, I really dislike what I would term as 'chronic complaining'. From personal experience, these chronic complainers, or constant malingerers, are notoriously difficult to pacify. Attempting to build these people up by showing encouragement seldom has the desired effect. In fact, even the most sympathetic responses to their excessive objections are largely ineffective when dealing with a battle-hardened complainer.

A few of my friends are atheists, agnostics, or at least don't have a visible faith in God. I don't view them as sinners, any more than I see myself as a sinner. I enjoy their company, finding them generally encouraging, uplifting, and even enthralling to be around. To be honest, I would rather spend my time with a positive, uplifting non-believer than a groaning, moaning and dispiriting Christian.

Some years ago, I came across 'The Paradoxical Commandments'. This set of profound guidelines for achieving personal fulfilment was written by a young visionary college student, Kent M. Keith:

People are illogical, unreasonable, and self-centred.

Love them anyway.

If you do good, people will accuse you of selfish ulterior motives.

Do good anyway.

If you are successful, you will win false friends and true enemies.

Succeed anyway.

The good you do today will be forgotten tomorrow.

Do good anyway.

Honesty and frankness make you vulnerable.

Be honest and frank anyway.

The biggest men and women with the biggest ideas can be shot down by the smallest men and women with the smallest minds.

Think big anyway.

People favour underdogs but follow only top dogs.

Fight for a few underdogs anyway.

What you spend years building may be destroyed overnight.

Build anyway.

People really need help but may attack you if you do help them.

Help people anyway.

Give the world the best you have and you'll get kicked in the teeth.

Give the world the best you have anyway.

I don't view the Paradoxical Commandments as morbid or disheartening – more as an encouragement or a challenge with the reassurance of all that is wholesome and true, and with the message that you will often remain unappreciated for your contributions.

But if you can find personal meaning without the world's applause, you are liberated.

I feel blessed to have the freedom to do what makes sense to me, whether others appreciate it or not.

I feel privileged to have the freedom, as well as the opportunity, to be what God intended me to be. Free to find the meaning that many people ignore, in the knowledge that if I do what feels ethical and true, my actions will have their own intrinsic value. I would always find significance, and I certainly don't need the glory.

Every time I come across these words of profound wisdom, I ask God to forgive me for spending so much of my life in self-focus mode.

Am I too much of an idealist to think that it's possible to be genuine, honest and real, while still being warm-hearted and accepting?

And why is it that Western civilisation as a whole seems to struggle so with this?

If only we could cast aside our arrogance and pride, so that we are able to reach out to each other with unconditional love and acceptance, then I'm sure it would bring more peace and love in this fallen world of intolerance, injustice, and hatred.

I genuinely believe that the first step in living the Christian life is to focus on others, and in this way to become part of something bigger than ourselves. In most cultures and countries, throughout the centuries, people have discovered that loving and helping others gives them the greatest meaning to life.

Victor Frankl suggests that 'Self Transcendence' – looking beyond oneself – is the key to a healthy attitude.

He says: 'One must transcend oneself to find meanings that are larger and more noble. It is a little person who is bound up with only his or her needs. Believing in more than yourself (God, country, religion, group, spouse, your work, a cause) gives us the power to control our situation and our attitude.'

From what I have learned over the last few years, man has always tried to find meaning for his existence, and a counsellor can play a significant role in helping individuals travel down the path of understanding.

Oliver Wendell Holmes, the 19th century writer and physician, once said, 'The great act of faith is when man decides he is not God.'

It's not easy to be people-conscious all the time; we get wrapped up in our own issues in our own little world. Naturally, our own interests come to the fore, and it can be a real effort to keep them concealed.

There are many tormenting voices that enter the vulnerable mind, and I strongly believe that this is the source of temptation, discouragement, and accusation.

Satan will grab any ground given to him through a wounded spirit, and begin to accuse the believer. He is not called 'The Accuser of the Brethren' without sound reason. He is 'The Father of Lies' and he will communicate tormenting falsity to our soul and spirit.

Satan loves to rake up my past. He is always capable of doing a 'Watergate' on me. He loves to drag up a mass of reprehensible sins. He holds the master key that unlocks my old wardrobes, revealing cobwebbed skeletons that were hidden deep in my subconscious mind.

He loves me to doubt myself, questioning how I can possibly call myself a Christian when I have so much baggage littering my past. But I see this as a deceitful trick, for the very fact that I do fight against sin proves that I am filled with the Holy Spirit. If this were not the case, there would be no struggle deep within my soul and I simply would not posses this sensitive conscience.

It is a truth that I need to keep in mind whenever I am experiencing temptation. I'm sure that we are all continually haunted by past regrets, but we can always draw on our wisdom to get a proper perspective – I find it's beneficial to learn from my past so that it doesn't repeat itself, yet the real battle commences when I try hard not to dwell on it.

When living with regret, it is tempting to be sluggish and super-cautious, and it's then that we run the risk of missing out on the abundant life that Jesus promises us.

Regret limits our chances of taking a risk when opportunity presents itself.

Regret robs us of today.

Regret is an odd emotion because it comes only upon reflection.

Regret lacks immediacy, and so its power seldom influences events when it could do some good.

The reality is that life is just a series of events that unfold before us; some are wonderful and some are tragic, but it is sometimes necessary for us to experience the bitter in order to be able to enjoy the sweet.

By recognising the things we cannot change, I can be assured of the fact that if my regrets involve others, I am only responsible for my own actions – not for the actions of others.

After becoming a Christian, I began the arduous journey of living a humble and unpolluted life. It was then that the internal battle deep within my soul commenced between the Spirit of God and my fallen nature – a struggle in which I tried to obey Christ but invariably found my old strongholds and desires lurking in the background. These areas of my life are very much 'a work in progress', and still to be totally dealt with.

But this only underlines the ongoing reality of transformation in my life. Before I accepted Christ, I was a fairly consistent blasphemer. Not one of the 'every second word' type, but a fairly regular swearer nevertheless. Following my salvation, my bad language was practically halted in its tracks overnight, and my drinking was greatly reduced – if not totally eradicated.

Faith in God has to be sincere. There is no need to play make-believe games and act as if everything in our lives is perfect. God expects honesty, not pretence.

When we live in denial, we are attempting to use our own strength to accomplish something that only God can accomplish.

God increases our faith – not our self-importance.

If any Godly person were to take me aside and lecture me about being 'unequally yoked' for spending so much time with non-Church goers, then I would like to say to them that there have to be Christians willing to walk into places that are devoid of faith – and I am one of them.

I frequently find myself in situations where I can represent Christianity in the company of people who may look at me and see someone they can relate to and identify with, but never someone who is more virtuous than they are. I trust and pray that God will never allow me to act so holy and pious that people will no longer be able to identify with me. I am passionate in all that I feel strongly about. I may appear outgoing, but I can be very shy …

If people have genuine questions and concerns, and are not in a Jesus-mocking or Christianity-bashing state of mind, then I am more that willing to listen to what they have to say. I will never have all the answers that they seek but hopefully I will always be able to point them in the right direction.

I never worry about being a 'text book witness'. People may think that I'm a bit peculiar because I am not hyperventilating about

'The Good News' all the time. However, I've talked to many people about God, but I know full well that proselytising with rare enthusiasm isn't exactly a favourable method of approach for the restrained and reticent residents of this area of Scotland where I am fortunate to live.

There are Christians who cocoon themselves in their own safe holy huddle, distancing themselves from mainstream culture. They withdraw from secular society because they seem to be aware of people out there who are doing atrocious things, and so feel more secure by keeping away from them.

I understand why Christians seek only their own company, but the bottom line is that Jesus was present with the iniquitous and disadvantaged of society, and we are called to shape our lives and work according to His example.

The word became flesh and dwelt among us.

Jesus didn't cocoon himself. He was always a loving presence in the face of greed and hatred, which means He wasn't just doing combat with society, He was transforming it in a way it had never been done before. This reassures me; He didn't just go along with the fashionable ways of the world.

People of faith are neither misguided nor necessarily filled with more wisdom than the average Joe Soap. People of faith are those who have tasted the mundane fruit that this world has to offer and have asked themselves, 'Is there anything more to this life than work, sleep, play, bills; more work, and more play? Is it possible that there is something more tangible and meaningful?'

I view genuine faith as simply a spiritual pilgrimage of discovering the Divine. It is much more than a rigid list of dos and don'ts. It is much more than what many non-believers perceive Christians to be: brainwashed Jesus freaks or Bible thumpers.

Faith is simply a belief in the unseen.

It's our search for the real meaning to life.

The late John Wimber, one of the founder leaders of the Vineyard Movement, once said, 'Faith is spelt: R-I-S-K'. It has become blatantly obvious to me that Church attendance, or membership, is not in itself the basis for genuine Christian faith.

By this I mean, if a person of faith is not haunted or at least greatly challenged by the profound injustices in this world – the pain and misery to which millions are subjected, the human fallibility and cruelty – then that person must be blind to both the world and his or her faith.

I have literally lost count of the amount of times I have heard say that 'Religion is the cause of all wars'. This sweeping statement, even without a great deal of research, seems to be a gross generalisation – and it sidesteps the need to analyse why, throughout history, mankind has twisted and contorted religion to serve his selfish and power-hungry motives.

Ultimately, either we allow ourselves to be indoctrinated through cultural impurity, or we choose to be free thinkers, living with love in our hearts – as the Lord Jesus taught us.

Secularism and Atheism have not stemmed the tide of conflict. The history of the 20th century should provide adequate examples of this fact, with some 40 million deaths attributed to Mao and another 20 million to Stalin.

The abuses of human rights, atrocities and massacres in the Soviet Union, Nazi Germany, Red China, North Korea, Eastern Europe, Uganda, and Cambodia, were the inevitable results of rejecting God's Law.

The simple fact is that mankind will either be governed by God's Law, or ruled by tyrants.

Some extreme forms of religion have been more prone to violence than others, including Christianity, but to tar them all with the same brush is overly simplistic. People, who blame Religion for every worldly conflict clearly demonstrate an unwillingness to be open-minded enough to genuinely consider alternative viewpoints.

Countries that have enjoyed great civil liberties throughout the centuries are generally those where the Gospel of Christ has penetrated the most. It is too easy to ignore the fact that genuine unity is a fruit of the Holy Spirit borne of God's truth, and that it's never a man-made unity, planned to the detriment of the truth.

Through the desire of the Church to avoid offending anyone, these truths seem to have taken second place because we allow ourselves to be captivated and seduced by our culture of materialism and contemporary trends.

Many people say they believe in God but don't go to Church because they think the churches are filled with hypocrites. Paradoxically, they are spot on! When our actions contradict our beliefs, we become hypocritical, and that has happened to everyone at some time or other. It is far too easy for a Christian to pretend to be Godly, but nothing will turn people off God more than an overtly hypocritical Church member.

Jesus himself denounced religious hypocrites. So, if hypocrisy turns your stomach, you may be more Christ-like than you thought.

But to make this claim stick, you must adopt Jesus' attitude to hypocrites: He forgave them ...

If people don't want to go to Church, because they don't believe in God or what is written in the Bible, then of course they are free to choose that, but to make hypocrisy the excuse is pretty lame. Let's face it, we can all be a shade hypocritical, but that's no reason to avoid Church like the plague – just like it's no reason to avoid going to the bank if we see the bank manager at the bookmaker's, or to stop going to our local butcher's after hearing that he is a vegetarian!

A true Christian says, 'I want you to reach your full potential and if this means that you'll then become a finer all-round person than I am, all the better.'

A true Christian knows that following Christ is not about being self-absorbed.

A true Christian doesn't say, 'Do this because I do it, for I am such a paragon of virtue that I am worth emulating.'

A true Christian accepts the fact that he or she is a sinner in need of forgiveness.

A true Christian says, 'Do this because Christ would have you do it, for He is the perfect example, not me.'

If there were one wish I could ask God to grant me in an instant, it would be to have a greater degree of patience. I can only stand back in wonder when I witness the patience of some people I come across during the course of a hectic day, whether it be a busy check-out girl in a supermarket, a Christian friend supporting a challenging person, or a support worker looking after someone with demanding behaviour.

I know I cannot excuse my own lack of patience by saying it belongs to my personality. Therefore, I must make a great effort to change from an impatient person into a patient one.

Solomon wisely states: 'A man of quick temper acts foolishly,' and this is certainly a piece of Scripture that I need to keep in mind when I'm driving behind a slow or indecisive driver, or when my computer screen freezes and I'm about to throw a temper tantrum.

Sometimes, when I am tired, stressed, or frustrated with my lack of progress, I can get irritated at an incident that is in itself quite trivial. But afterwards I'm always angry at myself for getting uptight about next to nothing. I realise that I can also be too hard on myself, and that is something I need to constantly work on.

It is frustrating for me when change takes so long to come about, and the history of Israel illustrates just how quickly one can revert back to old habits and behaviour patterns.

My anger used to erupt at fairly trivial things, and I was rather prone to the occasional emotional outburst. In those days, I relied solely on my own 'great' opinions, as there was no room in my life for any God-given revelation. My opinion reigned supreme in my own mind when insecurity was king of my castle.

I am slowly learning to live in the present. This is something I find challenging, since it's really easy to take the present for granted. By using my time wisely, I know that I am constantly making a better future for myself.

There is no point denying the past, for no matter how hard you bury it, it will resurface time and again – like an old betamax video! Many people I come across appear to have no real conscience regarding sin. They frequently justify their behaviour by saying: 'I did no harm to anyone,' or: 'Everybody does it,' as they brush their sins aside with barely the blink of an eye.

Of course, I'm not suggesting that all non-believers have absolutely no conscience – there are many well-meaning atheists and agnostics who have a high-principled philosophy to life – but I strongly believe in the Spirit of God that dwells deep inside the heart of a committed believer, and I'm sure that a transcending secular conscience is tepid by comparison.

Like most other people, I can occasionally feel despondent. Thankfully, though, feeling this way never lasts for more than a few hours, or at the very most a couple of days. Suffice to say, it's not a pleasurable feeling and is adverse to my primarily optimistic nature.

Some of the despondency may come from hurt pride – typical after the break-up of a relationship, a business failure, or even saying or doing something that I know was wrong.

Some days I can be too busy for God, and this is when I seem to lose focus. I tend to have to learn things the hard way.

My personal healing began when I finally felt accepted by God as the person I am, and I can now see myself in a positive light. I have come to know what it is like to be effective at something, and to experience what it is like to be cherished and valued by my Creator.

We all carry a certain amount of emotional baggage and preconditioning from previous experiences, but slowly the blood of Jesus washes away all our shame, guilt and self-condemnation.

I am fully aware that my imperfections have accounted for many memorable moments in my life. Most of the amusing stories I have shared with anyone I have encountered have partly been the result of acting inappropriately in a given situation. Misjudgement and error are a large part of what made me the person I am.

Everyone needs encouragement, and I always make a conscious effort to surround myself with encouragers and uplifters. I feel privileged to be in a position whereby I just have to pick up the phone to be able to talk to someone, or pop in to see friends and acquaintances who can advise and reassure me every now and then when I have been buffeted by the storms of life.

Since I have become a Christian, I have suffered the sadness of losing a special relative, the pain of a broken engagement, and the stress of a bitter legal dispute, among other things. But I would have to say that the trials I have faced have helped build my faith, strengthened me in my journey, and increased my understanding of the Lord.

There is no promise of "A Bed of Roses" type of life for the person who commits himself to follow Jesus. I think it's easy to misinterpret Jesus' promise of an abundant life to mean a flawless life, with constant happiness and perfect health.

If that really were the case, we would almost create Heaven on earth! But surely we need the tough times and character-building to prepare us for eternity? In common with most other people, I don't particularly enjoy being criticised, but I realise that disapproval is an unavoidable experience of life. Every Prime Minister, business director and Church leader in world history has been vilified, disparaged, belittled, ridiculed and scorned, to some extent. That same critical spirit inevitably filters down to every work place, every home, and every social relationship.

Whenever I receive criticism, I first of all have to ascertain whether it is a correction or an attack. As German poet, Johann Wolfgang von Goethe, once said: 'Correction does much but encouragement does much more' – which leaves me with the question: Is correction always purposefully beneficial and restorative? Discerning where the root of the criticism is coming from is, in my opinion, essential to the correct way of handling it.

If I feel that someone is continually criticising me unfairly, due to their own insecurity, resentment, or simply the need to feel superior, then I will still pray for them. I will erase what they have said from my mind, but at the same time I will make no further attempt to seek their company. I strongly believe that a person needs to earn the authority to speak to me about my life. By that I mean that he or she needs to know me well enough to be able to voice a fair opinion about me, or my behaviour.

There have also been times when I had to prove I was right, which robbed me of opportunities to show grace and allow God to deal with others. Being right was almost insignificant when my attitude was wrong.

What I need most, when I inevitably make a mistake, is mercy – not judgement. If I ever find myself in the unenviable position of being the one impacted by someone else's actions, and I am tempted to revert to defensive and point-scoring mode, God softly reminds me of the last time I deserved justice but received mercy instead, and I am humbled before Him.

I need to be forever mindful that Jesus taught us to look at the plank in our own eye before we try to remove dust from someone else's. I remember looking at the notices on the walls of the session room at my local Church and being confronted by an imposing poster that has stuck in my mind ever since. It featured a coloured photograph of a policeman, pointing accusingly at me with the words, 'If you were arrested tomorrow and charged with being a Christian, would there be enough evidence to convict you?'

This was certainly aimed at the right person, for the words hit me like a slap across my face.

I dare say, there would have been times when I could have puffed out my chest and accepted all charges against me with pride, but I also knew full well that there had been times when I would not have had a leg to stand on if the authorities had come knocking at my front door.

When I get too comfortable, God stirs things up. I frequently evaluate my life and what I want it to represent. Sometimes, I try to imagine what it would be like if God were to grant me a long life and I were to see myself as an old man. What would I be like? Would I be bitter? Resentful? Would I be hardened with the adversities that life has thrown at me – shuffling about with a victim mentality and a sour look on my face all the time, looking as if I had been weaned on a pickle? Or would I be gracious, forgiving, humble, and appreciative of the life that God had granted me?

I know, deep down, that I only have one choice to make, and part of that choice process is to become a reconciler of the breach.

I don't want to look through the rear-view mirror of life and still see various unhealed relationships. I must swallow my pride and reconcile any broken relationships, regardless of the fact that I may have been the victim rather than the perpetrator.

In some ways I miss the innocence that came with being a new Christian. The fresh revelation, awe inspiring, being totally unashamed in the presence of those around me. Why does it all seem to fade as years go by? The ways of the world are always a temptation. I pray earnestly to recover my initial awe and enthusiasm ten fold before I reach eternity.

Years ago, I heard it said that most people fall out because of hurt feelings and misunderstandings, rather than major issues. I have no control over whether people like or even love me, but I do have total control over how I feel about them – and how I treat them.

I know that God has blessed me with an open heart and strong character traits that can help give encouragement, hope and comfort to all kinds of different people I may encounter throughout my life – hopefully, also by way of this book, and any other publications that I aim to write in the future.

Character is a word that was often used by two people I greatly admired when I was growing up. One was my mother, who would never tire of telling me that 'my character was all I had'. This was her regular response to any trouble I seemed to attract like a magnet. I still feel a tinge of sadness when I realise she only lived long enough to see too many examples of my flawed character, rather than my more favourable autumnal attributes.

The most profound definition of character I have ever heard is: 'Character is the person that you are when no one is watching you.' The other person I greatly admired was Jock Wallace, who was manager of Rangers when I was growing up in the 1970s. His frightening growl and gruff voice often belied his soft centre. My abiding image of him is that of a clenched fist in the air, his reaction to the adoration he received from legions of supporters, signifying the character he built into his teams – character and spirit, which emanated from the man himself.

Jock Wallace believed in a tough approach and was renowned for being a fitness fanatic, who often made his players run up and down the Gullane sand dunes, in Ayrshire, until they practically collapsed with exhaustion. He was said to have learned his brutally punishing training methods from the great Australian athlete and world mile record holder, Herb Elliot. Such was the incredible high level of fitness and durability he instilled in his footballers that most of them played into their mid to late thirties.

When Jock sensationally resigned as manager in 1978, after winning all three domestic trophies, I was in a state of shock. Like many other supporters at the time, I had heard various rumours – but that is all they remained, as he did not want to bad-mouth the club that meant so much to him.

He could easily have sold his story to the newspapers, or run to the nearest publisher, but selling his soul for money just did not come into the equation for such a loyal and dignified man. His reasons for leaving were between himself and the club and remained so.

Years later, even as he fought, and ultimately lost, the biggest battle of his life against Parkinson's disease, Jock displayed both the dignity and the character for which I will always remember him.

In his book, *The 7 Habits of Highly Effective People*, Stephen Covey relates a touching personal experience on the New York Subway that taught me a lot about patience and compassion.

The passengers were sitting quietly in the train when a man entered with children who were extremely noisy and active. To Covey's surprise, the man (who was obviously their father) sat down and closed his eyes, totally ignoring his noisy, out of control children. It seemed as if he was oblivious to them! The children's behaviour was way out of line, and everyone was getting agitated ... except the father.

Finally, Covey leaned over and spoke to the man about his children. The father opened his eyes and seemed to finally grasp the situation.

'Oh, you're right. I guess I should do something about it. We just came back from the hospital where their mother died about an hour ago. I don't know what to think, and I don't know how to handle it either.'

Steven Covey's experience, however extreme and unlikely it may seem, reminded me how easy it is to leave compassion out of my daily life, and that I should always look past initial appearance.

It was not until I became a Christian that God softened my heart enough for me to feel compassion for someone who was living a desperate life as a homeless drifter.

I had first seen this woman vagrant in Tenerife, perhaps seven or eight years ago. Because of her appearance – a tangled mass of unkempt hair, tattered clothing and hardened weather-beaten face – it was initially hard to figure out what sex and age she was.

Everything about her screamed homeless and destitute, as she frequently appeared in different places on the Island. I found her such a sad and pathetic sight that I could only give her a brief glance before walking past.

Just after I had become a Christian I saw her again, and I started to think about her life. I thought to myself: long ago, or perhaps not all that long ago, this woman was just a little girl – someone's child – and now she could be someone's mother, sister, or grandmother. But even in her sad desperate state, which may or may not have been of her own choosing, she was a creation of God, and still very dear to Him.

More recently, whilst out for a walk along the pathway that runs along the top of the old cemetery in Portsoy, I noticed that the metal gates were open, and a couple of kids from the nearby caravan site were playing innocently near the old historical well, known locally as St Colms.

This well, dating back to the 7th century, is hidden in an earth mound and is now covered by a stone cupola with an arched entrance. With the water still flowing peacefully, it provides the perfect backdrop for our early morning Easter Service.

It was a glorious midsummer's evening, and although dusk was nearing I was in no desperate rush to head home. The open gates seemed to invite me in, perhaps reminding me that it had been a while since I had paid my respects to my parents.

I made my way slowly downhill, taking time to savour the magnificence of God's creation as I watched the sun slowly setting against the backdrop of a spectacular pink and grey skyline.

As I entered the locally named New Cemetery, adjacent to the older burial site, I became instantly aware of the presence of Almighty God. It was so real, yet difficult to define, but I felt God was guiding me through His Spirit. I had visited the cemetery many times but never before had I sensed such a distinct unearthly presence.

With not a soul in sight I became overwhelmed with emotion, but at the same time a reassuring calmness came over me. As I slowly walked past the various gravestones, I felt a heavy sense of sadness for all the families of the young people who, because of different circumstances, had not been allowed to reach their full potential here on earth. I knew these families personally. I prayed for them, and trusted that their loved ones were in a better place.

As far as my parents were concerned, although they had died relatively young, they had still witnessed and experienced much of life, but I felt a divergent sorrow for these infants, teenagers, and young adults in their twenties and thirties – taken away too early from the people who loved them.

One particular gravestone I came across really moved me. As I approached the recently erected stone, I was jolted by a memory, seeing the name of Andrew Malpas engraved there. This 11-year-old boy had died in a tragic accident involving a lorry, while cycling home from school, in 1974. He was a former classmate of mine. Tears welled up in my eyes as I read the poignant messages from his family.

It felt strange – almost as if it was a recent death and I was meant to be there to show my respects. The new headstone seemed to give a freshness to the memory of this young lad to whom I had given little or no thought over the last three decades.

Andrew had been at Portsoy Primary School for only a while when his young life was cut tragically short. As I read his inscription, my mind flashed back to my Primary 6 days and a blond-haired waif of a boy who had neither been my friend nor someone I had even taken the time to get to know.

I began to pray for peace for Andrew's family, while I tried to comprehend the deep sense of loss they must have felt all these years. It was so moving to realise that not one day had passed since his premature death that Andrew had not been missed by his loving family.

Going back in time to that day, I clearly remember how shocked my classmates and I had been by his death. One normal day Andrew was my classmate, and the next there was just an empty chair where he used to sit ... At the age of eleven, I was not able to fully understand or comprehend the scale of loss and devastation that Andrew's death caused to his family.

I would never have thought that God could begin the process of renewing my mind and softening my hard heart, thus enabling me to see things so differently. He started with my mind, and then it was time to work on my heart.

When God began to work so powerfully in my heart I felt a great need to give something back to Him.

I feel that the depth of my relationship with Christ can sometimes depend on the amount of my life I am willing to share openly with other people. Such openness, I acknowledge, can bring me anguish as well as joy.

The Kingdom of God is still a mystery to me – it always will be. Who can understand it by the mind of man alone? He's up there and we're down here. What is real up there is so vastly in excess and so greatly superior to what I know down here.

But I do know that Christ died on the cross so that we would be given the Holy Spirit – the Counsellor who would lead us all to the ultimate truth.

The implications of the life and resurrection of Jesus Christ are massive. This incredible historical event has formed such a massive paradigm shift in my thinking that it helps me to build the foundations of a world perspective that should shape my reasoning in every area of my life.

Mahatma Gandhi wrote: 'Jesus died in vain if He didn't teach us to regulate the whole of life by the eternal law of love: how to forgive, be thoughtful, and considerate, and understanding and courageous; how to trust, how to defer, and serve, and give, and receive, and help, and encourage and support.'

I first came across this wonderful poem several years ago, and even though I have no idea who wrote it, I find myself regularly reading it and reflecting on what it really means.

THE MEASURE OF A MAN

Not 'How did he die?' But 'How did he live?'
Not 'What did he gain?' But 'What did he give?'
Not 'What was his station?' But 'Had he a heart?'
And 'How did he play his God-given part?'
Not 'What was his shrine?' Nor 'What was his creed?'
But 'Had he befriended those really in need?'
Not 'What did the piece in the newspaper say?'
But 'How many were sorry when he passed away?'
Was he ever ready with a word or good cheer,
To bring back a smile, to banish a tear?
These are the units to measure the worth
Of a man as a man, regardless of birth.

In *Wild at Heart*, John Eldredge challenges the reader with these words: 'The world offers a man a false sense of power and a false sense of security. Be brutally honest now – where does your own sense of power come from? Is it how pretty your wife is – or your secretary? Is it how many people attend your Church? Is it knowledge – that you have a knowledge that others come to you, bow to you? Is it your position, degree, or title? A white coat, a Ph.D., a podium, or a panelled office can make a man feel like pretty neat stuff.'

What really is the true measure of a man?

Should we measure him by his title – King, Prime Minister, Managing Director, or Doctor of Philosophy?

Is he measured by his wealth and power?

Or do we measure him by the colour of his skin, his intellect, or by the simplicity of his life?

I think the best answer to that question can be summed up by Martin Luther King:

'The ultimate measure of a man is not where he stands in moments of comfort and convenience, but where he stands at times of challenge and controversy.'

A boat is safe in a harbour, but that is not what boats are built for.

An aircraft is safe in its hangar, but that was not what it was built for either.

We, too, feel safer when we can avoid having to take risks, or are side-stepping controversy, but that was not what God created us for.

We all seek comfort, security, stability and familiarity in our lives, yet, at the same time, many of us aim to accomplish great things, and wish to be respected and admired.

We want to live a life of purpose and value.

Unfortunately, we can't have it both ways.

But it is always wise for me to reflect on the life of Jesus of Nazareth and ask myself whether at times in my life my short-sighted self-imposed values and insatiable quest for personal glory was done for the greater good of mankind.

Only when I make my final roll call in this transitory existence, will I be able to look back – hopefully as a more rounded person – and rightfully answer that universal question: What is the true measure of a Man?

LEARNING TO PRAY

I have always prayed to God. However, in my annoyance with prayer over the years, I often focused on God's lack of intervention. Why won't He do what I would ask? In reality, many of these frivolous prayers were birthed out of self pity and selfishness: 'Father please give me a heatwave for my school holidays,' when, at the same time all the local farmers were praying desperately for rain to protect their livelihoods : 'Please Lord, let Rangers beat Celtic on Saturday.' 'Please God, make that girl who smiled at me at the weekend fancy me, and want to go out with me.'

Prayer is something that I have always been pitifully inept at, even since I came to faith. Conscious of the fact I was more akin to a Prayer wimp than a Prayer warrior, I felt that God was leading me to become involved with the Prayer ministry team at my local Church. This was confirmed when I was given the opportunity to join the Prayer ministry team at Clan Gathering.

It was only when the penny finally dropped that I realised that I had in my transcendental arsenal one of the most powerful weapons in the shape of prayer for the daily spiritual warfare against the enemy, and that I had scarcely scratched the surface of its mighty potency.

I would regularly visit my good friends Murray and Caroline Farquhar for a time of prayer and reflection. In this safe environment I felt comfortable enough to pray openly, forming a discerning trilateral bond of discretion and trust which in time helped me with my confidence in prayer.

It wasn't that there was no complexity involved in making

prayer something as straightforward and vital as eating my daily bread, but I was finding it all incredibly challenging. Most of this awkwardness and embarrassment that I would often feel in a group situation came about because I was so focused on finding the correct God-inspired words that I inadvertently disregarded, allowing myself to be led by the power of the Holy spirit. It's not just that I had to learn to intercede, I myself had to become intercessor.

If prayer is that intimate place where God and His Creation meet, then I felt I had a responsibility to find out more about the ancient art of praying.

Philip Yancey, in his book *Prayer; Does It Make Any Difference?* asks these perceptive questions regarding the perplexity of prayer:

'I write about prayer as a pilgrim, not an expert. I have the same questions that occur to almost everyone at some point. Is God listening? Why should God care about me? If God knows everything, what is the point of prayer? Why do answers to prayers seem so inconsistent, even capricious? Does a person with many praying friends stand a better chance of physical healing than one who also has cancer, but with only a few people praying for her? Why does God sometimes seem so close and sometimes far away? Does prayer change God or change me?'

I was also finding it a real struggle to fit praying in to my own frenetic life style. There were several reasons for this. Sometimes I was too tired, or just lazy and not disciplined enough in my walk with the Lord. But, because I always seemed to have so many issues on my mind at the same time, I did not know how to pray, or what I should pray for, whether it was something personal, local, national or global.

The apostle Paul obviously knew that I was still prone to over-complicate the simple act of prayer when he said: 'We do not know what God wants us to pray for'. Paul again reassured me of this when he writes: 'The Holy Spirit helps us in our weakness. He prays for us with groanings that cannot be expressed in words. And the Father who knows all hearts knows what the Spirit is saying, for the Spirit pleads for us believers in harmony with God's own wil.' (Romans 8:26-27 NLT).

When Jesus said, 'And so I tell you, keep on asking, and you will receive what you ask for. Keep on seeking, and you will find. Keep on knocking, and the door will be opened to you' (Luke 9:11 NLT), I often followed this principle but did not find doors opening. Did that mean that Jesus was calling my bluff? No, not at all, it simply meant that my one or two pithless knocks was not enough.

If I was really earnest or badly in need of something I would have kept knocking until my knuckles bled and the door was opened. That would at least have shown God that I was desperate about my need. Without a shadow of doubt, God honours such desperateness in His children. It is often only then that He will answer our prayers. In other words: God does not answer my or anyone else's wishful thinking. He honours persistent pleading. Those of us who are really in need will keep on knocking. Christ encourages fervency and constancy in prayer. We must come for what we need.

As George Bernard Shaw, the Irish born dramatist, once remarked: 'Common people do not pray; they only beg.'

However, we know it's not always that simple. Why are some prayers answered and others not? Why does God answer a prayer for a lost ring, but appear absent in the face of tragedy? Has it anything to do with our lack of faith or even the current sin in our lives? I really don't know. All I can do is accept the paradox.

Philip Yancey offers this sobering view of what would happen if the God of Heaven were to answer every single one of our prayers:

'By answering every single prayer, God would in effect abdicate, turning the world over to us to run. History shows how we have handled the limited power granted to us: we have fought wars, committed genocide, fouled the air and water, destroyed forests, established unjust political systems, concentrated pockets of superfluous wealth and grinding poverty. What if God gave us automatic access to supernatural power? What further havoc might we wreak?'

In my own life, I can reflect on numerous instances of unanswered prayer, especially in relationships where if God had consented to grant me my deepest desires, I would have been married about half a dozen times ... to the wrong person!

We all know what it feels like to beg, plead and even bargain with God but still fail to get what we've asked for – the addiction is not beaten, the relationship still ends, or the person we love still dies. Yet, most of us who have endured suffering know what it's like to have prayer answered in the most amazing and extraordinary fashion, believing beyond any shadow of doubt that God's healing hand was on our life.

Many times when I pray faithfully, God will not say: 'No,' but: 'Wait'.

There is always a proper time for answered prayer, and it's very seldom in my time. Sometimes God needs to wait until I am ready for the answer, or perhaps others need to be made ready first. Sometimes a delay is necessary for my wish to fit into God's overall plan.

Daniel learned this lesson. For sixty years, Daniel prayed for the return of Israel to Jerusalem, for the rebuilding of the city of God which lay in ruins. It seemed that there was no answer from God. Then Daniel discovered the word of the Lord to Jeremiah, which had said that there would be a wait of seventy years before the captives of Israel could return to their city. (Jer. 29:10)

With this knowledge, Daniel went to the Lord in fervent prayer. I believe his prayer is one of the great prayers of Scripture. (Dan. 9:3-19)

When Daniel began to pray, about sixty-eight of the seventy years had already passed. In answer to Daniel's prayer – and in keeping with God's timetable – the Book of Ezra records the return of Israel to its ancient land and capital city.

So, delay in answering prayer does not mean that God has not been listening to us. But that doesn't mean that I am patient enough to wait sixty years for an answer to prayer!

Speaking or praying in tongues, from all indications in the New Testament, is the consequence of the baptism in the Holy Spirit. There was an initial utterance in tongues, bearing witness that the tongue had been sanctified and empowered by God for His use. But my understanding is that speaking in tongues was not necessary for the salvation of those people.

Fifty days after the resurrection of Jesus, God began His New Testament Church with an event that has caused controversy ever since. It was on the Day of Pentecost. The disciples were filled with the Holy Spirit and began to speak with other tongues and magnify God.

This one event brought the wisdom of God's Kingdom full circle and appears to have been resisted, scorned, ridiculed and misunderstood ever since. It appears, due to this controversy, that throughout the centuries the Church has backed away in fear, using the lame excuse that it might cause offence. This has been evidenced by myself over the last six years, as I have had the distinction, on more than one occasion, of being accused of not being a 'real' Christian for not having received the gift.

I find it deplorable as well as dumbfounding that just proudly wearing the helmet of salvation is not enough for some people in the Church. I can assure you that when it has taken you 40 years to encounter the living God, you feel dreadfully downhearted to be told that you need extra 'add-ons' to become a 'real Christian'.

Of course, depending on someone's Church background, this issue of tongues is either a mystery, a big deal, or a non-issue. Although praying in tongues is significant in some people's Christian experience, I don't believe it is a gauge of someone's competence, credibility, or devotion as a follower of Christ.

It's easy for me to understand why an affluent, sophisticated person is repelled by the thought of a need to pray. After all, no proud person likes to think that they have to beg for anything. Many people, that is those with any level of moral conscience, prefer to persevere in their own strength or hard graft to get what they want. We, as a society, would rather settle for less because we don't want to lower ourselves to the position of a suppliant. Some of us would prefer to go without rather than to have to ask God or anyone for help.

Perhaps this is illustrated by the fact that the Titanic was built by experts while the Ark was built by amateurs!

There is nothing to hide when in quiet supplication we are reaching into the deepest part of ourselves, admitting our needs and failures. In so doing, our hearts are quietened and pride is stripped so that we can fully enjoy the presence of God.

To the cynic, praying is just a delusion and a total waste of time. Whether, of course, that same person would still be as dismissive if they were on a sinking ship or an aircraft hijacked by terrorists, only they and the One they are rejecting could possibly know.

There is no doubt that praying to an invisible God is a bit more complicated than conversing with close friends or opening up to a trained counsellor whom we can at least see nodding their heads in understanding. It is easy therefore, perhaps understandable, if in troubled times we were to ask: 'Is anyone really listening?'

Yet, as I return to God in prayer over and over again, the way becomes clearer, more familiar, and the relationship I find there begins to mature.

That doesn't mean that the mysticism of His divinity, transcendence and omnipotence will ever make sense to me. When news reports of the horrific Asian tsunami of 2005 reached the rest of the world, 'experts' were quick to seize upon the disaster as proof of either of God's power or of God's non-existence. When something as horrendous as that happens, we want someone to blame – in fact we need someone to blame. When that awful event is a natural disaster, there's often no one left to blame but God. Earthquakes, hurricanes, tornadoes, tidal waves, lightning strikes – the insurance companies still call them 'acts of God'.

When tragedy and misfortune falls on the righteous as well as the unrighteous, prayer appears so futile and ineffectual. This uncomfortable reality makes it difficult for us to reconcile such obvious unfairness with the existence or justice of an intelligent divine being.

I realise that the most meaningful prayer needs to be borne out of not only true repentance but also utter dependency. It is not enough for any of us to attend a Church or house group, only to pray a bland, uninspiring, stereotypical prayer. The Holy Spirit speaks and calls to the spirit within us. We don't need to go far to experience the divine presence of God that is all around us.

God searches my heart. He understands every motive behind my thoughts. He refuses to answer prayers that have wrong motives. Prayers must be in harmony with what He has revealed to be His plan for all of the people of the world that He created in His own image. These petitions must be in agreement with God's holy and righteous character.

What I desire from God must be in the best interest of others as well as myself. On more than one occasion I have listened to open prayer in a house group or Church building, where I have even heard people telling God what to do, combined with thinly veiled hints on how others present should conduct themselves.

We as a nation can hardly pray with sincerity, 'Give us this day our daily bread,' when most of us live in 'the land of plenty' where we can open any jumbo fridge freezer in our modern fitted kitchen and find enough provisions from outlets such as Marks & Spencer's to last us months. We discard almost as much of our daily bread as we use. In Scotland alone, experts estimate that we waste 1 billion pounds worth of food every year.

Thankfully, intellectual intelligence does not make one nano bit of difference to our capacity for faith and the ability to pray. It is the power of thorough consecration, the grace that comes with humility, an absolute losing of one's self in God's glory, and an ever-present and insatiable yearning to seek all the fullness of God that makes the difference. Men and women can set the nation ablaze for God – not necessarily in a yelling, eccentric, attention-seeking fashion, but with an intense purposeful passion that moves everything for the God of Heaven.

John Welch, a wondrous Scottish 17th century preacher, thought the day ill-spent if he did not pray for eight to ten hours. He kept a plaid that he might wrap himself with when he arose to pray at night. His wife would complain when she found him lying on the ground weeping. He would reply: 'O woman, I have the souls of three thousand to answer for, and I know not how it is with many of them!'

There have been many mighty men of God in the Scottish Church. They adorn its proud history; they are the forefathers of our Church's legacy. Their remarkable example has been a real blessing to me. I continually pray for more mighty men like these in the Church today.

I know Satan dreads such prayers, for one of his main concerns is to prevent the saints from praying. He trembles when we pray as a united army of God. He fears nothing from prayer-less studies, prayer-less work and prayer-less faith. He laughs and sneers at our misfortune and mocks our failures as believers.

Many times I have turned to prayer feeling enclosed. The repeated 24 hour tragedies on Sky news constantly remind me of human misery and injustice.

There are countless things that could foster stress and anxiety if I were to sit down and really contemplate the wounds of a broken world. Added to this is a more personal concern that I have for family, friends and neighbours. So many of them are battling addictions, relationship problems, poor health and financial burdens – amongst other things.

To my shame, trivial interruptions in my own life often blot out these concerns: getting engrossed in scanning the football news online, opening that innocuous-looking e-mail, and once again feeling condemned by it's pornographic content; missing another dental appointment ...

Even when I confess my sins to God, there is almost a subliminal voice saying : 'These are the same sins that you confessed last week, last month and last year!'

God's Spirit speaks to me of my own selfishness, of an often judgemental nature – my own shortcomings that others, through a deeper and more intimate understanding of the Father, treat with love, grace and mercy.

The Gospels make it abundantly clear to us that Jesus desires that all His people experience the love of the Father, because He devoted His whole life to spreading that message. Jesus desires physical healing and good health for us. This is shown by the fact that He never once turned down a request for physical healing. Despite this, millions of people around the world still experience poor physical health.

Does this tell of a God who has abandoned us?

I know God envisioned a world of beauty and harmony, and He created it, making every part an expression of His freedom, wisdom and love. (Gen 1:1-25 NLT). This means that something must be interfering with His great plan for this planet, but it does not disprove His love for us.

It's so easy to mock and criticise others and their method of searching for meaning. At the same time, we may secretly wonder if maybe they know something we don't. Apart from the need for companionship, we also long for a relationship where we feel safe to draw close; to be with someone who understands and loves us and appreciates our love for them.

Only in the person of the Lord Jesus Christ can we achieve that. This very second, people all around the globe are praying to false gods. This world is brimming with sects, cults, religions, philosophies and movements, all of which claim to be the right way or the only path to God. How can we determine which one is true?

In fact, what makes me so convinced that I pray to the correct God?

Well, in Jesus Christ, unlike other gods, prophets and idols, we have the unique mediator between man and the Creator of the universe, because He is the only person who is both God and man. History is littered with stories of men attempting to be God, but there is only one true story of God becoming man.

The Christian God is both our Creator and our Redeemer.

What would it confirm about me, if I concluded that this planet had no Creator, simply because I couldn't contact Him about any personal dilemma? Surely the reality of His existence has nothing to do with whether or not He returns my prayers? Neither does His existence have anything to do with the fact that there are those who have experienced miracles and physical healing, seen visions, or heard His audible voice. After all, as I once heard someone say, the sun doesn't exist because we see its light, or because we feel its heat. Nor does it cease to exist because a blind man is not conscious of its reality. Its existence has nothing to do with any human testimony. The sun exists, period.

The existence of God isn't dependent on the Bible or its authenticity. It isn't dependent on the existence of the Church, the prophets, or even Creation. God existed before the universe came into being; long before the Scriptures were even written.

Even if someone could prove the Bible to be fraudulent – and there have been plenty futile attempts to do that – God would still exist.

THE MISSION FIELDS OF SCOTLAND

Not long into my Christian walk, I developed a strong desire to become involved in outreach. It had come to my notice, even before I gave my life to the Lord, that there were divisions within the body of the Church with little fellowship and cooperation between many of the different denominations, not to mention the obvious barrier that existed between Christians and the outside world.

I felt led to play my part in bringing Churches together by organising several quiz nights in different Church venues in Banff, Portsoy and Gardenstown. I was grateful for the leadership and administrative staff at the Riverside Christian Church for giving me the freedom and support to develop my ideas.

As I was attending all three Churches I was able to help bring people together for these enjoyable relaxed evenings. I was just as encouraged to see that they were supported by many non-Churchgoers as well as some of my secular friends. This meant a lot to me, convincing me that there was not an insurmountable barrier between the Church and secular society. Considerable amounts of money were raised as people gave generously to worthy Christian causes, both at home and overseas.

Although I enjoyed organising these outreach events, I felt that the Lord had a greater calling for me. I knew it was selfish and even sinful of me to be comfortable and cosy with my own salvation as a back-seat believer and that, if Jesus was in the process of transforming my life because people cared about and prayed for me, I was duty-bound to do the same for others.

I had a great desire to be doing more for His Kingdom but was not sure what His plans were. Even praying regularly never seemed to give me a clear vision of where I was being led. I was open to all possibilities, especially evangelism, and even overseas missionary work.

In the midst of all this praying and searching I was subtly challenged one night in Church. I was attending an evening service at Gardenstown Kirk when the minister, Rev Donald Martin, produced a copy of an American publication called 'Pentecostal Evangel' with the front page headline of: 'It's Sunday in Scotland and the pews are empty.' The poignant photo on the front cover was of a solitary man sitting with his back to the camera in an otherwise empty Church.

I instantly felt a deep sense of sadness that the Church had become such a low priority in life, as well as being viewed in such a negative and pitiful manner by people visiting from another country.

In July 2005, I attended Clan Gathering – a week-long Christian conference in St Andrews – for the very first time. I was delighted to be invited to spend four days in that historic town with my minister, Iain Sutherland, his wife Heather and their two young children, Grace and John. It was there that I began to learn more about Scotland's proud history as a once mighty God-fearing nation.

One of the key speakers that week was Dr Jack Deere, an author and pastor from America, and I found myself being deeply moved by his sermon on 'The Great Reformers of Scotland' with its reference to John Howie's eighteenth century book *Scottish Worthies.*

Jack Deere went on to recount incredible, true stories of the Protestant Martyrs; our heroic forefathers, who paid the ultimate price for demanding that Jesus was elevated to His rightful position as Head of the Church.

This rekindled a real sense of patriotism that had lain dormant within me for many years. I had always felt great pride in my heart when Scotland qualified for the World Cup finals, when Alan Wells won his Olympic gold medal at the Moscow Olympics, and when

Jim Watt boxed his way to becoming a world champion, but many years had passed and I had lost much of this national fervour and pride, reasoning that it was too conceited to feel any great passion for my country.

In the free time we had in the afternoon, between all the praise and worship, I felt drawn to make a short daily pilgrimage to the various historic monuments in this town that had played such a central role in establishing our Church heritage. It was an incredibly moving and humbling experience to visit the exact place where fearless men of God, such as George Wishart and Patrick Hamilton, laid down their lives for Christ.

When I returned home from St Andrews, and was back working in my painting business, I became more observant of our Church's sad decline as I drove along the coastal and rural roads of the North East of Scotland.

I began to feel a sense of sadness while passing the numerous old Churches and meeting halls that had been so fundamental to the fishing and farming communities. Many had been closed when membership dwindled because worshippers died, left the area, or simply turned their back on God.

Churches that had once been places of great comfort and significance in our communities found themselves teetering between ineffectiveness and extinction.

In 2006, I flew with my then girlfriend Julia to Florida for the first time. It was marvellous to see so many warm, inviting, brightly coloured Churches of all shapes and sizes scattered along the vast stretches of road as we visited places like Orlando and Lakeland. Even though we were thousands of miles from home, it was so reassuring that I was in a part of the world where the name of our Lord Jesus was revered and lifted high.

However, I couldn't help thinking how much of a contrast this was to what I had become familiar with back home. Those abandoned once-vibrant places of worship were either lying empty or were being used as stores for farmers and small businesses. Some had even been converted into homes, restaurants and nightclubs.

Although I still had issues with the traditional Church, particularly with legalism, status, and over-structure, I was still saddened by its evident demise. As I passed one or saw one in the distance, I instantly felt connected with its emboldened past – its ministers, most now deceased, its ever changing congregation, and the fundamental role it must have once played in that particular community. I was now being spiritually nourished by good gospel preaching, and although I could connect with my Lord more effortlessly participating to contemporary worship from song writers like Robin Mark and Brian Doekson, I was finding that some older hymns, written by the likes of Charles Wesley and Fanny Crosby – unless they are played at funeral procession pace – could also be uplifting to me.

In a similar but more personal way than I mourned the death of the corner shop and the trusting community spirit of the 60s, 70s and 80s, this nostalgic romanticist saw all these old Victorian Church buildings as confirmation that the Christian faith was in decline.

I began to wonder if in this first decade of the 21st century many of our traditional Churches had become too drab and too colourless – both inside and out – to attract people of all ages who badly needed to feel the love, comfort and forgiveness of Jesus Christ.

All through my teens, twenties and thirties, my own perception and experience of the Church had been of a boring, outdated and irrelevant institution.I reasoned that many people of my generation and younger must have felt the same way.

It was becoming glaringly obvious to me that during the last thirty years there had been a steady erosion of our Christian values and way of life. I began to despair at some of the issues that were being highlighted through the media; an indication that our traditional faith was in danger of retreating into history.

The abandoning of the nativity play at Christmas in some schools, and a national airline's employee being banned from wearing a crucifix made me deeply concerned about where my country was heading. Secularism and humanism has clearly been creeping into many Churches, while affluent lifestyles were making many of us apathetic and complacent about our faith.

As I travelled regularly to Edinburgh to visit Julia, we found ourselves doing a bit of Church 'hopping' before we could find one that really made us feel both welcome and comfortable.

We attended services in some traditional Churches but the congregation appeared to be a bit on the self-righteous "hoity-toity" side, devoid of genuine warmth. It was only after the twenty-minute car journey to Holy Trinity Church in Wester Hales that I really felt at home in a welcoming, vibrant Church.

I felt a strong pull towards this community Church, situated in one of the less affluent parts of the city. I loved being in the company of its cross-section of worshippers of all ages who, despite their obvious life challenges, had created an atmosphere in which I felt a real presence of the Holy Spirit.

It seemed to be the kind of Church in which everyone was accepted, regardless of their background and social standing, and I found that refreshingly appealing. In addition, I never left the building feeling less than mightily challenged by the preaching of minister Kenny Borthwick – in my view a truly anointed man of God.

July 2007 was a very hectic time of year for me with many business commitments, but as Clan Gathering approached I felt a deep yearning to be present again. So, I hurriedly made last minute plans to attend the Sunday and Monday sessions, trying to cause as little disruption as possible to my forthcoming week's work schedule.

My good friends Laurie and Meg Harris, who owned a holiday cottage across the street from me in Portsoy, were kind enough to offer me accommodation for the two nights. I made arrangements for the forty-five minute journey from their home in Letham, Angus, to the site on the outskirts of St Andrews.

Even the treacherous conditions underfoot, caused by the

torrential rain the previous day, failed to dampen my enthusiasm and sense of anticipation as I met up with my friends, John and Maggie West, at 9.30 a.m. when we took our seats alongside two to three thousand other worshippers in the main tent for the morning session. Such had been the level of rainfall that straw was used on top of what was a quagmire inside to help absorb the mud.

Although R.T. Kendall – an author I greatly admired – was preaching in the morning, it was actually a young Church of Scotland minister from the Outer Hebrides who really challenged me. He stirred up a passion in me that God had planted in my heart two years previously.

Using the platform of live satellite TV exposure through the God Channel, as well as the thousands of delegates inside the huge tent, Tommy McNeil grasped the opportunity to speak a powerful Word into the Church in Scotland.

He commenced with these prophetic words: 'There is a move coming to our nation that will surpass everything our nation has seen until this day. The next move of God is going to be nameless and faceless.'

Tommy firmly believed that God had been talking prophetically to the Church in Scotland for years. He continued: 'There will be no name associated with it, there will be no Church, there will be no movement, there will be no stream. It will be the Lord Jesus Christ and Him alone that will receive all the glory.'

From that moment on, I felt completely overwhelmed with the power of the Holy Spirit. The hairs on the back of my neck stood up as I became glassy-eyed with emotion and renewed pride for my country.

I felt a burning desire stirring up within my heart to go and help make a difference in the lives of the lost and spiritually destitute in my community, and also my country.

Struggling to hold back the tears, I began to envisage such a wonderful scenario. I became resolute in my belief that our Christian heritage should not be looked upon as a relic of the past but rather as achievements that would inspire us all in the future.

Tommy read from 2nd Kings 5:1 (NLT): 'The King of Aram

had great admiration for Naaman, the commander of his army, because through him the Lord had given Aram great victories. But though Naaman was a mighty warrior he suffered from leprosy.'

This man, ablaze with passion for God, made the comparison between the once proud, brave, mighty warrior and the once revered God-fearing nation of Scotland, for Scotland was now suffering from its own "leprosy" within the Church ... spiritual pride!

Tommy continued: 'We look here, there, and everywhere for change but the real change must come from in here' – pointing to his own heart.

Immediately I knew this to be a personal challenge to me as well as a timely reminder, for I had often been guilty myself of looking for change everywhere, and in everybody else's heart instead of my own.

Tommy McNeil, his voice swelling with emotion, went on to challenge the denominations within the Church in Scotland. He urged all the Churches of Scotland to unite; to stop comparing and judging each other's doctrine, theology and style of worship. He called for us not to look at other movements and revivals around the world but to live the kingdom life according to the unchanging word of God in the Holy Bible.

He preached passionately about how we were once respected and known around the world for being a nation of God – with the Covenanters and our proud Puritan heritage, with our famous missionaries, who paid an awesome price so that the name of Jesus would be honoured.

Tommy referred to the fact that people had come to the Island of Lewis, where he preached in a Church in Barvas, to visit the place of the famous Lewis Revival with Duncan Campbell in 1949-'53 and, although he met some wonderful people from every continent, it grieved his heart that people only wanted to talk about what had happened in the past rather than what was happening at present.

It was a captivating Word from God and one that came with heartfelt sincerity from a young minister who obviously cared passionately about the Church and the people of his country. He proclaimed that these were days of preparation for the Church in

Scotland and that we would experience revival, unprecedented in our nation's history, with tens of thousands coming to know Christ as their Saviour ...

At that moment, I felt an overwhelming surge of belief that Scotland would once again be that God-fearing nation it was always destined to be.

This was no cry of patriotic bravado, it was a prophetic word spoken directly into my heart. I knew instantly that this was my calling. This was where God wanted me to serve in His Kingdom. Here, in my own country, in my own community, where I could pray for, encourage, and reach out to the lost.

It was not the first time that I had heard a word for revival, for I had prayed for revival many times before. But such was the lack of real conviction and belief behind these prayers that I doubt if they had ever really got beyond the height of my bedroom ceiling.

In the weeks and months that followed, I began to study the past revivals of Scotland.

There was the Cambuslang revival, which peaked in 1742, and where crowds of 30 000 gathered to hear sermons, resulting in thousands of conversions.

Nearer to home, in 1859, Donald Ross led a team of fearless evangelists along hundreds of miles of deeply indented Moray Firth coastline in, arguably, the most significant and far-reaching spiritual awakening of modern times.

In the 1920s, Jock Troup, called from East Anglia, led a revival in the North East of Scotland whereby 10 000 Doric-speaking people accepted Jesus as their Saviour.

As the next great spiritual awakening dominated my thoughts, I began to get excited about a rebirth of the New Testament Church which was wonderfully warm and inspiring, and much closer to the biblical model as described by Dr Luke in the Book of Acts.

Reading about these remarkable revivals, I came to realise that they were all birthed after a dry, barren, dark period in Scottish Church history. It also became apparent to me that the Church had always been in an ever-changing cycle of growth, decline and renewal.

As I neared the end of writing this book, I became a keen student of Rodney (Gypsy) Smith, who adopted the name 'Gypsy' as he was raised on a Gypsy camp and never attended a school. Perhaps I saw some of myself in him, in his early years. He was a liar, a thief and even a competent salesmen, and his lightning-fast tongue and quicker leg-power got him into and out of many scrapes. In spite of this, he grew up to influence the lives of millions of people for God through his powerful preaching. He was converted in 1876 and the following year was invited by General William Booth (who founded the Salvation Army) to join him in evangelistic work. He served as an officer with the Salvation Army until 1882. He then began ministering as an itinerant evangelist working with a variety of organisations all over the world for more than 60 years.

His ministry, that spanned continents, was so enriched with countless inspirational quotes and words of profound wisdom; none more so than when he was asked how to start revival. He answered: 'Go home, lock yourself in your room and kneel down in the middle of the floor. Draw a chalk line all around yourself and ask God to start a revival inside the chalk line. When he answers your prayer, the revival will start.'

Somehow I don't think Gypsy would have taken any excuse from me – having a carpeted floor.

Tommy McNeil's views on the judgmentalism of the Church in Scotland had touched a raw nerve in me. I had encountered this kind of attitude long before I became a Christian and it only became more evident when I came to faith.

This was the first time I had heard a Church minister mention the fact that many Christians were quick to smugly criticise another Church, even though they had never set foot in it.

I felt strongly about the issues that Tommy shared with millions of viewers on satellite TV as well as with all of us at the conference. We should be less judgemental of the different structures within our diverse denominations, and that we should not criticise when we don't understand them.

I reckoned that it was blatantly obvious to any Christian that there was enough scorn and ridicule from the outside world without the sniping and whispering from our fellow brothers and sisters in Christ. Can it be that differences between denominations or congregations reflect the rich diversity of their social, cultural and temperamental backgrounds? But at the same time they should reflect the character of God, whose grace is 'multi-faceted'. If you belong to Christ – and I belong to Christ – then surely we belong to each other and we need each other.

Nothing should divide us. If the congregation is split, almost every opinion, no matter how right or wrong, is guaranteed to cause division. There are people within the Body of Christ who regard the Church as an exclusive organisation that should only welcome people who fit their own man-made criteria.

I don't know why I should ever be surprised about Church divisions as they are not a new phenomenon – they existed in the early Church and will no doubt continue to exist until the Saviour returns. People everywhere are starving for the Word of God, yet so many places of worship are engaged in contentious bickering, often over trivial matters. There appears to be little respect or encouragement for one another. Instead, there is an unhealthy attitude of self-interest, self-importance and self-preservation.

All the weighty spiritual qualities like faith, patience, humility, common courtesy and brotherly love are somehow set aside when a difference of opinion arises. Arguments, suspicion, rage and slander take over, making separations inevitable.

Well-known Scottish scholar, William Barclay, once wrote, 'One of the highest of human duties is the duty of encouragement.'

The world is full of discouragers, yet, we have a Christian duty to encourage one another. Many a time a word of praise, thanks, appreciation or cheer has lit up a person's day, including mine. Blessed is the one who speaks such a word.

The Apostle Peter also reminds us: 'Most important of all, continue to show deep love for each other, for love covers a multitude of sins. Cheerfully share your home with those who need a meal or a place to stay. God has given each of you a gift from His great variety of spiritual gifts. Use them well to serve one another.' (1 Peter 4:8-1 NLT). Encouragement is what I miss most about the Network Marketing business seminars, for it is something that seems to be in short supply in some Churches. That is why I love to read about Barnabas in the book of Acts. Barnabas is not remembered as a visionary leader or a spellbinding preacher. He is remembered for one thing: wherever he went, he encouraged people – that is, he put courage into the hearts of otherwise frightened and discouraged men and women.

The acid test of an encourager is surely the ability to let someone else take the lead and receive the credit. To recognise potential in a colleague and encourage him or her to move ahead without becoming envious or resentful – that's Barnabas.

In our Church in Portsoy, we are fortunate to have among us several encouragers in particular Paul Williams and Vera Lumsden; both are more thrilled about other people's successes than they are about their own. We need more Barnabas-type people in the Church of Jesus Christ today.

I once heard a preacher suggest that many Christians share the same blood-group ... B Negative!

There are so many things that discourage us and leave us with self-doubt. We desperately need unsung heroes like Barnabas to build up our confidence.

By giving generously.

By seeing and affirming the grace of God at work in the lives of others and giving them the chance to succeed.

By believing in people who've made mistake after mistake, who have experienced failure or rejection, and helping them to believe in themselves again.

I have no doubt that our Church leaders also need more encouragement. These men and women – many of whom have turned their backs on flourishing professional careers and healthy salaries to follow the call of God – need our prayers and support like never before. It is only natural that in these challenging days for the Church they occasionally feel the chill of discouragement, the sting of criticism and the pain of loneliness that often leads to isolation.

Many of us don't allow our leaders to experience any marital strife or discord. We do not allow them to deal with doubt and depression when it attacks them, mercilessly – as it did the great Baptist Preacher, Charles Spurgeon, for most of his life.

Our leaders must never have a bad day like us; they must never get angry. And just imagine how they would turn into the evaluator's dream target if ever they were to lose their temper in public.

We do not allow a minister's wife to miss a Church activity. She must appear to be super spiritual all the time. Oh, and she must be able to sing, play a musical instrument, minister to other wives and, of course, raise cherubic children.

And these children are invariably treated differently at school, for they are growing up under the community microscope. We make no allowances for their juvenile humanness. They are sitting ducks for those among us who expect ethereal human behaviour from those kids.

I don't think the minister needs to be outgoing, academic or have an encyclopaedic knowledge of the Scripture. But he does need to be approachable and have a real passion for making his Church a fellowship with a dynamic concern for helping to lift the load off humanity.

I used to be under the false impression that for the Church to be fully effective it only needed the minister's drive and enthusiasm; that he should always be the main man mentoring a Christian to reach their full potential. I now see this as the collective responsibility of the whole Church family. It is obvious to me that the quality and effectiveness of the Church leader depends a lot on his ability to delegate authority and assign responsibility.

If leaders assume their man-made role of "Lone Ranger" they will inescapably become overworked, detached, and exhausted. When they fail to encourage, appreciate or recognise the accomplishments of others, people become frustrated and disillusioned. As harmony within the fellowship degenerates, these people may even move on to pastures new.

We all need someone. After all, even the Lone Ranger needed Tonto!

In *A Child No More*, a challenging book about growing into Christian maturity, Mary Pytches states, 'There are those who control their environment and others from their advantageous position of leadership. Delegation is far too threatening, so they keep everything in their own hands. So long as they stay "top dog" they can control those around them. These people only feel secure, and of value when they are in charge.'

The natural consequence of this is that the body of Christ is weakened when its people are not allowed to serve.

In several traditional Churches that I have attended a familiar catch phrase appears to be: 'It has always been done this way' – or should that be 'our way'?

This commonly heard statement reinforces my view that the primary function of some traditional Churches is to perpetuate the past and simply exist. Change is always viewed as threatening, and stagnation can easily be interpreted as stability.

I ask the question, 'Do we want to be a Church of maintenance or one of mission?'

I feel that we, as Christians, are sometimes too busy propping up what we already have and pretending that we live in some glorious past rather than reforming, revitalising and reaching out in the way we are called.

It appears that the traditional Church model is so embedded in a certain mindset that any attempt to deviate from what feels safe and secure will meet with fierce opposition. Many of our Churches were built in a Dickensian era, in a prudish Victorian age, where even piano legs were deemed offensive and had to be covered with tiny pantalettes! Sadly, it seems that Victorian attitudes still exist in some traditional Churches.

Did Jesus really have bricks and mortar, denominations and traditions in His heart when He envisaged His glorious, victorious Bride, prevailing against the gates of hell?

I don't think so.

I may not have had an upbringing that would be a shining example to anyone, but as an ecumenical Christian I am relieved that I have not been brought up in a culture of suppressive Church rules or an environment of judgemental exclusiveness.

As long ago as the 1930s, George McLeod – viewed by many of his generation as a maverick within the Church of Scotland – argued that with the collapse of the Puritan ideal, Presbyterianism needed to work out a new framework.

He pointed out that in order to move forward the Church must first go backwards, to ransack the drawers of its own past and find garments that would fit today and tomorrow. He firmly believed that our future identity would depend upon how we choose to remember our past – being honest about what was wrong but also celebrating what was good.

In his book *Church of the Isles*, Ray Simpson warns, 'Third-millennium Churches need to relate to the third-millennium framework or they will become dinosaurs.'

According to evangelist J. John, the Church has been stuck in an archaic mindset which promotes an outdated model of evangelism.

He feels that the Church has always been seeking to "attract" people from the outside to join. He argues that this will fail. We must learn to work in reverse, for example, by befriending people, so that they feel they belong; they will be free to choose when and if they want to believe. There is no doubt in my mind that the primary human need is to be loved and accepted unconditionally.

I have noticed that the way traditional 'religion' offers the gospel does not seem to relate to many Postmodernists with all their questions and concerns about identity, meaning and purpose.

Is it wrong to suggest that our new generation of men and women are all seeking psychological answers, rather than a spiritual solution? I believe they recognise that anything real and spiritual must affect their psychological sense of being and identity in a dynamic day-by-day, moment-by-moment impact.

I recently read this piece by Edwin Orr, the great Baptist minister, lecturer and author. 'The Reformers were more evangelical than the Lollards; the Puritans more evangelical than the Reformers; the Revivalists of the 18th century were more zealous for soul-winning than the Puritans, whilst those of the 19th century were much more enterprising than their forerunners in the 18th; and ecumenists have conceded that 20th century Pentecostals outdo older denominations in zeal.'

I wonder how near we are to the model which Jesus envisaged for the Church? One of the reasons why Christians have given up on the conventional Church, is not because it demands too much from them but because it demands too little.

Jesus established His Church in order to meet the basic human requirement of nurture and support. It was never meant as a place to show our uprightness. The apostolic Church became a fellowship of believers committed to each other.

The minutes of the early Church read: 'All the believers devoted themselves to the apostles' teaching, and to fellowship, and to sharing in meals (including the Lord's Supper), and to prayer... all the while praising God and enjoying the goodwill of all the people. And each day the Lord added to their fellowship those who were being saved.' (Acts 2:42, 47 NLT)

The Bible reveals a dynamic early Church, which called men and women into a joyful fellowship with the Lord.

Many of our modern-day inventions were invented and formulated by Scots, which is a remarkable tribute to our original and creative spirit.

It was after the Reformation, however, that Scotland had its greatest impact on the world, although, sadly, today no one could deny that Scotland has become a very secular society in which Christianity has been pushed to one side.

This promise of God to Israel can rightly be claimed for Scotland:

'If my people, who are called by my name, shall humble themselves, and pray, and seek my face, and turn from their wicked ways, I will hear from heaven, and will forgive their sins, and restore their land.' (2 Chronicles 7:14 NLT)

Herein, surely, lies a guarantee that the Church will never die in Scotland – actually, I would go as far as to say that Church may well be about to enter into a new lease of vitality, power and prosperity, through which greater glory to God will be achieved in the future than has been yielded in all the past revivals throughout the centuries.

John Knox, the great Scottish reformer, uttered, 'God, give me Scotland, or give me death.'

His passion and faith were influential in changing Scotland from being one of the most 'sinful, irredeemable, and spiritually blind nations of all Europe' to becoming one celebrated for its honesty, piety and morality – centuries after his death.

Mary Queen of Scots once famously said that she feared the prayers of John Knox more than all the armies of Europe.

I am aware of the fact that people come to Church with all their hurts and worries. What they seek is a touch from God that will change their lives forever and when this does not happen they may feel let down, disappointed and disillusioned.

Some may not relate to the style of worship, the minister's sermon, or they may feel unwelcome. How different things might have been if they had met someone they could have related to – a listener; an empathiser who could tell them that Christianity is not about a building, a set of rules, or hymns and songs with words they do not understand.

Because of this negative experience, they may only attend Church once or twice - never to return - which is real tragedy.

This is an all too common scenario for many people who are searching. I know from my own experience that some non-Churchgoers still perceive the Church to be a privatised concern for the minority who want 'religion'. They do not feel that the Church is in tandem with their wholesome but non-religious aspirations.

People are more likely to turn to God in times of adversity than in times of prosperity. If they are anything like I was, God is viewed as a lucky rabbit's foot.

Joe Ewen, founder of Riverside Christian Fellowship, in Banff, shared a story with a house group I was attending. It was about a conversation he'd had with a Hungarian pastor who told him that when his country was under communist rule his Church was jam-packed, but when the Iron Curtain of oppression was brought down his Church was half empty in a matter of months.

A common problem in traditional Churches is that some senior members of the congregation, who have served and supported the Church for many years, want the status quo to continue, while most of the twenty to forty somethings want to ditch the organ and prayer-hymn-sermon type of structured service for a more informal, contemporary one. I can empathise with both stances.

I honestly believe that we will always struggle to gain acceptance from our teenagers and young adults, because their adventurous spirits loathe the perceived caution and predictability of the traditional Church.

Our inner spiritual fire is always in danger of petering out. It needs to be constantly poked, fed, and fanned into flame.

The idea of being on fire for Christ will strike some people as piteous emotionalism, but fanaticism is not what is intended here. Fanaticism is a turn-off for most rational people (out-with fans of our beloved national game!) because it is action without reflection.

What Jesus Christ desires and deserves from us is the consideration that ultimately leads to commitment. It is easy for us to view any sign of enthusiasm or evangelical zeal from another believer as naïve or fanciful. When someone's passion for the lost and heart for revival is considered to be a kind of personal eccentricity it is an indication that we ourselves are content with our own mediocre Christian life.

My simple answer to any cynicism of today, whether mine or anyone else's, is not to steer away from the pure doctrine and understanding of the Holy Bible in order to cater for our own needs or to fit in with the masses, but to intensify our efforts and to labour, like the Apostle Paul, to show every person we meet that he is loved and accepted by Jesus.

It is my firm belief that if the 21st century Church is carrying out its divine calling it is the only true conscience and sense of morality in our country.

That it is both the comforter and motivator of its people.

It also represents the only safe spiritual sanctuary that enables people of any age and ethnic background to relate to each other, to share, and to give encouragement as one family.

I'm sure this can still be done within the framework of a traditional Church, but it requires courageous leaders with vision and a congregation willing to pull themselves away from the comfortable traditions of the past. Birthed over five hundred years ago, the Reformation was the onset of the restoration of the Church returning to the pure Gospel message.

Martin Luther, who initiated the Protestant Reformation, wrote in his interpretation of the book of Galatians, as he looked back to the beginning of the reformation of the Gospel: 'Undoubtedly, this restoration process has now reached a decisive point in God's plan for the Church.'

For all confessing Christians, the Gospel has to be God's declared answer to all the problems of our hurting world.

If we, as the Church, have fallen short in this respect it is primarily because some of us have watered-down the Gospel and reduced its power through the wholesale adoption of philosophies, intellectually-pleasing methods, and self-help plans imported from all over the secular world we live in.

According to Mark Stibbe, leader of Father's House Trust, a Christian charitable organisation: 'There are two kinds of Churches in the UK. There is a compromising Church and a confessing Church.' He says that the compromising Church 'panders to fit in with the world'.

The confessing Church must also be the prevailing Church; not just in the battle of winning souls but also in the battle of changing the culture of the community where that Church is located – the Church that is making a dynamic difference in shaping that community, whether it be in the social, the educational or even the political perception.

The prevailing Church is one in which you see the

characteristics of a whole confession of Christ as being the Son of the living God. They literally live out that confession in the shadows of the gates of Hades.

The prevailing Church is one that's moving outward and then going beyond what is visibly safe and secure, taking on the spiritual battles for the souls of lost people, absorbing the knocks, accepting the criticism and ploughing through ridicule and resistance to ultimately win the battle.

That is exactly the vision that the Lord Jesus had in mind when he proclaimed '... and upon this rock I will build my church, and all the powers of hell will not conquer it.' (Matt. 16:13-18 NLT)

I write this chapter more as a student than an expert. My own journey with God, although brief, has convinced me that there are those who will never come to Church because they have such a negative perception of it, whether from past experience or from dry theological explanations. This, however, is no admission that the lost can't be reached or that souls can't be saved; it is merely a realisation that a more radical, unconventional approach is required to bring them the unchanging gospel of Jesus Christ in a new, fresh and relevant way. Radical models, such as 'Café Churches' and 'House Churches', may become the norm as we shift to an exciting, revolutionary paradigm of Church.

This phenomenon is sometimes referred to as 'The Emerging Church', with some even calling themselves 'Small Faith Communities'. There will no longer be a 'One model fits all' Church. The Café Church approach of exploring Christianity is one that involves interaction, creativity, and an opportunity to connect with people who may have different ideas, beliefs and values to your own.

Although we live in an age of continuous change and unanticipated consequences, we will still have traditional granite-built Churches, but more House Churches will spring up for those people who are disillusioned with mainstream Church.

I would imagine that we will see mega Churches built in our larger towns and cities, as well as outdoor ones, and Churches that meet regularly online.

I hope we will also see Churches that focus on the desperately poor, the physically and mentally handicapped, and other minority groups.

Nobody can say exactly what the Church will look like in the future. I'm sure there will be multiple models, not just one stereotypical Church, like we've had from the end of World War II until the early 1980s, when the Church growth movement popularised Church planting by pioneers and visionary leaders. That modification resulted in the planting of hundreds of newfangled Churches, led by entrepreneurial Church leaders.

This is what I believe will happen again but this time in greater numbers and with an expressive imprint that will be even more innovative and far-reaching than those of the last 30 years.

I realise that God is not a God of methods and formulas, and that powerful evangelism will be the main outreach used to continue to rejuvenate the Church in Scotland in a way that we could never have contemplated.

I firmly believe that we are at the start of an exploration of one of the most exciting missions on the face of this earth: re-discovering what it means to be the living, corporate expression of Jesus Christ in the post-modern world.

In his book *Churchquake!*, Peter Wagner writes that the fastest growing movement in the world is the 'New Apostolic Reformation'.

He says that this is a God-restoring first century Christian leadership and government, and that without both the restoration of Apostles and first century Church principles for appropriate and effective discipleship there is little hope of bringing this glorious vision into being!

More than two millenniums have passed since Christ was born, but that event and the life it ushered in have not lost their attraction through the long lapse of time. On the contrary, it's a case of Christ being born anew among us; His life and ministry are being enacted over again in as much as it may be said with truth that the Hero of the gospel story is better known around the globe today and more intelligently esteemed than He ever has been since the first century Church in Corinth was planted.

In no way do I feel that the faith I profess is a worn-out exclusive club, a spent force, or a religious movement, which has run its course and is about to take its place alongside the now extinct Dodo Bird.

Jesus commanded His disciples to go into the world preaching the gospel and making disciples, 'teach these new disciples to obey all the commands I have given you.' (Matt 28:20 NLT)

As I travel all over the country to various Churches, conferences, seminars, men's breakfasts, prayer rooms, spiritual retreats and Christian music concerts, I am both reassured and inspired by the growing number of God's people who are no longer content to settle for stagnation and decline within our Church, and who are desperate for Him to do something in these days of spiritual hunger and emotional despair.

I am drawn to the vision of Jim Ritchie who was called to birth 'The Scotland Trust', after successfully leading Oldmachar Church in Aberdeen for eight years. As Jim says: 'At the heart of The Scotland Trust is a desire to see revival in our nation and to encourage churches in our land to become all that God has destined them to be.'

The Trust's vision is to encourage a grassroots movement in Scotland that will bring about radical spiritual and social transformation of this nation. The life of Jesus Christ is without doubt the turning point of all history. The ordinary calendar that hangs on our walls evolved from His birth.

Adopted by a simple carpenter named Joseph, He spent the first thirty years of His life in relative obscurity, swinging a hammer with His dad. But the impact He made during His three years of ministry is still reverberating around the globe.

Today, Christianity is still spreading like wildfire in many countries such as China, Africa and South America – in stark contrast to the apathy and complacency in our own country, which I feel is principally created by pluralism and materialism.

In recent times, *The Da Vinci Code*, by Dan Brown, has been a bestselling book bringing the name of Jesus to the fore in secular society – at least its success has made people want to know more about this man, Jesus.

The difficulty is that the narrative grapples with a few facts and a plethora of fabrication, then seamlessly extrapolates them into the realms of fantasy, which paints a completely wrong picture of Jesus, of God, and of His Church.

Indeed, Christianity has been twisted and warped to such an extent by authors like Brown that I suspect even Jesus Himself would struggle to recognise it now. Going by my own personal experience, the true Jesus is exciting and inspiring, and far more compelling than any contorted worldly version.

Anyone who wants to argue for a heresy, non-Jewish, non-prophetic and non-messianic Jesus has a herculean case to make, with the burden of finding proof sitting heavily on their shoulders.

Surely, if we profess to be Christians we must be willing to challenge secular, postmodern society rationale that uses the name of Jesus more as a curse than a word that radiates love, hope and compassion.

I wonder how peculiar it would sound if, when missing an easy putt, a golfer were to moan 'Robbie Burns!' Or, when an electrician accidentally gave himself an electric shock, he'd scream 'William Wallace!'

It's a damning indictment on our society as a whole that Muslims appear to have more respect and awe towards Jesus than most of us in this once respected 'Christian' nation. Even though they get it wrong by relegating Him to a mere great prophet of God, I doubt if they would ever break the third commandment and use His name in vain. There is no doubt our nation has been in a moral and spiritual decline.

The traditional Church appears to be in crisis – the nation that God has blessed for so long has been turning its back on Him. This saddens me, but it hurts God a lot more; just as it would if any of us were rejected by someone we loved deeply.

At times, before Clan 2007, I mourned that if we did not turn

Scotland around spiritually and seek God's wisdom and love, there would have been be a real danger of our country's faint heartbeat petering out.

We need to develop a new sense of loyalty inside the Church. A fresh undertaking is what is required to support all that is gracious and divine within its fellowship; a recognition of all the good that is being done quietly and zealously in the name of Christ.

Above all, we need commitment from all within its fold, to respect and maintain its redeeming name as the chosen instrument of God to save the soul of Scotland. My gut feeling is that if the traditional Parish Church is to confront the often complex transformations required to reach the young people of this country, it would need to go through radical change. However, I believe that the Lord has set before us an open door to cultivate that change.

There are many good things happening within the Church, and we do have many assets. I am convinced that Scottish society is now more open to the Gospel than it has been for many years. We are beginning to witness good practice with good results in our quest to re-Christianise our nation.

Am I too much of an idealist, dreaming about a united Scottish Church that would make possible St Columba's vision of the never-changing gospel of Jesus Christ being carried to a pagan nation in a way that radiates the love, acceptance and humility of our sovereign King? That King of Kings who came 'to seek and to save what was lost', and gave His life as a ransom for us all.

LAND OF BOOZE

When I reflect on my father's life, I realise he didn't not grow up thinking, 'I want to be alcohol dependent some day.'

That was never his intention.

This can be difficult to visualise, but it is said that once you cross a 'line', drinking is no longer a matter of choice. He believed alcohol to be his friend, but, on the contrary, it was his enemy, and became his ruthless taskmaster. The liquor was controlling him, and over time he was literally driven to take that next drink. In reality, the relationship was a classic one of love and hate.

Alcohol became my dad's refuge when he just couldn't face the world. It helped him to sleep. It blotted out all his painful memories – that is, until he woke up the next day to find these memories still there. Little by little it eroded pieces of his life, and ultimately his self-respect because he had started to compromise standards that used to mean everything to him. He became lost in the wheels of confusion.

Although I believe his primary intentions were sincere, he still picked up that whisky glass again, and as this relationship continued it became harder and harder for him to quit.

All the while the habit was forming a well-worn groove in his behaviour, for the addiction was gaining momentum. His eyes turned bulbous and yellow. His speech became slow and slurred with the onset of Korsakoff's syndrome – an alcohol-related brain disease that causes irreversible memory loss.

Forget the preconception that, individually, many Scots have a drink problem, and reconsider the hard evidence that Scotland as a whole has a major drink problem.

Once rightly regarded as the 'Land of the Book', Scotland could now justifiably be called 'Land of the Booze', and it would be typical of our Scottish macho pride if we were to boast about drinking every other country in the world under the table.

Just think about the many lives that are devastated by alcohol addiction; the weeks, months and years of a routine of weekend or even daily drunkenness. The conflict, the days off work, the marriages strained or wrecked, the family embarrassed, the children ignored or assaulted. Then follows the self-loathing, the pounding headaches, the laughing off of the offensive night before, the bragging, the exaggerating and, of course, the vomiting.

Those are the cold facts of the sheer human misery caused by the personality-altering effects of Scotland's addiction to alcohol. Earlier, I mentioned the late George Best's unsuccessful battle with alcohol addiction, yet his mother Ann's tragic descent is less known. Her rapid decline into chronic alcoholism is all the more saddening when you consider the fact that she was staunchly teetotal until she was 44. She passed away, prematurely, ten years later from heart-related problems believed to have been triggered by her alcoholism.

My father told me more than once that he seldom touched a drink until he was 21 – a claim that can be backed up by his National Service Certificate which shows this report about him: "A quiet, well mannered soldier who is honest and sober in his habits." I feel we must further encourage a culture change to overcome the macho attitude towards heavy drinking as well as the embarrassment and stigma that young men feel about seeking help, particularly with mental health problems.

Alcohol is a depressant drug that relaxes you, thus reducing social inhibitions. Taken in moderation, it is a relatively harmless and enjoyable private or social pastime. Unfortunately, we Scots appear to view drinking as part of a 'Scottish way of life' while in many other European countries it is done more sensibly. If we really see alcohol in terms of being part of our lifeblood, or "the excuse", then what does this say about Scottish society?

I certainly don't underestimate the scale of the challenge in Scotland. Cirrhosis rates are falling across Europe – even in traditional wine-growing areas such as France and Italy – while in Scotland they are spiralling. In the past 50 years, the mortality rate due to cirrhosis has grown six-fold in Scottish men, and four-fold in Scottish women.

Every year in Scotland, almost 500 women die directly from alcohol-related causes. Alarmingly, in England the death rate among women is now higher than among men. And it is not just one specific age group that is at risk; Scots of every generation have drinking problems.

It is gallingly self-evident that alcohol abuse has taken the lives of too many men and women in this small country. If that sounds apocalyptic, it is because the problem in Scotland really is that bad.

As F. Scott Fitzgerald, whose brilliant life was cut short by booze, said: 'First the man takes a drink, then the drink takes a drink, then the drink takes the man.'
There is an exhaustive list of celebrated Scottish sportsmen who failed to conquer their self-destructive drinking addiction that eventually destroyed flourishing careers.

The history of Boxing, despite its stimulating excitement, is littered with such weakness. In the long run, even the victors end up vanquished – as is tragically evidenced by Benny Lynch in the 1930s and alarmingly mirrored by a visibly tormented Scott Harrison in the present day.

World champion Lynch's boxing career was over by the time he was 25, and he battled against alcohol dependency for the rest of his short life. This man, blessed with so much God-given talent, died in 1946, from malnutrition brought on by pneumonia. He was 33, a lonely misfit in the city of Glasgow that once loved him but ultimately broke him.

While idling about in Tenerife I recall opening a British newspaper, only to be met by the sad news that former Big Country singer and songwriter, Stuart Adamson, had taken his own life in a hotel room in Hawaii.

Following the initial shock, my mind instantly drifted back more than 15 years to a time when I myself was depressed and afraid. Back then I was enduring a rough time from a local bully and Stuart Adamson comforted me through his music. When he sang with his soaringly powerful voice, my troubled mind was carried off into an idyllic world – a place where my soul could delight in the vast landscapes and tumultuous skies that Stuart painted so poignantly.

For me, Adamson evoked both the sacred splendour and blue-collar drudgery of Scotland with his unique lyricism.

During the 1980s I was drawn to Big Country's heavily accented anthemic Scottish folk and warrior-like music style, skilfully engineered by their guitar sound to resemble traditional instruments like bagpipes and fiddles.

Alcoholism appears to be a malignant affliction that can often resurface, and Stuart Adamson was an example of this.

In 1985, on the very day that Big Country were part of the Live Aid concert, he told friends of his intention to quit alcohol, and for a number of years he stayed true to his word. Sadly, he slipped back into his old pattern of heavy drinking and drifted into such a deep depression that he felt there was only one solution. An untimely loss to his family, friends, the people of his home town of Dunfermline and the Scotland he deeply loved.

A nation hooked on the escapism of alcohol must be one that is profoundly uninspired by life as well as being disengaged from the real world. Perhaps this sounds a bit rich coming from someone with my binge drinking history, but give me the 'crutch' of Christianity any day.

It used to be said that Scotland had a 'tough nut' drinking culture. Those days have changed. Nowadays, women are involved in the 'lad and ladette' binge-drinking culture too.

Just a generation or two ago, the popular image of a hard-drinking Scot was predominantly male but the new map suggests that the hard-drinking Scottish female is now not very far behind.

I once read a story about a minister who was completing a sermon on teetotalism. With great passion he said, 'If I had all the beer in the world, I'd take it and throw it into the river.' With even greater emphasis he continued, 'and if I had all the wine in the world I'd throw it into the river.' He sat down. The worship leader then stood up very cautiously and announced with a wry smile, 'To close this morning, let us sing Hymn 347: "Shall we gather at the river?"'

The perplexing mixed message being sent out in this parable typifies the confusion that many Christians have with the issue of drinking alcohol.

Whether to drink or not to drink.

When I look at the Bible for answers we can see very clearly that drunkenness is a sin. However, drinking in moderation is not. Jesus was not opposed to the drinking of wine in Cana – He supplied it. And to demonise alcohol would be pointless and potentially counterproductive.

From personal experience, I am only too aware of the devastation caused by alcohol abuse behind closed doors. It could concern normal youngsters, manipulated by the commercialism and sweet taste of Alco Pops, but just as vulnerable are the neglected housewife, bored bachelor, or the lonely widower – who all seek solace in drinking alone.

When I see someone I care about undergoing a personality change when drinking alcohol – turning from an easygoing placid person into an irrational, angry and aggressive one – it is almost enough to make me a staunch advocate of teetotalism.

And yet ... Alcohol is not always detrimental. Consumed in moderation it helps us relax, and it is pleasurable when socialising. It is hard to beat a glass of Rosé when enjoying a nice meal in the company of good friends, or that pint of ice cold cider after a lengthy walk in scorching Tenerife.

I see nothing in the Scripture which forbids the drinking of alcohol, although there are plenty of warnings as regards to over-indulging. Sometimes the decision of whether to drink at all needs to be based on the ability to resist the temptation to drink too much. Not long after I became a Christian, a clearly intoxicated lady approached me in one of the local pubs, poked an index finger into my face and told me I shouldn't be drinking because I was 'all religious'. I don't accept the concept of religion in that context, for

I felt that as a Christian, God could trust me to consume a couple of drinks sensibly. I sometimes get the feeling that I must break every man rule in the religiosity rule book!

Scotland's love affair with alcohol is deep-rooted and complex. There is, without doubt, a self-destructive drinking culture within society. This is reflected in the number of alcohol-related deaths, which in some areas of Scotland is now between five and seven times higher than the UK average.

Alcohol is a perceptive antagonist, widely available in places we frequent – pubs, off-licences, supermarkets, restaurants and petrol stations – which seems to give it a certain level of respectability.

Sadly, as a country we have reaped what we have sown over the last three or four decades, when we have trampled disrespectfully over God's Word and largely turned our back on God. In my lifetime, I have seen alcoholism, drug addiction and depression escalating to reach epidemic proportions.

God has been thrown out of our living rooms, work environments and classrooms, while we continue to live a life with little meaning and no real purpose.

The devastation caused by this process is the very reason why anyone with a drinking problem who is attempting to recover deserves immense credit for having the courage to confront their addiction.

I WANNA BE A MACHO MAN

I recently watched *Just a Boy's Game* again, on DVD – a shocking and yet strangely endearing drama, in which we follow the life of a young Greenock 'hard man', Jake McQuillan, played convincingly by poker-faced and gravel-voiced soul singer, Frankie Miller.

Set in the late 1970s, written by Peter McDougall, and directed by John MacKenzie, this was one of the most disturbing, poignant and dark dramas television has ever produced. With its trademark caustic one-liners and grimly honest observations on life, this hard-hitting play perfectly captured the hard man culture of the west of Scotland but could also easily have been synonymous with more rural settings.

Caught up in the same perpetual cycle of violence that consumed his grandfather and caused his father's death, Jake is isolated by and entangled in his own formidable reputation. Young pretenders view him as an impressive scalp and want to take his crown.

Jake's sole aim, fostered by his dead-end environment, is to appear to be as tough as the grandfather he hates. His best mate is Dancer, who carelessly breezes through life, seemingly without a care for anything or anybody, including his wife and children. However, in spite of all his glaring shortcomings, Dancer is a likeable character whose whole existence appears to be interspersed with humour and misfortune. He is work-shy, and edging ever closer to full-blown alcohol dependency. This unlikely partnership trawls through seedy bars, shipyards, snooker halls and run-down housing estates – with violence always just around the corner.

This drama speaks volumes about the mentality of the archetypical working-class Scottish male of 30 years ago. After all, only Scotland could have produced Irn-Bru, a soft drink aimed squarely at hard men, with its slogan: 'Made from Girders'!

As the whole of Scotland shivers in minus temperatures in any January or February, you only need to tune into a football match on TV to witness the incredible sight of bare-chested men on the terraces, while some of those a little less macho will be wearing a short-sleeved top.

A football stadium seems to be the ideal venue to stage symbolic struggles between rival working-class communities, testing macho identities. Young men (and sometimes not so young men) "defend" their own, their town or city's reputation against the opposing team. Having been part of a generation of Scotland's working-class male culture that would have viewed men who did not work with their hands as sissies, skivers or even snobs, what do you think our view would have been of a man singing hymns or Christmas Carols?

At school, dare a macho boy take up skipping, hockey, piano playing, or even home economics which involved cooking. Indeed, it was a cardinal sin to leave school and not find a job that toughened up your hands, or at least put some dirt under your finger nails.

Imagine, nowadays, someone telling celebrity chef Gordon Ramsay that he is 'a big sissy'!

I think it's easy to confuse machoism with the healthy masculine traits that God bestowed on every Alpha male.

Machoism is charged with the struggle for dominance over others.

Machoism is like a theatrical performance to cover inadequacy in some form or other.

Machoism is masculinity's poor imitator, while masculinity is simply manly character. It is a positive God-given trait that is nurturing and generative, not wounding and destructive.

When a society rejects the gospel message, it ceases to provide specific inaugural pathways and the individual male psyche is naturally left to initiate itself. Lads of my generation were not influenced by adults but mainly by members of the macho youth culture who were at most three or four years older than us – then we, in turn, became the macho role models for the next impressionable generation.

The induction into manliness usually manifests itself in the shape of "normal" adolescent accomplishments such as: drawing back a fag, getting legless with drink, flashing large wads of bank notes, losing your virginity, and serial sexual conquests. The tragedy is that 20-30 years later some men are still living in this adolescent time-warp, and are still searching for what it means to be a real man.

The true image of the Scottish industrial hard man is of someone who has corrupted, tainted, and even brutalised parts of our society for many a year. Yet we never tire of reinventing a Jake McQuillan or a Rab C Nesbit stereotype and celebrate the dim, inarticulate, insensitivity it encourages.

Sadly, the power of today's television plays down to the lowest common denominator of intellectualism and panders to their beliefs. It sends out the wrong message to the maladjusted, telling them what they want to hear, which is, that it's okay to be like this.

Most hard men lived in the 'Walter Mitty' fictional world where stories of fearless bravado bolstered their deep-seated feelings of inadequacy, often cruelly spawned by parental rejection and emotional deprivation. The distinct absence of affirmation for boys, to validate their value and ambitions, turned them into the emasculated men of today.

I believe the real danger arises when their fictional world becomes reality to them. While those crazy-for-recognition severely deprived types were never emotionally tough, they react violently in this state of mind, rather than respond to stimuli rationally.

In living out their dreams, they become caught in the web of tough-guy hysteria where they feel compelled to prove their worth as individuals, and in the seemingly safe and cosy environment of the group they seek to excel through brutality and notoriety.

Tony recounts the times when, as a skinny, scrawny kid, he came home battered and bruised from beatings from the much bigger neighbourhood kids, only to be berated by his father who told him to go back out and not to bother coming home until he had won his fight.

Is it any wonder that the Tonys of this world become angry young men, whose lives descend into a world of constant strife and discord? Kids that have been hurt often grow up to hurt other people.

No one wants to be a pushover but, with a wounded heart, a young man's life can take several different routes. Those youths can either over-compensate for their hurt by becoming angry violent men, or they can shrink back into themselves to become passive pipsqueaks. Sometimes it can even be the potentially dangerous combination of both.

When masculinity can no longer define itself in hard work, it inevitably identifies itself with the "hard man" for whom torment, cynicism and violence are the only way he sees possible to salvage that lost dignity of hard graft.

We baby boomers saw the irresponsibility of our teenage years as a brief escape from the adult life that awaited us. Many of our fathers appeared to be in boring, monotonous jobs, for which their employers and the government expected them to be eternally grateful. An age in which a culture of mechanised mass production of every conceivable thing removed much of the skill and individual responsibility that had been fundamental to the pride of the working man.

Every man was once a boy. And if he was anything like me, he had dreams – big dreams: of being a champion; beating the bad guys; accomplishing amazing feats, like playing for a famous football team; leading an expedition; becoming an astronaut; and maybe of rescuing a damsel in distress from the clutches of evil.

But these dreams get eroded, and as we are buffeted by the storms of life we settle for so much less. Many of our young generation are conditioned to have low ambition, passion, and achievement. Perhaps even forever, that young person is wounded by some significant adult – possibly his father, his older brother, his teacher, or his best friend, saying to him: 'That's ridiculous, you can't do that.'

Every boy on his journey to become a man takes a few sharp emotional blows that pierce his heart – and they come quite often from his own father. Like so many men of his generation, I feel that my father never faced and worked through the emotional wounds that blighted his own childhood.

One evening, my father was in a foul mood after coming home from work. I was eleven or twelve at that time – a critical and delicate age in my masculine journey. 'Shut up, you damned fool,' he snapped angrily at me because I was humming a song as I lay sprawled on the sitting room floor, reading a boy's comic. The door to the kitchen door was ajar but I assumed my mother had not heard him. That was the cue for me to retreat to my bedroom and sulk for the rest of the evening.

I nodded off, then woke up abruptly by the penetrative shrill of my mother's voice: 'I am sick to death of you starting on him. He can never do anything right in your eyes. You are turning like your own father ... an ill-natured auld b... ...'

Her tirade was met with the predictable response: Silence ...

My father could hurt me with his silence. Sometimes, in the evenings during the week, he could go for hours on end with barely a word spoken. I would often pray that he would go down to the pub for a while, to return home more like his mellow unagitated self.

In fairness, I can also recall various instances when Dad dropped his guard and portrayed himself in a more supportive and positive light, most notably when I overheard him enthusiastically telling a friend who was visiting him that I had been picked for the North of Scotland army cadet football team. Another such occasion was when I noticed him watching me play for the local amateur football team, from the driver's seat of his car.

I believe that we as a society sometimes misunderstand that what is generally termed as adolescent rebellion could be just a cry for approval and acceptance. In my case, I can't use that as an excuse, but I did always yearn for my father's affection and approval.

Every man carries a relationship hurt. I have yet to meet a man without one. Regardless of how impressive our life may look from the outside, we live in a hurting world with broken people. I once heard Don Williams, founding pastor of the Coast Vineyard Christian Fellowship in California, mention on a CD that he read a survey where it stated that 96% of us were brought up in dysfunctional families, a figure that, he argued, was 4% inaccurate.

The perfect family of the 1970s was exemplified by television shows such as 'Little House on the Prairie' and 'The Partridge Family'. The warm, caring, understanding characters in these serials left many of us feeling cheated out of that fantasy model of the "perfect" childhood.

Perhaps our parents quarrelled, had money problems or sometimes lashed out at us in anger, and it's little wonder that many of us now struggle through life a little damaged and confused.

But what we often fail to realise is that this media-generated, stereotypical family image is a myth, and always has been.

Our parents struggled to raise us without scripts, self-help books, and quite often without God's guidance. Yet, we expected them to be perfect in every way – almost superhuman. Instead, they often set a bad example, gave us poor coping skills, weren't always there when we needed them, and never showed enough love – in other words: they were all too human!

There seems to be no middle ground in our perception of our parents, and of our fathers in particular. Each boy had a father with a distinctive worldly identity. This may have been in terms of being a workaholic, a hard man, a loner, a quiet guy, a Churchgoer, a perfectionist, a sportsman, a drinker, a gambler, or even a work-shy hypochondriac. We either see them as wonderful or woeful, when in reality they were neither. Failing perfection, they were flawed beyond redemption. They were inadequate, overbearing and ineffectual. Attaining perfection, they were flawless, unblemished, and incomparable.

Despite all the Freudian analyses about our parents being at the core of much that has gone wrong in our lives, I believe we ultimately have that thinking and discerning capacity that eventually lets us decide for ourselves which route to take as we get older, with the distinct possibility of a liberated life with a happy, God-inspired ending.

It's the imitation self we often carry around, the same false self that I experienced, but we have a Heavenly Father who offers to initiate us into building our masculinity – even giving us a new identity.

We all carry our own emotional scars - from a stinging remark, from a failed relationship, or a mentor-defector who himself had no model of positive or ethical leadership.

God offers to take us into the adventure.

The first battle worth fighting is the battle for our manhood. There is a danger that we in Scotland will continue to produce passive, domesticated, predictable men willing to live in denial of being the person God made them to be: unshackled risk-takers, embracing adventure beyond their control; being men of God to be reckoned with.

As children, surely, we would rather have spent time with an adventurer instead of a parent, uncle or grandparent, whose routine cautionary advice was, 'Be careful,' or 'Stay here, where it's safe.'

As a result, we all struggle to understand and to establish our real identity as men – especially as Christian men who aspire to be leaders. Many good men have grown up in the traditional Church, but some of these veterans of the pews come to Church not because they desire to be transformed by Jesus, but because they enjoy participating in consoling rituals that have changed little since their childhood. Church attendance becomes a duty, a habit, or a way of maintaining their status in society.

How did our great Faith, founded by a sinless revolutionary and His twelve-man motley crew, become so fashionable with women but such a turn off for most men?

The first century Church in Corinth was a sponge for alive young men to soak in the power of the Holy Spirit. Christ's impregnable leadership, blunt honesty, and fearless commitment mesmerised wary grown men. A five-minute sermon by Peter (Yes, the same Peter who had previously three times denied knowing Jesus) resulted in the conversion of three thousand men.

One of the lessons I have learned from the heroes of the Old Testament, Abraham, Isaac and Jacob, is that masculinity is passed down from father to son right through the generations.

Unfortunately, the tendency today is to pass on our uncertainties and insecurities, rather than our strengths, so nowadays boys grow up trying to validate who they are by what school football team they play for, what type of mobile phone they use and which designer trainers they own. Later, by what job they do, their salary, and the car they drive,

It seems obvious to me that though masculinity has been marginalised within Christianity, it cannot be expunged from human society. If detached from Christianity, it reappears as a substitute religion, with harmful and even horrific consequences.

The value of the Church, too, seems to be diminishing through its unmanliness; its spirituality becoming individualistic, more leaning towards theological doctrine and mysticism.

In his powerful book *Wild at Heart*, John Eldredge states: 'Guys are unanimously embarrassed by their emptiness and woundedness, and for most of us a tremendous source of shame, but we do not need to be. From before the fall and the assault, ours was meant to be a desperately dependent existence.'

Christ, who said: 'I am the Vine; you are the brances. Those who remain in me, and I in them, will produce much fruit.' (John 15:5 NLT), is not berating or mocking us. He is not even saying with a sigh: 'I wish they would get their act together and stop needing me so much.'

Looking at myself today, I still question whether I have what it takes to be a real man of God, but I am soon reminded that victory over self-doubt comes when I have no other rock upon which to stand. It comes when Jesus alone is my Fortress. When He is my all.

There's a deep sense of security that derives only from resting in Him. It calms the deep confusion of my soul. When He is my life, nothing can shake me.

My fear for many years was to be revealed as an imposter – not being authentic as a real man. To be found out; to be exposed as insecure and inadequate.

It did not take me long to observe that while male ministers come and go, women seem to provide a faithful continuity in our congregations. Women appear to be the devoted ones who build their lives around their commitments to Christ and His Church. From my experience, they are more likely to volunteer and serve in Church, and are the greatest participants in outreach activities.

I pray earnestly that the Church will turn the tide with the men of Scotland. History indicates that it will. During the last 500 years there have been times like this when the Church in Scotland has been imbalanced and in danger of losing much of its masculine spirit. When the Church appeared to be at its lowest ebb, God raised a fearless warrior – a John Knox, a Thomas Guthrie, a Robert Murray McCheyne, or a Duncan Campbell – to draw men back to the Church.

Jesus built His Church on twelve Spirit-filled men who changed the world. We must do the same: We cannot have a thriving Church without a core of men who are true followers of Jesus Christ. If the men are lifeless, the Church remains unbalanced and stagnant. Jesus was a magnet to men. But today, few men are living for Christ.

Why, I ask, do rival faiths inspire male allegiance, while ours breeds male indifference?

David Murrow, author of *Why men hate going to Church,* presents this view: 'When men need spiritual sustenance, they go to the wilderness, the workplace, the garage, or the corner bar. They watch their heroes in the stadium or on the racetrack. They plunge into a novel or sneak off to a movie. Church is one of the last places men look for God.'

I would estimate that more than 80% of Scottish men believe in God, or at least have a God conscience. Perhaps half of them would call themselves Christians, but probably less than one in ten would attend a place of worship on a Sunday morning. Tens of thousands of men would not argue against the reality of Christ, but most of them would see little point in attending Church.

Men deliberately reject the Christian faith. Many are proud and would rather be their own Supreme Being. Most men hate to admit imperfection, impoverishment or insecurity. Multitudes of decent ordinary guys are held captive by addiction and sin and incredulity. They find their divinity and sense of identity in their passion for clubs, sports teams and organisations that prevent a genuine commitment to Christ.

God has balanced His Church many times throughout history and He will undoubtedly do so again. To confront this glaringly evident gender gap has to be part of the calling of the post-modern Church. We need to understand and accept the cause of this unevenness, as well as have the courage to remove the barriers that discourage and demoralise men.

I can assure you, however, that my passion and focus is not for male dominance in the Church, but simply for a male resurgence. In fact, I see in the Bible both a masculine and feminine God. However, as I write this book, I struggle to find the appropriate pronoun to express this, because my language is so restricted. That is why I have humbly settled for the masculine Him and He, although I am aware that this never does justice to His great diversity and deity.

Every earthly man needs a band of brothers. Jesus began His ministry by assembling such a team. They trained together, worked together, and suffered together. Men cannot succeed as followers of Jesus without a team surrounding them. No matter how inspiring the minister's sermon is, I firmly believe that men will not come to full maturity in Christ without a band of brothers and a spiritual Father to guide them. One of the most common stereotypical views of the Christian life – and a view that I held myself for many years – is that it is too upright and straight-laced to have any fun or enjoyment. Men are drawn by vision and purpose; by achievement and power. Churches that attract enthusiastic men do so by embracing the big picture; by taking risks and by bringing a measure of adventure back to the Christian life.

I believe that men can find Christ in any place or any situation, and that is more likely to happen when they are doing something they enjoy or that challenges them. Men need to feel appreciated and valued. They must be encouraged to use their gifts, even if these gifts don't fit in with the traditional Christian service. Church leaders must let men plan adventures and do 'masculine' things together. That is why I would like to see group activities, such as five-a-side football, ten pin bowling, fishing, white water rafting, hill walking and mountain climbing added to the serving outreaches of voluntary car washing, grass cutting and DIY work – which some Churches already partake in – to become a regular part of Christian life for men.

I firmly believe that men of all ages are drawn to risk, challenge and daring. While the official mission of the Church is one of service, the actual mission of some congregations is to make people feel comfortable and safe. Church leaders have the power to block anything challenging or innovative because it might make themselves feel uncomfortable or unsafe.

This caution may well keep the peace in the short term, but it drives men and young adults away over the long term.

I purchased *Man of Steel and Velvet,* by Aubrey Andelin, in my early days in Network Marketing. I recall reading a couple of chapters of this bland looking book and quickly dismissing its principles and teachings as too 'preachy' and old-fashioned. It seemed, at this time of my life, that most men, including myself, had too much of one and not enough of the other, making us either insensitive macho-men or effeminate weaklings, where the term 'Man of Lead and Linen' would have been a more apt description.

Several years later I picked it up again and started reading it. I then found it to be a powerful book on masculinity, based on timeless Biblical principles, which held up Abraham Lincoln as the perfect modern-day example of a man of steel and velvet.

With no formal schooling available to him, the young Lincoln set out to shape his own character. Without the visual media of today, he developed himself through continuous reading. Conscious as he was of the limitations of his rural environment, he might have used reading as an escape – yet, he did not. Instead, he read for discipline. He read, not only to learn what others had thought and said, but also to find out how they achieved things.

Andelin begins by describing Lincoln's steel-like qualities, such as being a protector and provider, as well as his self-assurance. He states: 'These principles will not change and are the foundation upon which a man must build his masculinity and make the most of his life.'

Of course, Andelin then rounds off by mentioning Lincoln's velvet qualities, such as: attentiveness, gentleness and humility. Moral integrity occupied the core of the kind of person Lincoln made himself. Financial honesty represented one important aspect of this integrity. When his partner in a grocery business, William Berry, died in 1835, leaving behind serious debts, Lincoln worked long and hard to pay off not only his own share but Berry's as well, going beyond his legal obligation in doing so.

Lincoln carried his financial honesty into his politics, as well as his personal life, earning himself the nickname 'Honest Abe'. He demonstrated how a person can possess both a will of iron and a heart of tenderness.

Nothing deterred the president during the American Civil War from his 'noble' cause, and few persons have ever endured more criticism and detractors than Lincoln. Yet, he was no more a man of steel than one of velvet.

When General Robert E. Lee surrendered his army, Lincoln sent an unexpected message to the enemy commander. 'Tell your men they may keep their horses; they'll need them for ploughing,' said the president. Then this: 'Tell your men they may keep their rifles; they'll need them for hunting.'

When Lee read those words he wept.

For each of us there is a time for toughness and a time for tenderness. A time for resolve and a time for compassion.

An iron will is not as effective as an iron spirit.

While writing this chapter, I attended a conference in Perth held by the Alcohol Focus Scotland charity. A quote from one of the speakers there really stuck in my mind. He suggested that our biggest strength is our vulnerability. He believed that there can be no real depth of compassion without that vulnerability. Like most people, I used to think of vulnerability as being synonymous with getting hurt or being emotionally wounded.

What is genuine strength? I ask myself. Well, I suppose there could be hundreds of variations. Fashionable culture appears to promote the idea that strength is cold, unyielding, insensitive, muscle-bound, brutal – even deadly. This is an incredibly simplistic idea of strength. I firmly believe that strength of the spirit involves true courage under difficult circumstances.

Some people may view strength as a masculine quality, and vulnerability as a feminine one. I feel that both of these definitions are based on fear, for I don't see vulnerability and strength as direct opposites. As far as I'm concerned, they go together like two sides of a coin.

At its best, to be vulnerable means to be open and not overly defensive – something only a strong person has the courage to be. Because vulnerability and strength are so entwined, I feel it's right to cultivate them at the same time.

From tragedy and misfortune I can take lessons in both vulnerability and strength. I can appreciate how much we all depend on each other. We can discover the joy of compassion.

I am aware that my own feelings of vulnerability can take me deeper into my self, much deeper than I have gone before. There I will sense a new strength: the power to yield confidently and comfortably – my vulnerability transformed into graceful openness.

Jesus was a man who also faced choices between power and vulnerability. During the short stretch of His life, He came into contact with power on countless occasions and had to make choices.

Jesus took a blind man by the hand and restored his sight.

He fed a crowd of thousands with loaves and fish.

He even had the good grace not to exclude people who were collaborating with the Roman empire.

How often have you seen effeminate images of Jesus? In His early thirties, He is portrayed as a man of slim angelic appearance, probably bearded, and with eyes that are mournful and piercing.

This is how the world and quite often the Church like to depict the most masculine man that ever lived, even though the prophet Isaiah tells us: 'There was nothing beautiful or majestic about His appearance, nothing to attract us to Him. (Isaiah 53:2b NLT)

All this tells us that Jesus was just like any other man – He was just an ordinary-looking bloke.

So, if the Word of God says that He is ordinary-looking, why is it that He is portrayed as that traditional Sunday School 'sissified' Jesus?

In his book *American Jesus*, Stephen Prothero asserts that the effeminate 'Sunday-School Jesus' was, in fact, a 19th century creation. The real Jesus was not a 'sissy'. On the contrary, He was a man who was accustomed to hard physical work and outdoor living. Throughout his adolescence and young manhood He worked as a carpenter (Mark 6:3 NLT); and He did so in the days before power tools!

During the years of His ministry, He and His disciples walked the dusty roads of Galilee, Samaria and Judea, often camping out under the stars, without the convenience of a cheap B & B to tide them over for the night.

I sometimes wonder if Jesus would get more respect from the masses in this country if we changed His image yet again, giving Him the biceps of Popeye, the rebelliousness of Che Guevara, the Argentinian Marxist revolutionary – complete with the sex-appeal of 1950s actor and 'Rebel Without a Cause', James Dean.
We can rest assured that the real Lord Jesus Christ is not some feeble, ineffectual, pathetic, effeminate weakling with long hair.

To the born-again believer, He is truly indescribable.

He is more.

He means more than human language can adequately express.

As Christians, we should be above being advocates of social stereotypes of "real men" and "real women", especially when this can be so hurtful to those who don't measure up.

As believers, we should appreciate the wonderful diversity that God has created in us, some of which has to do with the diametrical blend of masculine and feminine gifts that we find in each and every one of us,

When I first became a Christian, my image of Jesus Christ was of a gentle meek and mild comforter. The Christmas Story also reminds us that He came meek and mild; born as a child in a humble stable, not as a powerful king and mighty warrior.

During His ministry and, as He entered Jerusalem on the first day of the week, He also came meek and mild; riding on a humble donkey, not astride a noble steed of battle.

Jesus may be meek and mild in His initial calling, but once we have heard the call, He expects and demands that we heed His call to follow where He leads.

To many of the people He encountered – common, virtuous people – He was considered a trouble maker, and even a disgrace. He publicly argued with moral crusaders and religious leaders. In fact, He condemned the religious leaders of His day for making a profit off the poor. In the temple in Jerusalem, when Jesus saw them buying and selling items (and price-gouging the people who had to buy things for worship), He made a whip and went through the temple, turning over their tables. (So much for that meek and mild image of Jesus!)

It seems to me that He wasn't even very popular among His peers. He had little regard for what people thought of Him. He associated with women of questionable moral background, and with corrupt businessmen who used their positions to manipulate and use people for their own personal gain.

Jesus stood up to his disciples to set thing straight.

He was assertive.

Yes, Jesus was meek and mild, and He was gentle, but He could also be assertive when He needed to be, and we should seek to follow His example.

John Eldredge encourages men to recover their masculine hearts.

He states: 'Jesus is no capon priest, no pale-faced altar boy with his hair parted in the middle, speaking softly, avoiding confrontation, who at last gets killed because he has no way out. He works with wood, commands the loyalty of dockworkers. He is the Lord of hosts, the captain of angel armies.'

Of course, Jesus will always be my ultimate example of a Man of Steel and Velvet. He wasn't a hard man, but He told it like it was.

Jesus was a Good Guy.

He was a real masculine man.

David Murrow reminds us of the fact that Jesus promised to make us fishers of men, but in today's Church we catch relatively few! Perhaps it is time to cast our nets on the opposite side of the boat?

The disciples overcame their scepticism, and conformed to the teachings of Jesus. In turn, they were rewarded with an exceptional catch.

I believe that in our nation today there are countless men ready to walk with their Maker. This can only happen if we, as God's people, are able to cast aside our apprehension in order to welcome the adventurous, rebellious, masculine spirit back into our Churches.

Being insensitive, thoughtless, harsh, and sharp-tongued – all of that comes naturally to us men! But it is the supernatural work of God through the Holy Spirit that cultivates the fruits of the spirit in a man: love, joy, peace, patience, kindness, goodness, faithfulness, gentleness, and self-control – in other words: to become more like Christ.

FREE TO FORGIVE

I had just given my testimony in the Baptist Church in Buckie when a man approached me from the back of the Church looking extremely distressed. He introduced himself only as 'Davie'. (Name changed to conceal his real identity out of respect for his family.)

'I really related to your testimony just now,' he sobbed, dabbing his cheeks with his handkerchief. He went on to relay a burden of painful personal issues, punctuated with sniffs, as I listened intently to his desperate plight.

Davie had been doing some relief driving work for my friend Yvonne's family Fish Merchants business and had shared some of his problems with her. Yvonne had invited him along to hear my testimony in the hope that he would be able to relate to what God had placed in my heart and receive some encouragement from other Christians.

He was clearly in the midst of great emotional turmoil and I could not help but feel intense sympathy for this troubled man. Although I was not in a position to give him any practical advice, I was reassured by the fact that he was in close contact with Yvonne. I promised him that I would keep him in my prayers and that I would get back in touch when I returned from Tenerife.

I did pray for Davie but, sadly, I never saw him again. Less than three weeks later, I went to the crematorium, near Buckie, with Yvonne and another two Christian friends, to pay my last respects to this 'lost soul' who had taken his own life during the time I was away.

It goes without saying that this tragedy brought back all the painful memories of my father's death. I even wondered if it had been God's plan to bring us together that evening in Buckie ...

It felt strange, attending a funeral service of someone I had only met during one brief encounter, but I knew it was the right thing to do. The logical side of my nature rushed to ask why I mourned a practical stranger, but in my heart I felt an overwhelming sadness for the loss of a man who had made a connection with me.

Almost two years later, in April 2006, I was stunned by the news that James Alexander, a young man I knew reasonably well, had returned to his house in Fraserburgh after a night out and had committed suicide. He was only 36.

Jamesie, as he was known to his friends, was Gamrie born and bred and a close friend of Michael Ritchie. I had enjoyed several nights out with him, most notably in Fraserburgh. If the tragic news shocked me, I could hardly begin to comprehend how his loving mother, family and many close friends must have felt.

He was a person who engaged with almost everyone. I had always found him easy-going and confident. His eyes twinkled with mischief when he'd had a few drinks and I recalled one night in a Fraserburgh waterfront bar when he cheekily pinched the bottom of a guy who was standing next to me, only to sneak away to make it look as if I was the culprit! Jamesie was someone who appeared to have had so much to live for.

After struggling to grasp the real shock of his death, I turned my thoughts to his distraught family. His mother, Mary, was a painting customer of mine and I knew his sister Rosemary and husband George through their involvement with the local Church.

Mary was a sprightly, humorous lady who had already experienced great loss in her life – having been widowed twice – but her attitude belied the trials she had lived through and the hardships she had endured. I had spent enough time in her company to know how she felt about her James – to lose her only son in such tragic circumstances would absolutely devastate her.

I did not sleep well that night. I tried to grasp the magnitude of the loss that Jamesie's family would be feeling. Once again, I found my mind drifting back to the aftermath of my father's death all those years ago.

Several days later, Gardenstown was a village united in grief as several hundred mourners packed into every available seating area in the Kirk to pay their last respects to one of their own. I was ushered into a side room, where the reverent hush was occasionally interrupted by a muffled sob.

Reverend Donald Martin spoke earnestly about a gamut of emotions we were all going through – ranging from shock and disbelief to anger and extreme sadness. His moving words pierced my heart in a way that gave a fresh dimension to what I myself had been feeling after Dad's suicide.

A short while later, taking my place on a steep grass embankment, I looked over a vast sea of grieving people at the graveside, crossing every denomination and generation. I could feel both sympathy and empathy for Jamesie's heartbroken family, huddled together, sheltering from the blustery spring weather. And I realised that nothing I or anyone else could say or do would offer much comfort to them.

I was fully aware of the fact that the funeral service was just one pinpoint in time on the painful path that this family must now walk. There would be unimaginable days ahead when the grief, anger, and perhaps even unjustified guilt, would inevitably trip them up, bruising their already fragile emotions.

Later that evening, I went through to my bedroom and knelt down to pray. My reddened eyes stared into the emptiness around me.

I broke down.

Somewhere amidst my tears I felt the powerful presence of God telling me to finally forgive both myself and my father. It was as if He looked me in the eye and said: 'Its over now. It's safe to forgive. Move on, but never forget the decent father he was.'

It was a defining moment ... A real watershed. I was incredibly humbled by God's grace and mercy towards me, but a sadness still remained that one of God's own creations had chosen to end his life so prematurely.

Waking up the following morning with my eyes full of tears, I cried. In fact, for the next eight days I would frequently break down and weep. But these were not tears of despair; they were a long overdue release from the anger, guilt and confusion I had lived with for fourteen years.

I had carried these pent-up emotions with me because I had never allowed myself to experience the appropriate amount of natural grieving over what had happened. My feelings had alternated from loss to anger and from compassion to resentment in the months and years following my father's suicide. Once the total forgiveness came, the natural grief and sadness were allowed to flow freely.

Being trapped in the bondage of guilt, blame and an unforgiving attitude, leaves us truly 'stuck' and prevents us from moving forward with our lives. Instead, we remain in a chasm of loneliness, despair and hopelessness.

The guilt I felt towards his suicide for many years was extremely strong; partly because of the harsh words exchanged the last time I ever saw Dad alive, but also because of the fact that I had not always done or said the right things when he was at his lowest point.

Church leaders had made casting our cares upon Jesus sound simple but in reality I found freeing myself from the shackles of guilt very complex, because when I finally laid my guilt at my Redeemer's feet, it forced me to relinquish a part of myself that I had found difficult to give up.

I had frequently taken the 'guilt trip down memory lane' and I think I used it as a type of masochistic punishment. Since there was no way to make things right with my father, I felt justified in accepting guilt as punishment for my words and actions – it served as some sort of pseudo-atonement for a wrong I could never make right.

I have learned, though, that withholding forgiveness makes us victims of our circumstances and removes our control of well-being, just like we experience pins and needles when the natural blood flow to our feet is obstructed. I believe this resentment I felt blocked God's love and compassion, thus preventing it from flowing through me fully and freely.

When someone says that forgiveness isn't easy – they're right. The underlying difficulty is usually this question: 'Who takes the initiative?'

Yes, who does take the first step in forgiveness?

This is surely at the heart of the struggle most of us have with showing mercy.

And why don't I always take the first step in forgiveness?

Often it has been because of my own pride. Sometimes I have been too scared of the person's potential reaction to be able to phone them or even write them a letter. At times, I have wished for the mistrust or silence to end, but I wanted the person who I felt had wronged me to go through the embarrassment of reaching out to me, rather than risking humiliating myself.

Christian author and editor of *Christianity Today*, Philip Yancey, suggests that forgiveness is an act of faith – the belief that God can take care of the fairness problems. It is not fair just to pretend that something hasn't happened.

It did happen. It still hurts. It still stings.

Forgiveness is not fair but forgiveness is a way of lifting that burden from us and giving it to God to bear, who is fair.

To survivors like myself I would say that we must stop blaming ourselves. The guilt that we inevitably carry around with us is soul-destroying and can even be slightly masochistic ...

Only when I was confronted by God about it could I finally accept this undeniable truth.

Friends of mine, Jim and Lorna Singleton, kindly gave me the gift of a book called *The Lost Art of Forgiving*, by Steve Chalke. This book has been a real blessing to me, as it not only challenged me to explore a side of my nature I still had to work on, but also humbled me to tears – reading how ordinary men and women could overcome acts of almost unspeakable evil with so much love, grace and compassion.

It was full of personal accounts of people who, against incredible odds, had found the strength to forgive those who had caused devastation in their lives – Gordon Wilson, for instance, whose daughter was killed by an IRA bomb at Enniskillen.

I'm thinking also of Phan Thi Kim Phuc, whose photograph as a burned naked nine-year-old, caught up in the ravages of the Vietnam war, was one of the most iconic images of the 20th century.

You have probably seen this heart-wrenching photograph before. It has been described as a photo that changed the world. It made Kim an international figure who symbolised everything that was wrong with war in general, and the Vietnam war in particular.

Did Kim survive? Where is she now?

Kim is married with two children. She is a Christian who lives out the principles of her faith.

In a commemorative ceremony for the Vietnam War, she publicly forgave the person who had launched the napalm bombing in her village in Vietnam. Ever since, she has dedicated her life to promoting peace - and to this end she founded the 'Kim Phuc Phan Thi Foundation'. This foundation helps children everywhere, who are victims of war, by providing medical and psychological help to surmount their traumatic experiences.

Gordon Wilson was a man of great Christian faith. He attended Enniskillen Methodist Church and studied at Wesley College, Dublin. He came to national and international prominence through an emotional television interview he gave to the BBC in which he described his last conversation with his daughter, Marie, a nurse, as they both lay buried in rubble in the aftermath of the Enniskillen Remembrance Day bombing by the IRA, in 1987.

He expressed forgiveness to his daughter's killers and pleaded with Loyalists not to take revenge for her death. In the interview, Mr Wilson spoke with anguish about his last conversation with his daughter, and of his feelings toward her killers:

'She held my hand tightly, and gripped me as hard as she could. She said, "Daddy, I love you very much." Those were her exact words to me, and those were the last words I ever heard her say.'

To the astonishment of the listeners, Wilson went on to add: 'But I bear no ill will. I bear no grudge. Dirty sort of talk is not going to bring her back to life. She was a great wee lassie. She loved her profession. She was a pet. She's dead. She's in Heaven and we shall meet again. I will pray for these men tonight and every night.'

As historian Jonathan Bardon recounts: 'No words in more than twenty-five years of violence in Northern Ireland had such a powerful, emotional impact.'

In this new season of my life, from my experiences as a former voluntary addiction counsellor, I can say with all honesty that my approach to dealing with my father's depression and alcoholism was more from the 'Jim'll fix it' manual than by the person-centred model, shown during my training.

There are things that I might have done differently, but they may not have made any difference. However unsuitable this approach may have been at times, I can look back with the benefit of hindsight secure in the knowledge that I did my best as the person that I was at that time.

After all, no one can be expected to take complete responsibility for someone else's life. Inner healing, ultimately, is what this chapter is all about. The old adage, 'Time heals all wounds,' is not necessarily true for survivors of a loved one's suicide. Mourning can be a lengthy process and should not be confused with inner healing, which can last a life-time.

There came a day when my lamentation did no longer consume my whole life. However, the length of time it took to come to some kind of healing had to be up to God rather than any pre-conceived notion that I or anyone else may have had. Grief is a universal human experience and one that is unique to each person. Both our mortality and our need to connect with others make all of us vulnerable to loss.

A close relationship with Jesus can comfort anyone dealing

with suicide, but an element of pain will always remain. Jesus is not a magician with a magic wand. It is nearly impossible to totally forget horrific experiences, but God is faithful in making those memories more bearable for us.

I once heard it said that, 'A Christian's practical theology is often his hymnology.' Many of us could testify to these words of wisdom as we recall some deeply moving experience – perhaps a tragic loss – in conjunction with a simple old-fashioned hymn that has been used at countless funerals to comfort people.

Such a hymn is, 'What a friend we have in Jesus'. Its simply stated message has brought immense solace and comfort to countless grieving souls since it was first written in the middle of the 19th century.

So relevant to the basic spiritual needs of people are these words that many missionaries state that this is one of the first hymns taught to new converts. The very simplicity of the text and music has been its appeal and strength.

I occasionally imagine my father enjoying a peaceful retirement, spending time with his grandchildren in the natural rugged beauty of the Moray Firth coast – perhaps doing a bit of his first love, fishing.

I'd like to think that a healing conversation might have been possible and that we could have made up for the often strained relationship between us. There is a deep desire in me to understand him more.

I ask myself: Was his alcoholism brought on by tragic life experiences – the premature deaths of his mother and Alan, the brother he was closest to – or as a comforting mechanism to cope with the day-to-day stress at work and the overall pressures of life with problems that he could only bottle up and keep to himself?

I also wonder if my dad grew up with an orphan heart in a home where he felt unloved and undervalued by a father who was viewed by many as a difficult and cantankerous man. Despite being blessed with a warm and tender mother, this environment may have created an emotional stronghold, therefore making it difficult for him to express real love and affection for his own sons later in life.

I don't deny that life had dealt my dad some cruel blows, but with a stronger will to survive he could have had times of joy with his grandchildren just a few years down the road. Sadly, suicide was his permanent solution to what I believe to have been only a temporary situation.

I have come to realise that I will never find a totally satisfactory explanation –and even if I could, my father would still not be alive. Although I have gone through the whole spectrum of emotions since his death, I have now been able to feel natural grief and genuine love for my dad. The anger I felt towards him for giving up on life and allowing himself to slide into a deep decline following my mothers death have long since subsided.

Much healing took place when I examined my father's life and began to truly comprehend the pressures and pains that led him to his dreadful decision. I didn't agree with him though, when he said he had nothing to live for. Certainly, it was difficult for him, but there is nearly always hope. Life is too valuable a commodity to give up during a dark period in life. There is no second chance.

It is a lot harder on those left behind, who have to live with the fact that their loved one was in so much inner pain that they no longer wanted to live.

The Bible tells of six self-killings. The best known is that of the betrayer, Judas, as recorded in the book of Matthew. The Biblical writers neither condemn nor commend those whom they record as having taken their own lives, thus the actual views of the Biblical narrators regarding the suicides of Samson, Saul and Judas cannot be ascertained.

An examination of our Biblical and Church history discloses different degrees of tolerance towards suicide. For some it is always wholly condemnable, while for others it may be an understandable response in exceptional circumstances.

The historical discussion provides some guidance on facing current dilemmas. Modern medicine can occasionally artificially extend the time scale of death – a fact that has generated heated debate about situations in which suicide might be acceptable, especially in cases involving aged or terminally ill people.

While in the process of writing this, I purchased several books that covered the experiences of suicide survivors. Most of those were guilt-, blame- and bitterness-saturated narratives that offered no hope and little comfort to the reader.

As my greatest desire for this book has always been to offer genuine hope and comfort, I was thankful that I was led to three enlightening publications of 'gold nugget' proportions that I would comfortably recommend to anyone who is struggling to come to terms with a loved one's suicide – or indeed with a human loss of any kind.

Despite suicide remaining one of life's unfathomable mysteries, it is always comforting that through the experiences of others we can connect with them so that we can find meaning, solace and hope, which will aid the healing process of our pain, guilt and grief.

Grieving a Suicide, by Albert Y. Hsu, is a book that echoes many of my own experiences. Hsu has succeeded in doing what few can accomplish: he has created a thoughtful, empathic, spiritually ennobling, practical and helpful account of his response to the loss of his father by suicide.

Hsu never minimises the importance of grieving. 'Only when we actively mourn will we be able to receive the comfort that God and others offer,' he writes. 'Nevertheless, those without 'Christian' hope grieve in one way; those with hope grieve in another.'

The Christian way of grieving is Hsu's focus in the latter half of the book, where he surveys Scripture to deal with questions such as whether people who die by suicide can go to heaven; where God is when tragedy strikes; what can be learned from suicide.

Roses in December: Finding Strength Within Grief is a book written by Marilyn Willett Heavilin. Suffering the loss of a child is hard for anyone to imagine, but Marilyn and her husband Glen suffered the loss of not one child, but three of their children.

Marilyn journals the story of her struggles, anguish, grief, despair, hopes, and blessings. In this wonderfully comforting book, she covers personal suffering from many different angles.

Bereavement is a universal, inescapable voyage but it is also a uniquely personal one. *Living With Bereavement*, by Sue Mayfield, can help anyone on their unpredictable journey that will be so different for each of us. Whatever our point of view, many of us are still confused and uncertain about death. So much is unknown and surreal.

This book covers topics such as: Funerals and Ceremonies; Absence and Presence; Anger and Guilt; Regret and Relief; Loss and Despair; Energy and Sleep; Support and Comfort; Anniversaries and Remembrances.

When someone we love grows old and dies of 'natural causes' we find it easier to accept it as the way God has designed the creation – we accept there's a time to be born and a time to die.

So what is the answer?

Why is suffering so indiscriminate?

Why is it meted out to those who don't deserve it?

Why do the innocent suffer from actions and events over which they have no control and often cannot foresee?

Great Thinkers and philosophers have weighed in on the issue for many centuries, but they have all failed to provide satisfactory rational answers.

Yet, those who are suffering desperately need to have answers to their questions.

When Jesus Christ came to earth, more than two thousand years ago, He saw misery. He witnessed the plight of outcast lepers, widows in need, and people with debilitating physical and mental disorders. He reacted with compassion to alleviate misery.

Jesus proclaimed that part of His mission was: to heal the broken hearted, to bring Good News to the poor, that captives will be released, that the blind will see, that the oppressed will be set free. (Luke 4:18 NLT)

Such a time has not yet occurred for all mankind, but we can be comforted by God's promises that He will bring an end to suffering in general during Christ's millennial reign and will eventually banish it. (Revelation 21)

Although what my father did was wrong, I feel he did not

commit an unforgivable sin. What we all need to understand is that the suicidal person cannot be in a rational frame of mind when he or she takes their own life.

My strong personal belief is that when someone carries out the act of suicide under severe emotional duress or while experiencing a mental breakdown, he or she will be commended to God's mercy, not His wrath.

On reflection, there probably was an element of selfishness in my father's final act but, like many other people who commit suicide, there were plenty of occasions throughout his life – when he was depression free – that exemplified complete selflessness on his part. None more so, than back in 1976, when he displayed incredible grace and courage to sit down sympathetically with his good friend, John Smith, the driver of the car on that fateful day when his brother was killed, to break the news that Alan had passed away. John had suffered memory loss after being in a coma, lasting several weeks.

Not a morsel of blame did my father ever attach to his now severely disabled friend, and they remained close till the day my father died.

Despite its catastrophic social impact, especially in the North of Scotland, suicide is seldom spoken of in Churches. Even though there is a greater understanding of mental illness nowadays, suicide survivors are still living with shame and guilt without receiving any spiritual counselling or support.

Church leaders may air their views regarding abortion, homosexuality or any controversial social issue you can think of, but I have never heard a sermon on suicide. Yet, I genuinely believe that cultural and religious attitudes towards suicide are changing, and many churches are beginning to confront suicide rather than sweeping it under the carpet.

In the past, suicide used to be a taboo subject. When a family member took his own life, it was often concealed and rarely discussed. Nevertheless, there was always something left unsaid or unfinished.

I would like society to try and be especially understanding of families that have sustained suicides. It is appalling to a family unit when one of its members decides that he or she would rather depart this world than continue to share their company. Since no illness or accident is to blame for the killing, they are naturally consumed with guilt.

We seem to live in an era where a man is expected to be strong, fit, powerful and affluent, and where he is often ridiculed if he shows his true feelings. This can make men complex because they keep all feelings inside, which makes them seem hard-hearted and insensitive on the outside.

It may be unusual for a man in his forties to write with such strong emotion, but I believe I have been set free from a condition which one American writer described as 'approval addiction', making me assured enough now to express what I really feel.

According to Dan Kindlon, a Harvard lecturer and co-author of *Raising Cain: Protecting the Emotional Life of Boys*, young men don't ask for help because we don't allow them to.

'Parents encourage boys more than girls to "tough it out" if they fall over or suffer a disappointment, and they unconsciously encourage emotional conversations with their daughters, but discourage them with their sons.'

Kindlon continues: 'By the time he reaches school, these patterns have not only become more entrenched, but more brutal as well. In school a boy who shows a more effeminate side, or cries, or expresses his feelings, is open to a lot of ridicule and teasing, especially at these vulnerable ages when we see a lot of suicides.'

Kildlon's views are backed up by Dr Warren Farrell, author of *The Myth of Male Power*, who devoted a whole chapter of his book to the issue of suicide.

Dr Farrell believes that men commit suicide in far greater numbers than women when they feel unloved, unneeded or they feel they are a burden to society. Men have spent all their youth striving to become achievers, to be providers and protectors, and never learn the life skills to deal with the humiliation that comes with failure in any of these areas.

Whereas women are often encouraged to develop nurturing

skills, taught to help each other through life's traumas, men are rarely taught these skills. Instead, men are taught to be strong and go it alone.

Unfortunately, their problems are too great to handle alone. A teenager commits suicide and we shake our heads and say 'must have been drugs-related'. Then we wait for another one. We go through the whole shock process again, hoping that the next tragedy doesn't come too close to our own doorstep ...

I feel that we, as a society, will have to come to terms with our high suicide rate, and accept and understand the devastation suicide has on family, friends and whole communities. It seems to be one of the few deaths where ignorance is running rampant; there is so much confusion and there are so many misunderstandings.

Suicide in Scotland is in danger of reaching epidemic proportions – it is affecting almost every Scottish family, directly or indirectly.

It can strike a child, a brother, a friend, a parent or a co-worker.

It can strike someone from any background or creed.

It can strike at any stage of life, from childhood to old age.

No community is immune to suicide, no school or workplace remains unaffected by it. More young men aged between 16 and 24 are committing suicide than are killed in road accidents.

It is no secret that many who are suffering from self-esteem problems have become victims of substance abuse and tend to immerse their woes in alcohol or hard drugs. Drugs are so deceptive; they promise much but deliver nothing – except carnage.

Alcoholism and drug abuse are two of the major problems of our nation, much of which stems from a self-perceived lack of worth and lack of purpose. People use them in an attempt to fill a spiritual void in search of meaning to life.

Of course, there are numerous reasons why a person may have a low sense of self-worth. Self-deprecation is invariably driven by many emotional issues that may attract bullying and harassment, often leading to eating disorders.

I think this plague of low self-esteem may come, in part, directly from the atheistic evolutionary view of mankind with which society now seems to indoctrinate our young people from an early age. This deeply concerns me, for it means that school children are brought up with an inaccurate idea of self-worth. I wonder how many of our youngsters are being side-tracked from the discipleship of Christ – which requires losing their "selves" – because they are told, 'Feel good about only yourself', rather than being taught that there is a sinner inside all of us who needs to be put to death daily. A healthy and accurate view of self-esteem can, I believe, be found in the very Christian ethos that both secular society and much of our educational system appear to be rejecting.

Several people have told me that they feel that suicide is a selfish act. I can understand that, as it was my own initial conclusion too. But can anyone really say, 'I would never take my own life,' with absolute certainty? Do we know ourselves that well?

Or is there, in some corner of our minds, that question of doubt; a tiny piece of precariousness? While I can go some way to understand how someone who shared my father's natural melancholic personality could slide into a deep depression, it is more challenging to figure out why people of a more extrovert nature commit suicide.

Tony Hancock was a leading figure in television and radio comedy in the 1950s and 60s. Nevertheless, towards the end of his life he was to sink into an alcohol-fuelled depression, decrying it all as pointless. His suicide note said simply: 'Things went wrong too many times.'

David Sutch, better known as 'Screaming Lord Sutch', was a man who brought eccentricity, colour and humour to the often drab world of politics for over 20 years as leader of the official Monster Raving Loony Party. But despite this public image he suffered from depression for most of his adult life.

When he took his own life, by hanging, in 1999, he left a note which read: 'I can't cope any longer.' Even more baffling is the decision of a person to end his life despite having emerged victorious from past suffering and pain.

Lewis Puller Jnr, the author of *Fortunate Son*, lost half his body in the Vietnam war but, although having served as an inspiration to thousands of American war veterans, he shoots himself dead in the basement of his own house.

Terrence Des Pres survived the Holocaust to write his highly acclaimed book *The Survivor – An Anatomy of Life in the Death Camps*, which chronicles the nobility of human spirit in the face of utter hopelessness and despair. Yet he couldn't defeat the doubts within his own mind and took his life in 1987.

Among the list of great inventors who committed suicide are George Eastman, of Kodak camera fame; Albert Ballin, credited with the invention of cruise ships; Edward Howard Armstrong, who gave us FM radio.

Some high-profile suicides involving rock stars fascinate us because they are shrouded by intrigue and mystery. Rock star Kurt Cobain is elevated to the position of instant icon by shooting himself in the head at the age of 27 and John Simon Ritchie, better known as punk rock star Sid Vicious, dies of a heroin overdose after being arrested for the suspected murder of his girlfriend in1979, prompting numerous books and films featuring his troubled life.

Much of our lives, if we are willing to analyse them, are taken up by routine, pedestrian, everyday, habitual, and emotionally colourless stretches of time – a life on automatic pilot, casually cruising along.

And then there is the pain that we all go through: sorrow, shame, humiliation, dread, defeat and anxiety. When we experience these negative emotions over a period of time and to a heightened degree, it is only natural that psychological anguish and disturbance follow.

Many people have heard the tale of the man who, desperately ill, goes to a doctor in Hamburg, Germany, and tells him that he has lost his desire to live and is contemplating suicide. The doctor listens to this tale of despondency, then tells the patient that what he needs is a good old belly laugh. He advises the clearly distressed man to go to the circus that same night and spend the evening laughing at the famous Grock, the world's funniest clown. The doctor sums it up like this: 'After you have seen Grock, I am sure you will have cured the malady of your soul.'

The patient rises to his feet, looks sadly at the doctor, turns and ambles to the door. As he is about to leave, the doctor says, 'By the way, what is your name?' The man turns towards the doctor with sorrowful eyes. After a deep sigh he whispers, 'I am Grock.'

Even more so today, many of us are wearing the mask of the clown; outwardly confident, self-assured and successful, yet living lives of quiet desperation.

I should know what I'm talking about – after all, I was nicknamed after another famous clown: Coco!

One in ten adults in Scotland are on anti-depressants, according to reliable health service statistics. Our emotions can so easily lead us astray. However, the reassuring fact is that there are also thousands of people whose lives have been dramatically saved through the intervention of therapy by psychologists, psychiatrists, physicians, counsellors (both Christian and secular), suicide prevention workers, and many others.

It would be a sad misreading of this chapter to believe that in relation to suicide, and its admittedly dire consequences, there is not a gigantic place for realistic hope.

Aleksandr Solzhenitsyn first spoke to me, when I was still a susceptible, if somewhat obstinate, teenager through his short novel *One Day in the Life of Ivan Denisovich*.

Solzhenitsyn's fearless accounts of torment, torture and courage, against all odds in the Soviet Union's labour camps, riveted his countrymen whose concealed cruelty he exposed.

Denisovich's days were filled with backbreaking labour and slow starvation. On one particular day, the hopelessness of his situation became too much for him. He saw no reason to continue living, to continue fighting the system. He thought that the rest of his life was meaningless since he would most likely die in that Siberian prison. His life made no difference in the world. So he gave up.

Laying his shovel on the ground, he slowly walked to a crude work-site bench and sat down. He knew that at any moment a guard would order him to stand up, and when he failed to respond, the guard would beat him to death, probably with his own shovel.

He had seen it happen to many other prisoners.

As he waited, head down, he felt a presence. Slowly, he lifted his eyes and saw a skinny, old prisoner squat down next to him. The man said nothing. Instead, he drew a stick through the ground at Denisovich's feet, tracing the sign of the Cross. The man then stood up and returned to his work.

As Denisovich stared at the sign of the Cross, his entire perspective changed. He knew that he was only one man against the all-powerful Soviet empire. Yet, in that moment, he knew that there was something greater than the evil that he saw in the prison; something greater than the Soviet Union.

He knew that the hope of all mankind was represented in that simple Cross – and through the power of the Cross, anything was possible. I believe that holocaust survivor Victor Frankl's perceptive insights can be summarised as two key discoveries.

His first discovery was that in Auschwitz you needed a reason to carry on living. If you let that evaporate you lost the will to live and if you lost the will to live you perished. Of course, this insight was not unique to him, for it was Solomon who told us this thousands of years ago: 'Where there is no vision the people perish.' – When people do not accept divine guidance, they run wild. (Proverbs 29 v 18 NLT)

The barbaric conditions in the camp were designed to break not just the human body but also the spirit. They were so de-humanising that they turned the prisoners into the walking dead.

It was the second discovery, however, that changed Frankl's life with the force of revelation. The Nazis robbed the prisoners of every fragment of humanity – their possessions, their clothes, their hair, even their names – giving them numbers instead, tattooed on their arms. But he realised that there was one thing that the Nazis could not take away from them: the freedom to choose how to respond.

That one slender opening of hope in the walls of despair was all that remained. It was this tiny chink of light that a prisoner needed.

Frankl persuaded himself that he was not a prisoner in a

concentration camp but a psychotherapist taking part in an experiment. This allowed him to salvage a vestige of freedom and dignity.

He had found a purpose in life: to do all he could to rescue his fellow prisoners from despair. He did so by helping them to find a reason to live – a task short of completion, or work still in progress. For one prisoner, it was finishing a series of travel guides. For another, it was the thought of rejoining a child in Canada, who needed him.

He tells the story of one particular young woman in the camp, who was about to die. She was remarkably cheerful and she explained this uncommon cheerfulness in the following way:

Until her imprisonment she had never thought about spiritual matters but in Auschwitz she had nothing except a tiny window through which she could see a branch of a chestnut tree on which there were two blossoms. That branch seemed to speak to her: 'I am here – I am life, eternal life.'

And she was there to experience that.

I feel there is something profoundly sacred about Victor Frankl's work.

The self finds itself by attending to something beyond the self. Our reason to be comes in the form of that cry, that invitation, that calling, that mission; that silent voice of the beyond-within.

He observes: 'Our generation is realistic, for we have come to know man as he really is. After all, man is that being who has invented the gas chambers of Auschwitz; however, he is also that being who has entered those gas chambers upright, with the Lord's Prayer or Shema Yisrael on his lips.'

Philip Yancey also gives expert insight into many of the baffling and difficult issues surrounding the mystery of pain, whether emotional or physical.

In a moving sermon on the Virginia Tech campus, only two weeks after the massacre, Yancey ended with these words: 'Honour the grief you feel. The pain is a way of honouring those who died; your friends and classmates and professors. It represents life and love. The pain will fade over time, but it will never fully disappear.'

Yancey continues: 'Do not attempt healing alone. The real healing of deep connective tissue takes place in community.

Where is God when it hurts?

Where God's people are. Where misery is, there is the Messiah, and on this earth, the Messiah takes form in the shape of His Church.

That's what the body of Christ means.

Finally, cling to the hope that nothing that happens, not even this terrible tragedy, is irredeemable. We serve a God who has vowed to make all things new. J. R. R. Tolkien once spoke of "joy beyond the walls of the world, poignant as grief".

You know well the poignancy of grief. As healing progresses, may you know, too, that joy, a foretaste of the world redeemed.'

Undoubtedly, Yancey's most powerful discussion about pain comes near the end of the second section of his book *Where is God when it hurts?*

In a small chapter titled *Extreme Cases*, he discusses the responses of World War II concentration camp survivors. These survivors suffered not only physical pain but also a complete assault on their concept of humanity.

One of the most revealing moments is when he turns Romanian born Jew, Elie Wiesel's denial of God's loving presence into an affirmation of God's love and care.

One of Wiesel's most horrifying teenage memories was when the guards first tortured and then hanged a young Jewish boy, a child with a refined and beautiful face; a sad-eyed angel.

Just before the hanging, Elie heard someone behind him whisper, 'Where is God? Where is He?'

Thousands of prisoners were forced to watch the hanging.

Not heavy enough for the weight of his body to break his neck, it took the boy half an hour to die. Elie files past him, looking the corpse full in the face. He sees the boy's tongue still pink and his eyes still clear, and weeps.

Behind him, he heard the same voice ask, 'Where is God now?'

Wiesel writes: 'And I heard a voice within me answer him: "Where is He? Here He is – He is hanging here on the gallows."'

Elie Wiesel meant to imply that God was dead and powerless to help. As a result of his experience of the Holocaust he rebelled against God for allowing people to be starved, tortured, butchered, gassed and burned. But Elie Wiesel's words have another meaning. A meaning he never intended.

'Where is God when it hurts? Here he is – hanging here on the gallows.'

When applied to the cross of Jesus, Wiesel's words are truer than he could ever have envisaged ...

Where was God when Jesus died a cruel, shameful death?

Another Jew, the apostle Paul, says: 'God was there. God was in Christ, reconciling the world to Himself.' (2 Corinthians 5:19 NLT)

Fast forward more than half a century, and Elie Wiesel, now a celebrated author and former Nobel Peace Prize winner, appears to have softened towards God in an impassioned speech in the East Room of the White House – part of the Millennium Lecture series, hosted by President Bill Clinton and his wife, Hilary.

Sharing his concentration camp experience Elie states:

'Rooted in our tradition, some of us felt that to be abandoned by humanity then was not the ultimate. We felt that to be abandoned by God was worse than to be punished by Him. Better an unjust God than an indifferent one. For us to be ignored by God was a harsher punishment than to be a victim of His anger.

Man can live far from God – not outside God. God is wherever we are.

Even in suffering?

Even in suffering.'

To Elie Wiesel it is no longer a question of doubting God. God will always be God; it is not for any man to judge why He does things.

However, it is natural that we can still question His motives, for I now believe that suffering contains the secret of creation and the magnitude of eternity; it can be pierced only from inside.

Regardless of the nature of the parent-son relationship, or the

Colin and Dad

circumstances surrounding my parents' death, many powerful feelings and memories still arise when I reflect on their lives.

In reality, I was only an adult child when I lost them both. Having to deal with the immediate loss, as well as unresolved issues from the past, I was forced to reshape my life, which, in turn, led me to discover the reality of my own identity and mortality, and ultimately the relevance of my spiritual beliefs and values.

There appears to be anecdotal evidence that the spirit of our parents still lives within us. These unseen influences are part of our spiritual heritage, and how we live out those influences forms much of our character.

We can choose to embrace the influences that helped shape us.

We can also reject them.

Better still, we can modify them – as I hope I have done.

The pathway of life is narrow and rock-strewn. We know not why. Often the way is clear and bright, but at times we stumble and fall – and all seems lost. When we arrive at a fork in the road, we have a choice to make. By making the correct choice and by trusting in our Heavenly Father we can be assured that all detours eventually take us back on the right road again.

Even though I believe that it is God who should number our days, not us, I can now view my father's death in a more merciful and sympathetic perspective. I can now look back on his suicide as a valiant but ultimately failed battle against depression and alcoholism, and not as a depraved, selfish or cowardly act.

To be honest, conflicting emotions still rise to the surface when I think of my dad, because you never totally lose the surrealism and sadness, but I am no longer torn between compassion and resentment.

Often, when the realisation of my father's humanity hit me, a sense of disappointment and a feeling of disillusionment naturally followed. However, I now understand that he carried the same childhood expectations as I did.

He was just a kid who grew up to have kids of his own.

Dad and sister Alice

This disappointment in my dad may have been a stumbling block for me, knowing God as a Father, for it was my common tendency to relate to God as I related to my earthly father.

But God is not like an earthly father. Matthew 5:48 says that He is the Perfect Father, and that He loves us perfectly and unconditionally ...

I sincerely believe that if anyone through reading this book can find a way to let go of the hurt and disappointment that they experienced with their parents, it will bring a new freedom to them. A freedom that will allow us to receive the love that we have always hoped to receive from our own father, from the Perfect Father.

BIBLIOGRAPHY AND
RECOMMENDED READING

The Last of the Mohicans	James Fenimore	H.C. Carey & I. Lea Cooper
The Magic of Thinking Big	David Schwartz	Simon & Schuster Inc
Man's Search for Meaning	Victor Frankl	Washington Square Press
The Cross and the Switchblade	David Wilkerson	Fleming H. Revell Co
Run Baby Run	Nicky Cruz	Hodder & Stoughton
Out of the Maze	Noel Davidson	Ambassador-Emerald Int.
A Child No More	Mary Pytches	Hodder & Stoughton
The Lost Art of Forgiving	Steve Chalke	Plough Publishing House
One Day in the Life of Ivan Denisovich	Solzhenisyn	Signet Classic
Where is God when it Hurts?	Philip Yancey	Zondervan
Wild at Heart	John Eldredge	Thomas Nelson
Man of Steel and Velvet	Aubrey P. Andelin	Pacific Press
Grieving a Suicide	Albert Y. Hsu	Intervarsity Press
Roses in December: Comfort for the Grieving Heart	Marilyn Willet Heavilin	Harvest House Publishers
Living With Bereavement	Sue Mayfield	Lion Publishing Plc (Adults)
Purpose Driven Life	Rick Warren	Zondervan
Searching Issues	Nicky Gumbel	Kingsway
Chasing the Dragon	Jackie Pullinger	Hodder & Stoughton
Scottish Worthies	John Howie	The Banner of Truth

The Diary of Anne Frank	Anne Frank	Longman
What's So Amazing About Grace?	Philip Yancey	Zondervan
Failing Forward	John C. Maxwell	Thomas Nelson
The Power of Positive Thinking	Norman Vincent Peale	Ballantine Books
Church of the Isles	Ray Simpson	Scarecrow Press
Living on the Devil's Doorstep	Floyd McClung	W Pub Group
You See Bones, I See an Army	Floyd McClung	YWAM Publishing
The Life: A Portrait of Jesus	J. John	Authentic Media
The Dawkins Delusion	Alister McGrath	SPCK
Darwin's Angel	John Cornwell	Profile
The God you are Looking For	Bill Hybels	Thomas Nelson
Revival: Personal Encounters	Hugh B. Black	New Dawn Books
Total Forgiveness	R.T. Kendall	Creation House
The Heavenly Man	Paul Hattaway	Monarch Books